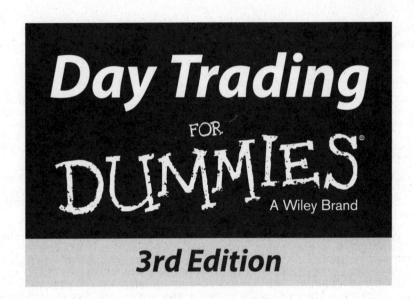

Day Trading

FOR

DUMMIES®

A Wiley Brand

3rd Edition

by Ann C. Logue, MBA

FOR

DUMMIES®

A Wiley Brand

Day Trading For Dummies® **3rd Edition**

Published by: **John Wiley & Sons, Inc.,** 111 River Street, Hoboken, NJ 07030-5774, www.wiley.com

Copyright © 2014 by John Wiley & Sons, Inc., Hoboken, New Jersey

Published simultaneously in Canada

For general information on our other products and services, please contact our Customer Care Department within the U.S. at 877-762-2974, outside the U.S. at 317-572-3993, or fax 317-572-4002. For technical support, please visit www.wiley.com/techsupport.

Wiley publishes in a variety of print and electronic formats and by print-on-demand. Some material included with standard print versions of this book may not be included in e-books or in print-on-demand. If this book refers to media such as a CD or DVD that is not included in the version you purchased, you may download this material at http://booksupport.wiley.com. For more information about Wiley products, visit www.wiley.com.

Library of Congress Control Number: 2013954192

ISBN 978-1-118-77960-6 (pbk); ISBN 978-1-118-80813-9 (ebk); ISBN 978-1-118-80808-5 (ebk)

Manufactured in the United States of America

Contents at a Glance

Table of Contents

Introduction

A lot has happened since the first version of *Day Trading For Dummies* came out. We've had a global financial crisis. Brokerage firms have introduced smartphone apps for trading. NASDAQ shut down for three hours due to a systems failure. A new currency, the bitcoin, was invented. The rules of trading have changed along with all the financial and economic upheaval, and savvy people looking for success in day trading need an up-to-the-minute reference like this new edition to steer them straight.

Day trading is a business in which you use real money to take on the markets. If you love the thrill of the markets and have the patience to sit and stare at a screen for hours, waiting for the right moment to get in and get out of securities, then day trading may be a great career option. But it has risks, too. Any day can be your best day, but it can also put you out of business forever. For that reason, day trading requires the right psychological makeup. Good day traders are patient and decisive, confident but not arrogant. They most certainly are not gamblers, although day trading attracts gamblers who discover it's a great way to *lose* money from home.

Day Trading For Dummies, 3rd Edition, is for people who are looking for a new business or who simply want to supplement their investment returns with new techniques. In this book you can find all the information you need to determine whether you're cut out for day trading, to lay out your home office, to research and plan trades, and more. (And even if you decide day trading isn't for you, you can still find lots of sound general advice about markets, trading, and investing strategies that you can benefit from. Plus you'll have saved all the money you would have otherwise invested on research and training, not to mention the trading losses!)

A lot of people make a lot of money selling services to neophyte day traders, claiming to be the best thing going. And maybe so — for some people. In this book, I give a wider perspective. Instead of telling you to use a particular trading strategy, for example, I help you research and evaluate the different day-trading methods available so that you can find one that works for you. And I also tell you up front that if you decide to day trade, this book shouldn't be your only guide.

About This Book

First, let me tell you what this book is not: It's not a textbook, and it's not a handbook for professional investors. Several of those are on the market already, and they're fabulous, but they're often dry and assume you already have a lot of knowledge about day trading.

This book doesn't make those assumptions. It contains straightforward explanations of how day trading works, how to get started, what the pitfalls are, and what some of the alternatives are for your portfolio and for your career. It's designed for you to be able to skip around and read the chapters or sections that interest you, without having to read every word that comes before them. This book has more than enough content to get you started — or to guide you to something that's a better fit for your sensibilities. If you really want to read some textbooks, I list a few in the appendix.

Oh, and I like to think this book isn't dry, either.

As for conventions, here are the basics: I put important words that I define in *italics*. I often **bold** the key words of lists to bring the important ideas to your attention. And I place all web addresses in monofont to set them apart.

During printing of this book, some of the web addresses may have broken across two lines of text. If you come across such an address, rest assured that I haven't put in any extra characters (such as hyphens) to indicate the break. When using a broken web address, type in exactly what you see on the page, pretending that the line break doesn't exist.

I also include sidebars in the book that you don't really need to read in order to follow the chapter text. With that stated, though, I do encourage you to go back and read through this extra material when you have the time. Many of the sidebars contain practice examples that help you get an even better idea of how some of the investment concepts work. Some of the information is pretty fun, too.

Foolish Assumptions

In writing this book, I made some assumptions about you, the reader.

- You're someone who needs to know a lot about day trading in a short period of time.
- You may be considering a career change, looking for a productive part-time retirement activity, or bored and looking for a challenge. Maybe you just want to know if day trading is a good way to supplement your

current investment program. Whatever your reason for considering day trading, you want to know how to decide whether it's the right option for you.

✔ If you already know that day trading is right for you, you want to know how to get started, from opening an account to setting up your computer monitors. (And yep, that's plural.)

✔ You have extra money to trade (whether it's yours or not) and you want to try day trading techniques to goose up your portfolio returns.

✔ You have some understanding of the basics of investing — that you know what mutual funds and brokerage accounts are, for example. If you don't feel comfortable with that much, you may want to read the latest editions of *Investing For Dummies* (by Eric Tyson, published by Wiley) or *Mutual Funds For Dummies* (also by Tyson; Wiley) and then come back here. I can wait.

Icons Used in This Book

As you read this book, you'll see icons scattered around the margins of the text. Each icon points out a certain type of information, most of which you should know or may find interesting about day trading. They go as follows:

This icon notes something you should keep in mind about day trading. It may refer to something I covered earlier in the book, or it may highlight something you need to remember for future investing decisions.

Tip information tells you how to invest a little better, a little smarter, and a little more efficiently. The information can help you make better day trades or ask better questions of people who want to supply you with research, training, and trading systems.

I've included nothing in this book that can cause death or bodily harm, as far as I can figure out, but plenty of things in the world of day trading can cause you to lose big money or, worse, your sanity. These points help you avoid big problems.

I put the nonessential (but often helpful) academic stuff here. By reading material marked by this icon, you get the detailed information behind the investment theories or, sometimes, some interesting trivia or background information.

Beyond the Book

In addition to the book content, you can find a free online Cheat Sheet that includes information on accounts, definitions, indicators, and performance calculation. Go to www.dummies.com/cheatsheet/daytrading to access this handy reference material, and then print it out and keep it by your side as you get started.

You can also access additional free articles that cover information I simply couldn't fit into the book. You'll find information on a day in the life of a trade. I also offer advice about chat rooms and Internet forums and a list of ten alternatives to day trading. You can find them at www.dummies.com/extras/daytrading.

Where to Go from Here

Well, open up the book and get going! If you have a particular area of interest, use the index and table of contents to go to the topic you want. If you're not sure, you can either turn the page and start at the beginning or flip through and see whether a topic catches your eye.

Need more guidance than that? Then allow me to give you some ideas. You may want to start with Chapter 1 if you know nothing about day trading. If you need to get set up to start trading, look at Chapters 11 and 12. If you want to know about some of the potential problems in day trading, turn to Chapters 4, 14, 15, and 16. If you are thinking about day trading as a career, Chapter 2 describes what day traders do all day. For ideas about developing strategies, whether you're going to hold for a few minutes or several years, go to Part II.

Bottom line: Anywhere you go, you'll find interesting and useful information.

Part I

Getting Started with Day Trading

getting started with

day trading

In this part...

✔ Get comfortable with the basic idea of day trading: the process of making a large number of short-term trades during a single day.

✔ Consider whether you have the steady temperament to handle day trading in treacherous markets. It is a business. Even part-time day traders need to approach the markets with the same seriousness as a business owner.

✔ Find out the basics of markets, trades, and strategies to help you get started — if day trading is right for you.

✔ Discover how to plan your trades so you can trade your plan and increase your chances for success.

Chapter 1

So You Want to Be a Day Trader

Make money from the comfort of your home! Be your own boss! Beat the market with your own smarts! Build real wealth! Tempting, isn't it? Day trading can be a great way to make money all on your own. It's also a great way to lose a ton of money all on your own. Do you have the fortitude to face the market every morning?

Day trading is a crazy business. Traders work in front of their computer screens, reacting to blips, each of which represents real dollars. They make quick decisions because their ability to make money depends on successfully executing a large number of trades that generate small profits. They close out their positions in the stocks, options, and futures contracts they own at the end of the day, which limits some of the risks — nothing can happen overnight to disturb an existing profit position — but those limits on risk can limit profits. After all, a lot can happen in a year, increasing the likelihood that your trade idea will work out, but in a day? You have to be patient and work fast. Some days offer nothing good to buy. Other days, every trade seems to lose money.

The individual human-being day trader is up against a tough opponent: high-frequency algorithms programmed and operated by brokerage firms and hedge funds that have no emotion and can make trades in less time than it takes to blink your eye. If you're not prepared for that competition, you will be crushed.

In this chapter, I cover what day traders do, share the advantages and disadvantages of day trading, list the personality traits of successful day traders, and give you information on your likelihood of success. You may find that day trading is a great career option that takes advantage of your street smarts and clear thinking — or that the risk outweighs the potential benefits. Either is okay: The more you know before you make the decision to trade, the greater your chance of being successful. If you decide that day trading isn't right for you, you can apply strategies and techniques that day traders use to improve the performance of your investment portfolio.

It's All in a Day's Work: Defining Day Trading

The definition of day trading is that day traders hold their securities for only one day. They close out their positions at the end of every day and then start all over again the next day. By contrast, *swing traders* hold securities for days and sometimes even months; *investors* sometimes hold for years. The short-term nature of day trading reduces some risks, because nothing can happen overnight to cause big losses. Meanwhile, many other types of investors go to bed thinking their position is in great shape only to wake up the next morning to find that the company has announced terrible earnings or that its CEO is being indicted on fraud charges.

But there's a flip side (there's always a flip side, isn't there?): The day trader's choice of securities and positions has to work out in a day, or it's gone. Tomorrow doesn't exist for any specific position. Meanwhile, the swing trader or the investor has the luxury of time, because it sometimes takes a while for a position to work out the way your research shows it should. In the long run, markets are efficient, and prices reflect all information about a security. Unfortunately, a few days of short runs may need to occur for this efficiency to kick in.

Day traders are speculators working in zero-sum markets one day at a time. That makes the dynamics different from other types of financial activities you may have been involved in. When you take up day trading, the rules that may have helped you pick good stocks or find great mutual funds over the years no longer apply. Day trading is a different game with different rules.

Speculating, not hedging

Professional traders fall into two categories: speculators and hedgers. *Speculators* look to make a profit from price changes. *Hedgers* look to protect against a price change. They make their buy and sell choices as insurance, not as a way to make a profit, so they choose positions that offset their exposure in another market.

As examples of hedging, consider a food-processing company and the farmer who raises or grows the ingredients the company needs. The company may look to hedge against the risks of price increases of key ingredients — like corn, cooking oil, or meat — by buying futures contracts on those ingredients. That way, if prices do go up, the company's profits on the contracts help fund the higher prices it has to pay for those ingredients. If the prices stay the same or go down, the company loses only the price of the contract, which may be a fair tradeoff to the company. The farmer raising corn, soybeans, or cattle, on the other hand, benefits if prices go up and suffers if they go down. To protect against a price decline, the farmer would sell futures on those commodities. His futures position would make money if the price went down, offsetting the decline on his products. And if the prices went up, he'd lose money on the contracts, but that loss would be offset by his gain on his harvest.

The commodity markets were intended to help agricultural producers manage risk and find buyers for their products. The stock and bond markets were intended to create an incentive for investors to finance companies. Speculation emerged in all of these markets almost immediately, but it was not their primary purpose.

Day traders are all speculators. They look to make money from the market as they see it now. They manage their risks by carefully allocating their money, using stop and limit orders (which close out positions as soon as predetermined price levels are reached), and closing out at the end of the night. Day traders don't manage risk with offsetting positions the way a hedger does. They use other techniques to limit losses, like careful money management and stop and limit orders (which you can read about in Chapter 2).

Markets have both hedgers and speculators in them. Knowing that different participants have different profit and loss expectations can help you navigate the turmoil of each day's trading. And that's important, because to make money in a zero-sum market, you only make money if someone else loses.

Understanding zero-sum markets

A zero-sum game has exactly as many winners as losers. And options and futures markets, which are popular with day traders, are zero-sum markets. If the person who holds an option makes a profit, then the person who *wrote* (which is option-speak for *sold*) that option loses the same amount. There's no net gain or net loss in the market as a whole.

Now some of those people buying and selling in zero-sum markets are hedgers who are content to take small losses in order to prevent big ones. Speculators may have the profit advantage in certain market conditions, but they can't count on having that advantage all the time.

So who wins and who loses in a zero-sum market? Some days, whether you win or lose all depends on luck, but over the long run, the winners are the people who are the most disciplined: They have a trading plan, set limits and stick to them, and can trade based on the data on the screen rather than on emotions like hope, fear, and greed.

Unlike the options and futures markets, the stock market is *not* a zero-sum game. As long as the economy grows, company profits grow, which in turn lead to growing stock prices. The stock market really has more winners than losers over the long run. That doesn't mean that any given day will have more winners than losers, however. In the short run, the stock market should be treated like a zero-sum market.

If you understand how profits are divided in the markets that you choose to trade, you have a better awareness of the risks that you face as well as the risks that the other participants are taking. People do make money in zero-sum markets, but you don't want those winners to be making a profit off you.

Some traders make money — lots of money — doing what they like. Trading is all about risk and reward. The traders who are rewarded risked the 80 percent washout rate. Knowing that, do you want to take the plunge? If so, read on. And if not, read on anyway, because you may get some ideas that can help you manage your other investments.

Being disciplined: Closing out each night

Day traders start each day fresh and finish each day with a clean slate. This daily regimen reduces some of the risk, and it forces discipline. You can't keep your losers longer than a day, and you have to take your profits at the end of the day before those winning positions turn into losers.

That discipline is important for day traders. When you day trade, you face a market that does not know and does not care who you are, what you're doing, or what your personal or financial goals are. There's no kindly boss who may cut you a little slack today, no friendly coworker to help you through a jam, no great client dropping you a little hint about her spending plans for the next fiscal year. Unless you have rules in place to guide your trading decisions, you'll fall prey to hope, fear, doubt, and greed — the Four Horsemen of trading ruin.

So how do you start? First you develop a business plan and a trading plan that reflect your goals and your personality. Then you set your working days and hours, and you accept that you'll close out every night. Both of these steps are covered in Chapter 2. As you think about the securities that you'll trade (Chapter 3) and how you may trade them (Part II), you'll also want to test your trading system (Chapter 16) to see how it may work in actual trading.

In other words, you prepare and have a plan. That's a basic strategy for any endeavor, whether you're running a marathon, building a new garage, or taking up day trading.

Committing to Trading As a Business

For many people, the attraction of day trading is that traders can very much control their own hours. Many markets, like foreign exchange, trade around the clock. With mobile trading apps, day trading seems like a way to make money while the baby is napping, during your lunch hour, or on just a few mornings a week in between golf games and woodworking.

That myth that day trading is an easy activity that you can do on the side actually does makes *some* traders very rich. Who are these traders? The professional traders who approach day trading as a business rather than a pastime. They make money when traders who are not fully committed lose their money.

But day trading is a business, and the best traders approach it as such. They have business plans for what they will trade, how they'll invest in their business, and how they'll protect their trading profits. Therefore, much of this book is about this business of trading: how to create a business plan (Chapter 2), how to set up your office (Chapter 12), tax considerations (Chapter 15), and performance evaluation (Chapter 16). If you catch a late-night infomercial about trading, the story will be about the ease and the excitement. But if you want that excitement to last, you have to make the commitment to doing trading as a business to which you dedicate your time and your energy.

Trading part-time: An okay idea if done right

Can you make money trading part-time? You can, and some people do. Successful part-time day traders approach trading as a part-time job, not as a little game to play when they have nothing else going on. A part-time trader may commit to trading three days a week or to closing out at noon instead of at the close of the market. A successful part-time trader still has a business plan, still sets limits, and still acts like any professional trader would, just for a smaller part of the day.

Part-time trading works best when you can set and maintain fixed business hours. Working on a fixed schedule helps your brain know when to go to work and concentrate on the market, because the habit is ingrained. The successful part-timer operates as a professional with fixed hours. Think of it this way: My son is a patient in a group pediatric practice that has some part-time doctors. These part-time doctors keep set hours and behave like the other doctors in the practice; the only difference is that they work fewer hours each week. They commit their attention to medicine when they are on the job, and patients only know about their part-time hours when it comes time to make an appointment. These doctors don't pop into the office and start giving shots during their lunch break from their "real" job, sneaking around so that their real boss doesn't find out.

If you want to be a part-time day trader, approach it the same way that a part-time doctor, part-time lawyer, or part-time accountant would approach work. Find hours that fit your schedule and commit to trading during them. Have a dedicated office space with high-speed Internet access and a computer that you use just for trading. If you have children at home, you may need to have child care during your trading hours. And if you have another job, set your trading hours away from your work time. Trading via cellphone during your morning commute is a really good way to lose a lot of money (not to mention your life if you try it while driving).

Trading as a hobby: A bad idea

Because of the excitement of day trading and the supposed ease of doing it, you may think that day trading makes a great hobby. On a boring Saturday afternoon, you could just spend a few hours trading in the forex market (foreign exchange) to make more money than if you spent those few hours playing video games! Right?

Uh, no.

Trading without a plan and without committing the time and energy to do it right is a route to losses. Professional traders are betting that plenty of suckers are out there, trading in just such a random way because that creates the losers that allow them to take profits in a zero-sum market.

The biggest mistake amateur traders make? Making a lot of money the first time trading and then assuming that all such successes will come as easily. That first success was almost definitely due to luck, and that luck can turn against a trader on a dime. If you make money your first time out, take a step back and see whether you can figure out why. Then test your strategy, using Chapter 16 as a guide, to see whether your strategy is a good one that you can use often.

Yes, I have two warnings in this section, and for good reason: Successful day traders commit to their business. Even then, most day traders fail in their first year. Brokerage firms, training services, and other traders have a vested interest in making trading seem like an easy activity that you can work into your life. But it's a job — a job that some people love, but a job nonetheless.

If you really love the excitement of the markets, you can find ways to invest on a hobbyist's schedule: You can spend your time doing fundamental research to find long-term investments (see Chapter 17 for information on that); you can look into alternative investments to help diversify your portfolio (head to Chapter 3); and you can trade with play money, either in demo accounts or in trading contests, to try trading without committing real money.

Defining the Principles of Successful Day Trading

Although you can day trade almost every asset with wild abandon, doing so probably isn't a good idea. Some traders spend their entire careers working with just one or two types of securities. This section covers the basics of success: working with just a few assets in one market, managing positions carefully, and concentrating on the work at hand.

Working with a small number of assets

Most day traders pick one or two markets and concentrate on those to the exclusion of all others. That way they can learn how the markets trade, how news affects prices, and how the other participants react to new information. Also, concentrating on just one or two markets helps a trader maintain focus.

And what do day traders trade? Chapter 3 has information on all of the different markets and how they work, but here's a quick summary, in no particular order, of the most popular assets with day traders right now:

- ✔ **Financial futures:** Futures contracts allow traders to profit from price changes in such market indexes as the S&P 500 or the Dow Jones Industrial Average. They give traders exposure to the prices at a much lower cost than buying all the stocks in the index individually. Of course, they tend to be more volatile than the indexes they track because they are based on expectations.

✔ **Forex:** *Forex,* short for *foreign exchange,* involves trading in currencies all over the world to profit from changes in exchange rates. Forex is the largest and most liquid market there is, and it's open for trading all day, every day. Traders like the huge number of opportunities. Because most price changes are small, they have to use *leverage* (borrowed money) to make a profit. The borrowings have to be repaid no matter what happens to the trade, which adds to the risk of forex.

✔ **Common stock and exchange-traded funds:** The entire business of day trading began in the stock market, and the stock market continues to be popular with day traders. They look for news on company performance and investor perception that affect stock prices, and they look to make money from those price changes. A similar asset is the exchange-traded fund, which trades like a stock but is based on a market index or strategy. The big drawback? Stock and ETF traders can get killed at tax time if they aren't careful. See Chapter 15 for more information.

Managing your positions

A key to successful trading is knowing how much you're going to trade and when you're going to get out of your position. Sure, day traders are always going to close out at the end of the day — or they wouldn't be day traders — but they also need to cut their losses and take their profits as they occur during the day. Specifically, they need to determine the size of the trade and the maximum profit or loss:

✔ **Determining what portion of their money they risk for any particular trade:** Traders rarely place all their money on one trade. That's a good way to lose it! Instead, they trade just some of their money, keeping the rest to make other trades as new opportunities in the market present themselves. If any one trade fails, the trader still has money to place new trades. Some traders divide their money into fixed proportions, and others determine how much money to trade based on the expected risk and expected return of the security they're trading. Careful money management helps a trader stay in the game longer, and the longer a trader stays in, the better the chance of making good money. Chapter 6 has more information on money-management strategies.

✔ **Protecting their funds by using *stop* and *limit orders:*** Stop and limit orders are placed with the brokerage firm and kick in whenever the security reaches a predetermined price level. If the security starts to fall in price more than the trader likes — *bam!* — it's sold, and no more losses will occur on that trade. The trader doesn't agonize over the decision or second-guess herself. Instead, she just moves on to the next trade, putting her money to work on a trade that's likely to be better.

Day traders make a lot of trades, and a lot of those trades are going to be losers. The key is to have more winners than losers. By limiting the amount of losses, the trader makes it easier for the gains to be big enough to generate more than enough money to make up for the losers.

Focusing your attention

Day traders are often undone by stress and emotion. Keeping a steady eye on what's happening in the market is hard when you're looking at screens all day and working alone. But as a trader, you have to be able to concentrate on the market and stick to your trading system, staying as calm and rational as possible.

Day traders who do well have support systems in place. They are able to close their positions and spend the rest of the day on other activities. They do something to get rid of their excess energy and clear their minds, such as running or yoga or meditation. They understand that their ability to maintain a clear mind when the market is open is crucial.

Traders sometimes think of the market itself, or everyone else who is trading, as the enemy. The real enemies are emotions: doubt, fear, greed, and hope. Those four feelings keep traders from concentrating on the market and sticking to their systems.

One of the frustrations of trading is that some days offer more opportunities to trade than you have time or money to trade. On these days, good trades get away from you because you simply don't have the resources to take advantage of every opportunity you see. That's why having a plan and concentrating on what works for you are so important.

Identifying the Personality Traits of Successful Day Traders

Successful traders are a special breed. They can be blunt and crude, because they act fast against a market that has absolutely no consideration for them. For all their rough exterior, they maintain strict discipline about how they approach their trading day and what they do during market hours.

The discipline begins with a plan for how to start the day, including reviews of news events and trading patterns. It includes keeping track of trades made during the day, to help the trader figure out what works and why. And it depends on cutting losses as they occur, reaping all profits that appear, and refining a set of trading rules so that tomorrow will be even better. No, this strategy isn't as much fun as just jumping in and placing orders, but it's more likely to lead to success.

Not everyone can be a day trader, nor should everyone try it. In this section, I cover some of the traits that the best day traders possess.

Independence

For the most part, day traders work by themselves. Computers and monitors are relatively inexpensive, high-speed Internet connectivity is easier to get, and many brokerage firms cater to the needs of traders who are working by themselves — all of which leaves the day trader at home, alone, stuck in a room with nothing but the computer screen for company. Being alone all day may be boring and make it hard to concentrate. Some people can't handle it.

But other traders thrive on being alone all day, because it brings out their best qualities. They know that their trading depends on them alone, not on anyone else. The trader has sole responsibility when something goes wrong, but he also gets to keep all the spoils. He can make his own decisions about what works and what doesn't, with no pesky boss or annoying corporate drone telling him what he needs to do today.

If the idea of being in charge of your own business and your own trading account is exciting, then day trading may be a good career option for you.

What if you want to trade but don't want to work by yourself? Consider going to work for a brokerage firm, a hedge fund, a mutual fund, or a commodities company. These businesses need traders to manage their own money, and they usually have large numbers of people working together on their trading desks to share ideas, cheer each other on, and give each other support when things go wrong.

No matter how independent you are, your trading will benefit if you have friends and family to offer you support and encouragement. That network can help you better manage the emotional aspects of trading. Besides, celebrating your success is more fun with someone else!

Quick-wittedness

Day trading is a game of minutes. An hour may as well be a decade when the markets are moving fast. And that means a day trader can't be deliberative or panicky. When it's time to buy or sell, it's time to buy or sell, period.

Many investors prefer to spend hours doing a careful study of a security and markets before committing money. Some of these people are enormously successful. Warren Buffett, the CEO of Berkshire Hathaway, amassed $54 billion from his careful investing style, money that he is giving to charity. But Buffett and people like him are not traders.

Traders have to have enough trust in their system and enough experience in the markets to act quickly when they see a buy or sell opportunity. Many brokerage firms offer their clients demonstration accounts or backtesting services that enable traders to work with their system before committing actual dollars, helping them learn to recognize market patterns that signal potential profits.

A trader with a great system who isn't quick on the mouse button has another option: automating trades. Many brokerage firms offer software that executes trades automatically whenever certain market conditions occur. For many traders, automatic trades are a perfect way to take the emotion out of a trading strategy. Others dislike this type of trading, because it takes some of the fun out of the job. And let's face it, successful traders find the whole process to be a good time.

Decisiveness

Day traders have to move quickly, so they also have to be able to make decisions quickly. You can't wait until tomorrow to see how the charts play out before committing capital. If you see an opportunity, you have to go with it. Now.

But what if the decision is a bad one? Well, of course some decisions are going to be bad. That's the risk of making any kind of an investment, and without risk, there is no return. Anyone playing around in the markets has to accept that.

But two good day-trading practices help limit the effects of making a bad decision. The first is the use of stop and limit orders, which automatically close out losing positions. The second is closing out all positions at the end of every day, which lets you start fresh the next day.

If you have some downside protection in place, you're more psychologically prepared to make the decisions you need to make in order to earn a profit. And if you're one of those people who has a hard time making a decision, day trading probably isn't right for you.

Seeing What Day Trading Is Not

So much mythology surrounds day trading: Day traders lose money. Day traders make money. Day traders are insane. Day traders are cold and rational. Day trading is easy. Day trading is a direct path to alcoholism and ruin.

In this section, I bust a few day trading myths. Someone has to do it, right? You find both good news and bad news in this section, so read it through to get some perspective on what, exactly, you can expect from day trading.

It's not investing

While swing traders hold positions for a few days, maybe even a few weeks, and investors hold their stakes for the long term, with some looking to hang onto their securities for decades and maybe even hand them down to their children, day traders never hold a position for more than a day.

Day trading is most definitely not investing. Day traders perform an important function to the capital markets because they force the price changes that bring the supply and demand of the market into balance. Day trading, however, doesn't create new sources of funding for companies and governments. It doesn't generate long-term growth.

Just because day trading isn't investing doesn't mean day traders don't have investments elsewhere. Many day traders withdraw their trading capital on a regular basis to put into investments, helping them build a long-term portfolio for their retirement or for other ventures they may want to take on. Still, because investing and trading have different mindsets, chances are the trader will have someone else manage this money.

It's not gambling

One of the biggest knocks on day trading is that it's just another form of gambling. And as everyone knows, or should know, in gambling, the odds always favor the house. That's not the case with day trading, however. Consider these points:

- ✔ **In day trading, the odds are even in many markets.** The options and futures markets, for example, are zero-sum markets with as many winners as losers, but those markets also include people looking to hedge risk and who thus have lower profit expectations than do day traders.

✔ **The stock market has the potential for more winning trades than losing trades, especially over the long run.** For this reason, the stock market isn't a zero-sum market, like options and futures markets. In the stock market, the odds are ever so slightly in the trader's favor.

In all markets, the prepared and disciplined trader can do better than the frantic, naïve trader. That's not the case when gambling, because no matter how prepared the gambler is, the casino has the upper hand.

People with gambling problems sometimes turn to day trading as a socially acceptable way to feed their addiction. If you know you have a gambling problem or suspect you are at risk, taking up day trading is probably not a good idea for you. Day traders who are closet gamblers tend to make bad trades and have trouble setting limits and closing out at the end of the day. They turn the odds against themselves. Chapter 4 has some information on the line between day trading and gambling.

It's not dangerous — if you use risk capital

A lot of day traders lose money, and some lose everything that they start with. Others don't lose all of their trading capital; they just decide that there are better uses of their time and better ways to make money. (For more on day trading success rates, head to the later section "Looking at Success Rates.")

A responsible trader works with *risk capital,* which is money that she can afford to lose. She uses stop and limit orders to minimize her losses, and she always closes out at the end of the day. She understands the risks and rewards of trading, and that keeps her sane.

Many day trading strategies rely on *leverage,* which is the use of borrowed money to increase potential returns. Leverage carries the risk of the trader losing more money than is in his account. However, brokerage firms, which don't want that to happen, will probably close a leveraged account that's in danger of going under. That's good, because it limits your potential loss.

It's not easy

Along with the relatively low rate of success, day trading is really stressful. Concentrating on the markets and knowing that real money is at stake takes a lot of energy. The profit amounts on any one trade are likely to be small, which means you have to be persistent and keep placing trades until the end of the day.

Some traders can't handle the stress. Some get bored. Some get frustrated. And some can't believe that they can make a living doing something that they love.

Looking at Success Rates

Given the participation of day traders in securities markets, researchers are always trying to figure out whether they make money. And the answers aren't good.

Yes, most day traders fail — about 80 percent in the first year, as I note earlier. But so do a large percentage of people who start new businesses or enter other occupations. That's why I've combed through several different reports and databases to show how well people do in other fields. (My sources are *Realty Times;* Barber, Lee, Liu, and Odean; American College of Sports Medicine; ACT; Ohio State University; and the National Center for Education Statistics.)

Field	*First-Year Failure Rate*
Real estate sales	86%
Day trading	80%
Training for a marathon	70%
College enrollment	33%
Restaurants	26%
Teaching	13%

If you understand the risks and keep them in perspective, you'll be better able to handle the slings and arrows of misfortune on the way to your goal.

Day trading is difficult, but it's not impossible. You can improve your chances of success by taking the time to prepare and by having enough money to fund your initial trading account. During the first year, you'll want to handle trading losses and still be able to pay your rent and buy your groceries. Knowing that you can cover your basic expenses will give you more confidence, and that can help your performance.

Negative numbers: The data on day-trading success rates

Here I review some of the literature to show you the current state of day trading success rates. Note that they are low. Few people who take up day trading succeed, in part because few people who take it up are prepared. And even many of the prepared traders fail. (Much of the research covers performance in the late 1990s, when day trading became wildly popular. It grew along with the commercial Internet, and it fell out of favor when the Internet bubble burst. The data is old, but it's the best we have.)

✔ *Do Individual Day Traders Make Money? Evidence from Taiwan:* This paper, written in 2004 by Brad Barber, Yi-Tsung Lee, Yu-Jane Liu, and Terrance Odean (and available at `http://faculty.haas.berkeley. edu/odean/papers/Day%20 Traders/Day%20Trade%20040330. pdf`) found that only 20 percent of day traders in Taiwan tracked between 1995 and 1999 made money in any six-month period, after considering transaction costs. Median profits, net of costs, were $4,200 (USD) for any six-month period, although the best traders showed semi-annual profits of $33,000. The study also found that those who placed the most trades made the most money, possibly because they were the most experienced traders in the group. This paper is one of the most cited on the subject because it remains the gold standard.

✔ *Report of the Day Trading Project Group:* In 1999, the North American Securities Administrators Association, which represents state and provincial securities regulators in the United States, Canada, and Mexico, researched day trading so that its members could provide appropriate oversight. The report does not include performance data. However, it cites several cases in which brokerage firms were sanctioned by regulators for misrepresenting their clients' performance numbers, including one firm that had no clients with profits.

✔ *Trading Profits of SOES Bandits:* Paul Schultz and Jeffrey Harris looked into the profits made by the so-called *SOES bandits,* day traders who took advantage of loopholes that existed in NASDAQ's Small Order Entry System in the 1990s. These people were the first day traders. Did they make money? The authors looked at a few weeks of trade data from two different firms. What they found was that about a third of all round-trip trades (buying and then later selling the same security) lost money before commissions. Only a quarter of the round-trip trades had a profit of $250 or more before commissions. The 69 traders in the study made anywhere from one to 312 round-trip trades per week. They had an average weekly profit after commission of $1,690; however, almost half of the traders, 34 of them, lost money in an average week. You can see the abstract at `http:// papers.ssrn.com/sol3/papers. cfm?abstract_id=137949`. The full article is available through many libraries.

Although day trading is tough, many day traders can't imagine doing anything else. The simple fact is that a lot of occupations are difficult ways to make a living, and yet they are right for some people. Every career has its advantages and disadvantages, and day trading is no different.

When you finish this book, you should have a good sense of whether or not day trading is right for you. If you realize that it's the career you have been searching for, you can find lots of good ideas in the coming chapters for how to set up your day-trading business and plenty of advice on how to increase your chances of success.

If you find that maybe day trading isn't right for you, I hope you get some ideas that can help you manage your long-term investments better. After all, the attention to price movements, timing, and risk that is critical to a day trader's success can help any investor improve his returns. What's not to like about that?

Chapter 2

Planning to Succeed As a Day Trader

*D*ay trading is sometimes presented as a profitable hobby. Anyone who buys a day-trading DVD course via infomercial can make money easily in just a few hours a week, right? Well, no. Day trading is a job. It can be a full-time job or a part-time job, but it requires the same commitment to working regular hours and the same dedication to learning a craft and honing skills as any other job.

The best traders have plans for their business and for their trades. They know in advance how they want to trade and what they expect to do when they face the market. They may, at times, find themselves deviating from their plans, due to luck or circumstance or changing markets, but in those cases, they understand why they're trying something else.

Trading comes in many flavors, and many of those who call themselves day traders are actually doing other things with their money. If you know in advance what you want to do, not only will you be less likely to panic or follow fads, but you'll also be in a better position to take advantage of opportunities in a way that suits your personality, trading skills, and goals. And that's why this entire chapter is devoted to planning.

Failing to plan is planning to fail. And if you can't remember that right now, don't worry. I repeat it several times in this book.

Planning Your Trading Business

The day trader is an entrepreneur who has started a small business that trades in securities in hopes of making a return. You can get your business off to a good start if you have a plan for what you want to do and how you're going to do it. With a plan, you know what your goals are and what you need to do to achieve them.

You can find a lot of sample business plans in books and on the Internet, but most of them are not appropriate for a trader. A typical business plan is designed to not only guide the business but also to attract outside financing. Unless you're going to take in partners or borrow money from an outside source, your day trading business plan is only for you. No executive summary and no pages of projections needed.

So what do you need instead? How about a list of your goals and a plan for what you'll trade, what your hours will be, what equipment you'll need, and how much to invest in the business? The following sections have the details.

Setting your goals

The first thing you need in your plan is a list of your goals, both short term and long term. Here is a sample list of key questions to get you started:

- Where do you want to be with your career and your life in the next three months, six months, nine months, year, three years, five years, and ten years?

- How many days a year do you want to trade?

- What do you need to know to trade better?

- How much do you want to make?

- What will you do with your profits?

- How will you reward yourself when you hit your goals?

Be as specific as possible when you think about what you want to do with your trading business and don't worry if your business goals overlap with your personal goals. When you are in business for yourself, the two often mix.

You may be tempted to say, "I want to make as much money as I possibly can," and forget the rest, but "as much as I can" isn't a quantifiable goal. If you don't know that you've reached your goal, how can you go on to set new ones? And if you don't meet your goal, how will you know how to make changes?

Finding volatility

You can day trade so many different securities and derivatives! Sure, you want to trade anything that makes money for you, but what on earth is that? Each market has its own nuances, so if you flit from futures to forex (foreign exchange), you may be courting disaster. But if you know what markets you want to trade, you have a better sense of what research services you need, what ongoing training you may want to consider, and how to evaluate your performance.

Chapter 3 covers different asset classes in great detail and discusses how you may use them. For now, the little cheat sheet in Table 2-1 lists asset classes that are most popular with day traders. Think about your chosen markets in the same way: What do you want to trade, where will you trade it, what is the risk and return, and what are some of the characteristics that make this market attractive to you?

Table 2-1	**Popular Things for Day Traders to Trade**		
Item	*Main Exchange*	*Risk/Reward*	*Characteristics*
Stock index futures	CME	Zero sum/ leverage	Benefits from movements of broad markets
Treasury bond futures	CBT	Zero sum/ leverage	Best way for day traders to play the bond market
Foreign exchange	OTC	Zero sum/ leverage	Markets open all day, every day
Corn	CBT	Zero sum/ leverage	An agricultural market liquid enough for day traders
Large-cap stocks	NYSE, NASDAQ	Upward bias	Good stocks for day trading; large and volatile
Exchange-traded funds	NYSE, NASDAQ	Depends on the fund's structure	Offer plays on indices and different market strategies

Key: CME = Chicago Mercantile Exchange, CBT = Chicago Board of Trade (a subsidiary of the CME Group), OTC = Over the counter, NYSE = New York Stock Exchange

What do *zero sum, leverage,* and *upward bias* mean? Well, *zero sum* means that for every winner, there is a loser. The market has no net gain. *Leverage* is the use of borrowed money, which increases potential return as well as risk. *Upward bias* means that, in the long run, the market is expected to increase in price, but that doesn't mean it will go up on any given day that you're trading.

The characteristics of the different markets and assets affect both your business plan and your trading plan. The business plan should include information on what you'll trade and why, as well as what you hope to learn to trade in the future. The trading plan looks at what you want to trade each day and why so that you can channel your efforts.

Many day traders work in several different markets, depending on their temperament and trading conditions, but successful traders have narrowed the field down to the few markets where they want to concentrate their efforts. Start slowly, working just one or two different securities, and consider adding new markets as your experience and trading capital grows.

Fixing hours, vacation, and sick leave

The markets are open more or less continuously. Although many exchanges have set trading hours, you can find traders working after hours who are willing to sell if you want to buy. Some markets, such as foreign exchange, take only the briefest of breaks over the course of a week, which gives day traders incredible flexibility. No matter what hours and what days are best for you to trade, you can find something that works for you. If you're sharpest in the evenings, for example, you may be better off trading Asian currencies, because those markets are active when you are. Of course, an always-open market can be a disadvantage, because no one is setting limits for you. Few markets are great places to trade every hour of every day.

If you want to, you can trade almost all the time. But you probably don't want to. To keep your sanity, maintain your perspective, and have a life outside of your trading, you should set regular hours and stick to them. In your business plan, determine when you're going to trade, how often you're going to take a vacation, how many sick days you'll give yourself, and how you'll know to take a day off. One of the joys of self-employment is that you can take time off when you need to, so give yourself that little perk in your business plan.

Trading is a stressful business. You need to take time off to clear your head, and you'll probably find that working while sick is a sure-fire route to losses. Build in some sick and vacation time — and read Chapter 14 for more information on how to manage the stress of the markets.

Getting yourself set up

Part of your business plan should cover where you work and what equipment you need. (Chapter 12 has some ideas on that subject.) What can you afford now, and what is on your wish list? Do you have enough computing equipment, the right Internet connection, and a working filing system? Determining what you have and how you'll get what you need is part of your plan for getting your business underway, so put some thought into your infrastructure.

And yes, setting up business space and investing in equipment are important. You don't want to lose a day of trading because your computer crashes, nor do you want to be stuck with an open position because your Internet service provider has a temporary outage. And you certainly don't want to lose your concentration because you're trying to work in the family room while other members of your household are playing video games.

Investing in your business

You won't have the time and money to do everything you want to do in your trading business, so part of your business plan should include a list of things that you want to add over time. A key part of investing in your business is continuous improvement: No matter how good a trader you are now, you can always be better. Furthermore, the markets are always changing. New products come to market, new trading regulations are passed, and new technologies appear. You need to continuously absorb new things, and part of your business plan should consider that. Ask yourself

- ✔ What percentage of your time and trade gains will go into expanding your knowledge of trading?

- ✔ Do you want to gain this additional knowledge by taking seminars or by allocating the time to simulation test (head to Chapter 16 for more on that)?

- ✔ What upgrades will you make to your trading equipment? How about to your programming capabilities?

- ✔ How are you going to set yourself up to stay in trading for the long haul?

It takes money to make money — another cliché. This maxim doesn't mean, however, that you should spend money willy-nilly on any nifty gadget or fancy video seminar that comes your way. Instead, it means that an ongoing, thoughtful investment in your trading business will pay off in a greater likelihood of long-run success.

Evaluating and revising your plan

One component of your business plan should be a plan for revising it. Things are going to change. Since the first edition of this book came out, exchanges have merged, the market has crashed, and high-frequency trading has become the norm. You may be more or less successful than you hope, market conditions may change on you, and you may simply find out more about how you trade best. So set a plan for updating your business plan to reflect where you are and where you want to be as you go along. At least once a year, and more often if you feel the need for a change, go through your business plan and revise it to reflect where you are now. What are your new goals? What are your new investment plans? What are you doing right, and what needs to change?

Business plans are living documents. Use your plan to run your trading business; as your business runs, use the results to update your plan. You can keep the old ones around to show you how much progress you have made, if you're so inclined.

A sample business plan

Not sure what should be in a business plan? Here's a sample to get you thinking about how to plan your trading business.

Where I Am Now

I am about to start a career as a day trader. I have $50,000 in capital that I can risk without affecting my livelihood. I will rely on my spouse's job to cover our family spending needs and our health insurance. This trading account will be used to meet our long-term goals: paying off the mortgage, sending the children to college, paying for our retirement, and ultimately buying a vacation house in the mountains.

This business plan covers what I need to get started.

My Business Goals

In three months, I will have spent $5,000 of my capital on a functional office and will have a tested trading strategy that works well in simulation.

In six months, I will be trading daily. I will have lost no more than $5,000 of my trading capital.

In nine months, I will be trading daily, and I will have more winning trades than losing trades.

In a year, I will have gained 10 percent on my account. I will withdraw $1,000 to pay toward our mortgage and another $1,000 toward an ergonomic chair and other office equipment upgrades. I will have learned to program, mastered my first trading system, and will be testing a second one in order to expand my trading opportunities.

In three years, my trading account will have $150,000 in it from my trading successes, after making investments in my business and paying an additional $10,000 in principal on the mortgage. I will be trading three different systems with satisfactory success.

In five years, I will have $300,000 in my trading account. I will have made enough money to have paid off our mortgage, after making regular payments on principal and interest every month, paying $10,000 in year three, and paying off the rest with the profits that I expect to earn between years three and five. I will be known as a successful trader.

In ten years, I will have a second house, and I will continue my record of trading success. I will take $100,000 out of my trading account to cover college tuition.

Markets Traded

My primary trading strategy will involve momentum trades on the E-Mini S&P 500 and E-Mini NASDAQ futures contracts traded on the Chicago Mercantile Exchange. I will put no more than 10 percent of my capital into any one trade, and I will close out positions each night.

I am interested in news-driven *swing trading* (holding for short periods of time but longer than a day) in large technology companies, so I will research and test strategies with those. I am also interested in trading Asian currencies, so I will make time to learn more about those markets and determine whether I can trade them effectively during my preferred trading hours.

Trading Hours and Days

Because my primary strategy is equity driven, I will trade only while the equity markets are open, from 9:30 a.m. until 4:00 p.m. Monday through Friday. I will spend an hour before the markets open researching current trends and news events so that I know what people will be looking for that day. I will spend an hour after the market closes doing paperwork and reviewing the day's trades.

I will take off three full weeks for vacation: the week of my children's spring break, a week in August for a family vacation, and the last week of December. I will also take off any day that I am ill so that I can maintain my health and my concentration.

My Business Setup

I work from a home office. I use my startup funds to purchase two monitors working off of one computer, with a second clone computer on hand in case something goes wrong. I have cable Internet access with a mobile application on my phone as a backup. I have a wireless router so that I can check my e-mail and instant messages through a third computer, a laptop, instead of through my trading computer.

I have an account with a full-service online brokerage firm that can offer me the necessary research services. I also subscribe to *Investor's Business Daily* and *The Wall Street Journal,* which I read each morning to help me gauge sentiment.

I track my trades on a paper form that I collect in ring binders. I collect my other paperwork in ring binders that I keep on the shelf in my office.

Investing in My Business

To stay successful in the long run, I need to keep my skills sharp. To do this, I will read one book on trading psychology or a successful trader's memoir each month. I will also work on simulation trading for swing trading in technology stocks because I plan to add that to my trading system.

As my trade profits grow, I will invest some of them in trying new trading techniques, knowing that I may have short-term losses until I understand a market better. I will spend one day at the end of each quarter on backtesting and simulation of new strategies.

My wish list includes a more comfortable chair for my office.

Evaluating My Business Plan

Before each vacation, I will read over this business plan. I will use the time away from the markets to think about what changes I need to make in it and will revise the plan upon my return.

Planning Your Trades

A good trader has a plan. She knows what she wants to trade and how to trade it. She knows what her limits are before she places the order. She's not afraid to take a loss now in order to prevent a bigger loss in the future, and she's willing to sit out the market if nothing is happening that day. Her plan gives her the discipline to protect her capital so that she has money in her account when the opportunities present themselves.

In this section, I cover the components of trade planning. When you start trading, you'll probably write notes each day to set up a trading plan that covers what you expect for the day, what trades you hope to make, and what your profit goals and loss limit are. As you develop experience, trade planning may become innate. You develop the discipline to trade according to plan without needing to write it all down — although you may find it useful to tape a list of the day's expected announcements to your monitor.

Like a business plan, a trading plan is flexible. The markets don't know what you've planned, and you'll probably end up deviating on more than one occasion. The key thing is knowing *why* you deviated: Was it because of the information that you saw when you were looking at your screen, or was it because you became panicky?

What do you want to trade?

The first step in your trading plan should also be addressed in your business plan: What do you want to trade? Many traders work in more than one market, and each market is a little different. Some trade different products simultaneously, whereas others choose one for the day and work only on that.

You need to figure out which markets give you the best chance of getting a profit that day, and this changes regularly. Some days, no trades will be good for you in one market, and you'll be better off sitting out. If you're too antsy to sit out, then find another market to keep you busy so that you don't trade just to stay awake. (Of course, many traders report that the big money opportunities are in the slower, less glamorous markets.)

As a day trader, you're self-employed. You don't answer to a boss, and you don't have to trade on any particular day if you don't want to. So if you have a headache, if no good trades are available to you, or if recent losses have gotten you down, take the day off and do something fun.

How do you want to trade?

Figuring out how to trade an asset involves a lot of considerations: What is your mood today? What will other traders be reacting to today? How much risk do you want to take? How much money do you want to commit? These considerations represent the nitty-gritty stage of trade planning that can help you manage your market day better.

Starting the day with a morning review

Before you start trading, take some time to determine where your head is relative to the market. Is today a day that you can concentrate? Are things happening in your life that may distract you, are you coming down with the flu, or were you out too late last night? Or are you raring to go, ready to take on whatever the day brings? Your mindset should influence how aggressively you want to trade and how much risk you want to take. You have to pay attention to do well in the markets, but you also have to know when to hang back during the day's activities. For example, many traders find that their strategies work best at certain times of the day, such as at the open or before major news announcements.

After you determine your own mindset, think about what people will be reacting to that day. Go through the newspapers and check the online news-wires to gather information. Then figure out the answers to these questions:

✔ Are big news announcements scheduled for today? At what time? Do you want to trade ahead of the news, or do you want to wait and see what the market does?

✔ Did something happen overnight? Will that event affect trading on the open, or is it already in the markets? Do you want to trade on the open or wait?

✔ What are the other people — those who trade the same future, commodity, stock, or currency that you do — worried about today? How are they likely to respond? Do you want to go with the market or strike a contrary position?

Drawing up a sample order

After you have a sense of how you're going to tackle the day, determine how much you're going to trade. Following are the key considerations:

✔ **Do you want to be long or short?** That is, do you want to bet that the asset you are trading is going up in price or down?

✔ **Do you want to borrow money?** If so, how much? Borrowing — also known as *margin* or *leverage* — increases your potential return as well as your risk. (I discuss margin, leverage, and short selling in Chapter 9.)

Some contracts, such as futures, have built-in leverage. As soon as you decide to trade them, you're borrowing money.

✔ **How much money do you want to trade?** Think about this both in dollars and as a percentage of your total account size. (I discuss money management in detail in Chapter 6.)

With these items detailed, you're in good shape to get started for the day.

Figuring out when to buy and when to sell

After you get insight into what the day may be like and how much money you want to allocate to the markets, your next step is to figure out when you'll buy and when you'll sell. Ah, but if deciding when to buy and sell were easy, do you think I'd be revising a book on day trading? No. I'd be too busy taking private surfing lessons in front of my beachfront mansion on Maui.

The very best traders aren't selling trading advice, because they're already retired. Everyone else is figuring it out as they go along, with varying degrees of success.

Many traders rely on *technical analysis,* which involves looking at patterns in charts of the price and volume changes (I discuss technical analysis in Chapter 7). Other traders look at news and price information as the market changes rather than looking at price patterns (you can find a discussion of this in Chapter 8). Still others care only about very short-term price discrepancies (covered in Chapter 10). But the most important thing, no matter what approach you prefer, is that you *backtest* and simulate your trading before you commit real dollars. That way, you have a better sense of how you'll react in real market conditions. You can find backtesting in Chapter 16.

Setting profit goals

When you trade, you want to have a realistic idea how much money you can make. What's a fair profit? Do you want to ride a winning position until the end of the day, or do you want to get out quickly after you make enough money to compensate for your risk? This question has no one single answer because so much depends on market conditions and your trading style. In this section are some guidelines that can help you determine what's best for you.

Your profit goals can be sliced and diced a few different ways. The first is the *gain per trade* on both a percentage basis and an absolute basis. The second is the *gain per day* on both a percentage basis and an absolute basis. What do you have to do to reach these goals? How many successful trades will you have to make? Do you have the capital to do that? And what is right for the trade you are making right now, regardless of what your longer-term goals are?

No one ever lost money taking a profit, as the cliché goes. (The trading business is rife with clichés, if you haven't noticed.) The newer you are to day trading, the more sense it makes to be conservative. Close your positions and end your day when you reach a target profit and then make note of what happens afterward. Can you afford to hold on to your positions longer to make a greater profit?

The language of money

Profits are discussed differently in different markets, and you may as well have the right lingo when you write your plan:

✔ **Pennies:** Stocks trade in decimal form, so each price movement is worth at least a penny — one cent. It's an obvious way to measure a profit.

✔ **Pips:** A *pip* is the smallest unit of currency that can be traded. In foreign exchange markets (forex), a pip is generally equal to one one-hundredth of a cent. If the value of the euro moves from $1.2934 to $1.2935, it has moved a pip.

   Note: Do not confuse a pip in the forex market with an investment scheme known as *PIP*, sometimes called People in Profit or Pure Investor. (The fraud also operates as *HYIP*, for High Yield Investment Program.) PIP has been promoted as a trading system with a guaranteed daily return, but it's really a pyramid scheme that takes money from participants and returns little or nothing. You can get more information from the SEC's website, `http://sec.gov/divisions/enforce/primebank.shtml`.

✔ **Points:** A *point* is a single percentage. A penny is a point, as is a 1 percent change in a bond price. A related number, a *basis point,* is a percent of a percent, or 0.0001.

✔ **Teenies:** Many securities, especially bonds and derivatives on them, trade in increments of ⅛ of a dollar. Half of an eighth is a sixteenth, also known as a *teeny.*

✔ **Ticks:** A *tick* is the smallest trading increment in a futures contract. It varies from product to product. How much it works out to be depends on the contract structure. For the CME Group's E-Mini S&P 500 contract, a tick is equal to $12.50, calculated as a 0.25 change in the underlying S&P 500 index multiplied by $50 multiplier. A tick on an E-Mini soybean contract is $1.25, calculated as ⅛ cent on a bushel of soybeans in a contract covering 1,000 bushels. You can get information on the tick size of contracts that interest you on the website of the offering exchange (exchanges are listed in Chapter 3).

Setting limits on your trades

Setting a *loss limit* along with a profit goal is a good idea. For example, many futures traders have a rule to risk two ticks in pursuit of three ticks. That means that they'll sell a position as soon as it loses two ticks in value and as soon as it gains three ticks in value. And for anything in between? Well, they close out their positions at the end of the day, so whatever happens happens.

Even traders who do not have a rule like that often set a limit on how much they'll lose per trade. Other traders use computer programs to guide their buys and their sells, so they sell their positions automatically. Brokers make setting limits easy by giving customers the choice of a stop order or a limit order to protect their positions.

You want to limit your loss per trade *as well as* your loss per day. If today is not a good one, close up shop, take a break, and come back fresh tomorrow.

Stop orders

A *stop order* is an order to buy or sell a security as soon as a security moves beyond the current market price. A *stop buy* order is set above the current market price, and it is used to manage a short position. A *stop sell* order is set at a price below where the market is now, and it is used to protect a profit or limit a loss on a security that you already own. If you want to make sure you sell a block of stock when it falls below $30 per share, for example, you can enter a stop order at $30 (telling your broker "Sell Stop 30"). As soon as the stock hits or goes below $30, the broker sells it, even if the price goes to $29 or $31 before all the stock is sold. This is often known as a *stop loss* order.

A version of a stop, known as a *trailing stop,* is used to help protect a profit. You can enter a trailing stop order at the current market with a stop loss price below the current market price. It would be set to trail, or automatically increase, as the stock price does. If you bought a block of stock at $30 with a trailing stop of $5, for example, the stop would kick in at $25. But if your trade was a good one and the stock went from $30 to $35, the stop would trail with it and rise to $30, a price $5 below the current market value.

Limit orders

A *limit order* is an order to buy or sell a security at a specific price or better: lower than the current price for the buy order (because you want to buy low, naturally), higher than the specific price for a sell order (because you want to sell high).

If you want to make sure you sell a block of stock when it's at $30 per share, for example, you can enter a limit order at $30 (telling your broker, "Sell Limit 30"). As soon as the stock hits $30, the broker sells it, continuing to place the order as long as the price stays at $30 or higher. If the price goes even a penny below $30, the limit is no longer enforced, and the broker stops selling your position. After all, no buyers are going to want to pay an above-market price just so you can get your order completed!

Stop-limit orders

A *stop-limit* order is a combination of a stop order and a limit order. It tells the broker to buy or sell at a specific price or better but only after the price passes a given stop price. If, for example, you want to make sure you sell a block of stock when it falls below $30 per share but you also want to make sure you sell it only when you'd have a loss, you can enter a stop order at $30 with a limit of $29 (telling your broker, "Sell 30 Limit 29"). As soon as the stock hits $30, the broker sells it as long as the price stays above $29. If it goes below $29, the broker stops selling. Stop-limit orders help you get out without maximizing your losses; the danger, of course, is that the stock goes to $6 and you could have gotten out at $28 without the stop-limit order.

Are you confused? Well, the differences may be confusing, but understanding them is important to helping you manage your risks. That's why Table 2-2 gives you a handy breakout of the different types of orders.

Table 2-2	Different Types of Orders		
Buy Orders			
	Stop Order	**Limit Order**	**Stop-Limit Order**
Order instructions	Buy Stop 30	Buy Limit 30	Buy Stop 30 Limit 31
Market Price ($)	**Action after the stock hits $30**		
28.50	Nothing	Buy	Buy
29.00	Nothing	Buy	Buy
29.50	Nothing	Buy	Buy
30.00	Buy	Buy	Buy
30.50	Buy	Nothing	Buy
31.00	Buy	Nothing	Nothing
31.50	Buy	Nothing	Nothing
Sell Orders			
	Stop Order	**Limit Order**	**Stop-Limit Order**
Order Instructions	Sell Stop 30	Sell Limit 30	Sell Stop 30 Limit 29
Market Price ($)	**Action after the stock hits $30**		
28.50	Sell	Nothing	Nothing
29.00	Sell	Nothing	Sell

(continued)

Table 2-2 (continued)

Market Price ($)	Action after the stock hits $30		
29.50	Sell	Nothing	Sell
30.00	Sell	Sell	Sell
30.50	Nothing	Sell	Nothing
31.00	Nothing	Sell	Nothing
31.50	Nothing	Sell	Nothing

Order cancels other

Also known as *one cancels other* or OCO, an *order cancels other* order is used with a limit and a stop-loss to set a trading bracket in a volatile market. The limit sets an automatic exit point when your position hits your price target, and the stop-loss kicks in if your trade moves against you in order to limit your losses. The broker will execute only the relevant order, cancelling the other order when that happens. If not, the other half of the order will be hanging out, waiting to be executed, causing you headaches.

Order sends other

Depending on who you talk to, OSO stands for *order sends order, order sends other,* or *one sends other.* They all mean the same thing: When one order is executed, another order is automatically entered into the system — and not a moment before. You use an OSO to enter a limit order or a stop-loss order as soon as your order to open a long or short position is executed.

What if the trade goes wrong?

No matter how in tune you feel with the market, no matter how good your track record, and no matter how disciplined you are with setting stops, stuff is going to happen. Just as you can make more money than you plan to, you can also *lose* a lot more. If you day trade, you have to accept that you're going to have some really bad days.

So what do you do? You suck it up, take the loss, and get on with your life. Yes, the market may have blown past your stops. That happens sometimes, and it's hard to watch real dollars disappear into someone else's account, someone you will never know. Still, close your position and just remember that tomorrow is another day with another chance to do better.

A sample trading plan

A trading plan may only be good for a short time, but having an idea of what to expect in the market and how you'll react goes a long way toward keeping trading discipline, which improves your likelihood of long-run profits. What does such a plan look like? Well, here's a sample to get you started.

What I'm Trading Today

Today I'll be trading the E-Mini S&P 500 futures. They closed down yesterday, but I'm expecting an uptick in the market today as companies report good earnings, so I am going to trade on the long side. My plan is to start the day buying two contracts with stop orders to sell if they decline more than three ticks each. These contracts will remain open until the end of the day unless the stop is reached. I will add a third contract if the market shows momentum in the morning and a fourth contract if it shows momentum in the afternoon. These two additional contracts can be long or short, depending on the market direction, although it is unlikely that the purchasing manager or home sales surveys will have a large effect on the market's direction. I will close all positions at the end of the day, if not sooner.

Because the margin on each contract is $3,500, my maximum exposure today will be approximately 28 percent of my total account, with no contract accounting for more than 7 percent of my account.

Today's Expected News Announcements

Before the open: Earnings announcements from ADM (expect $0.62), PG (expect $0.74)

10:00 a.m.: ISM Index — survey of purchasing managers — market expects 51.0

10:00 a.m.: Pending Home Sales — market expects up 0.5 percent

After the close: Earnings announcements from AAPL (expect $8.27), MET (expect $1.29)

5:00 p.m.: Auto Sales — market expects 5.1m

5:00 p.m.: Truck Sales — market expects 7.2m

My Profit and Loss Goals for the Day

My profit goal is five ticks or $62.50 per contract traded for a target of $250 if I acquire my planned maximum of four contracts, but I plan to ride my profits until the end of the day. If all four contracts decline in value, I will close when they fall three ticks apiece, for a maximum loss of $37.50 per contract or $150 for the day.

Tip: Set up a basic form or spreadsheet with all this information so that it's easy to fill out each morning. It might look like this:

What I'm trading today:

Assets: _____

Leverage: _____

Limits: _____

Expected news announcements:

Time: _____ Item: _____

Time: _____ Item: _____

Time: _____ Item: _____

Time: _____ Item: _____

Profit and Loss Goals: _____

_____

Don't hold in hopes of making up a loss. The market doesn't know what you own and will not reward your loyalty and best hopes.

After you take the loss and clear your head, see whether you can learn something for next time. Sometimes a loss can teach you valuable lessons that make you a smarter, more disciplined trader in the long run.

Closing Out Your Position

By definition, day traders only hold their investment positions for a single day. Closing out at the end of the day is important for a few reasons:

- Closing out daily reduces your risk of something happening overnight.

- Margin rates — the interest rates paid on money borrowed for trading — are low and in some cases zero for day traders, but the rates go up on overnight balances.

- Good trade discipline is what can keep you from making expensive mistakes.

But like all rules, the single-day rule can be broken and probably should be broken sometimes. In this section, I cover a few longer-term trading strategies that you may want to add to your trading business on occasion.

Swing trading: Holding for days

Swing trading involves holding a position for several days. Some swing traders hold overnight, while others hold for days or even months. The longer time period gives more time for a position to work out, which is especially important if the position is based on news events or if it requires taking a position contrary to the current market sentiment. Although swing trading gives traders more options for making a profit, it carries some risks because the position can turn against you while you are away from the markets.

A tradeoff always exists between risk and return. When you take more risk, you do so in the hopes of getting a greater return. But when you look for a way to increase return, remember that you have to take on more risk to do it.

Swing trading requires paying attention to some basic fundamentals and news flow. (Fundamental research is discussed in Chapter 7.) It's also a good choice for people who have the discipline to go to bed at night instead of waiting up and watching their position in hopes that nothing goes wrong.

Position trading: Holding for weeks

A *position trader* holds a stake in a stock or a commodity for several weeks and possibly even for months. This person is attracted to the short-term price opportunities, but he also believes that he can make more money holding the stake for a long enough period of time to see business fundamentals play out. Position trading increases the risk and the potential return because a lot more can happen over months than minutes.

Investing: Holding for months or years

An *investor* is not a trader. Investors do careful research and buy a stake in an asset in the hopes of building a profit over the long term. It's not unusual for investors to hold assets for decades, although good ones sell quickly if they realize that they've made a mistake or if the story changes. (They want to cut their losses early, just as any good trader should.)

Investors are concerned about the prospects of the underlying business. Will it make money? Will it pay off its debts? Will it hold its value? They view short-term price fluctuations as noise rather than as profit opportunities.

Many traders pull out some of their profits to invest for the long term (or to give to someone else, such as a mutual-fund manager or hedge fund, to invest). Doing so is a way of building financial security in the pursuit of longer goals. This money is usually kept separate from the trading account.

Maxims and Clichés That Guide and Mislead Traders

In this chapter, I cover a few of the many maxims traders use to think about their trading, such as

- The stock doesn't know you own it.
- Failing to plan is planning to fail.
- Your first loss is your best loss.

A lot more are out there.

Clichés are useful shorthand for important rules that can help you plan your trading. But they can also mislead you because some are really obvious — too obvious to act on effectively. Yes, everyone knows that you make money by buying low and selling high, but how do you tell what low is and high is? Here's a run-through of some clichés that you'll come across in your trading career, along with my take on what they mean.

Pigs get fat, hogs get slaughtered

Trading is pure capitalism, and people do it for one primary reason: to make money. Sure, a ton of economic benefits come from having well-functioning capital markets, such as better price prediction, risk management, and capital formation. But a day trader just wants to make money.

Get too greedy, however, and you're likely to get stupid. You start taking too much risk, deviating too much from your strategy, and getting careless about dealing with your losses. Good traders know when it's time to take a profit and move on to the next trade.

This maxim is one of those obvious but tough-to-follow ones. After all, when do you cross the line from being a happy little piggy to a big fat greedy hog that's about to be turned into a pork belly? Just know that if you're deviating from your trading plan because things are going so great, you may be headed for some trouble.

Here's a cliché that's related to "Pigs get fat, hogs get slaughtered": "Bears get fat, bulls get fat, and hogs get slaughtered." In other words, a savvy trader can make money whether the market is up or down, but a greedy trader runs into trouble.

In a bear market, the money returns to its rightful owners

A *bull* market is one that charges ahead; a *bear* market is one that does poorly. Many people erroneously think of themselves as trading geniuses because they make money when the entire market is going up. Making money by day trading was easy with Internet stocks in 1999, but it wasn't so easy in 2000 when the bubble burst. And when the markets turn negative, those people who really understand trading and who know how to manage risk are able to stay in until things get better, possibly even making nice profits along the way.

The corollary cliché for "In a bear market, the money returns to its rightful owners," is "Don't confuse brains with a bull market." When things are going well, watch out for overconfidence. It may be time to update your business and trading plans, but it's not to time cast them aside.

The trend is your friend

When you day trade, you need to make money fast. You do not have the luxury of waiting for your unique, contrary theory to play out. An investor may be buying a stock in the hopes of holding it for decades, but a trader needs things to work now.

Given the short-term nature of the market, short-term sentiment is going to trump long-term fundamentals. People trading today may be wrong about the direction of foreign exchange, interest rates, or stock prices, but if you are closing out your positions tonight, you need to work with the information in the market *today*. In the short run, traders who fight the market lose money.

There are two problems with the maxim "The trend is your friend." The first is that by the time you identify a trend, it may be over. Second, sometimes, going against the herd makes sense because you can collect when everyone else realizes their mistake. In such a situation, the psychology of trading comes into play. Are you a good enough judge of human behavior to know when the trend is right and when it's not?

Buy the rumor, sell the news

Markets react to information. That's ultimately what drives supply and demand. Although the market tends to react quickly to information, it can overreact, too. Lots of gossip gets traded in the markets as everyone looks to get the information they need to gain an advantage. And despite such things as confidentiality agreements and insider-trading laws, many rumors turn out to be true.

These rumors are often attached to such news events as corporate earnings. For whatever reason — good news, analyst research, a popular product — traders may believe, for example, that the company will report good quarterly earnings per share. That's the rumor. If you buy on the rumor, you can take advantage of the price appreciation as the story gets more play. When the earnings are actually announced, one of two things will happen:

 ✔ The earnings will be as good as or better than rumored, and the price will go up. The trader can sell into that and make a profit.

 ✔ The earnings will be worse than rumored, everyone will sell on the bad news, and the trader will want to sell to get out of the loss.

Of course, if the rumor is *bad,* you want to do the opposite: sell on the rumor and buy on the news. For more information on *short selling* — selling securities in hopes that they fall in price — turn to Chapter 9.

The problem with "Buy the rumor, sell the news" is that rumors are often wrong, and there may be more opportunities to buy on bad news when other traders are panicking, thus driving prices down for a few minutes before sanity sets in. But this rule is one of those that everyone talks about, whether or not they actually follow it.

Cut your losses and ride your winners

I mention earlier in this chapter that you need to cut your losses before they drag you down. No matter how much it hurts and no matter how much you believe that you're right, you need to close out a losing position and move on.

But the opposite — that you should ride your winners — is not necessarily true. Although good traders tend to be disciplined about selling winning positions, they don't use stops and limits as rigorously on the upside as they may on the downside. They're likely to stick with a profit and see how high it goes before closing out a position.

Note that this conflicts a little with the "Pigs get fat, hogs get slaughtered" maxim. (Trading maxims can be so contradictory!) To prevent overconfidence and sloppiness from greed, ride your winners *within reason.* If your general discipline is to risk three ticks on a futures contract to make five, and a contract goes up six ticks before you can close it out, you may want to stick with it. But if you also close out at the end of every day, don't give in to the temptation of keeping that position open just because it's still going up. Keep to your overall discipline.

You're only as good as your last trade

The markets churn on every day with little regard for why everyone trading right now is there. Prices go up and down to match the supply and the demand at any given moment, which may have nothing to do with the actual long-term worth of an item being traded. And it certainly has nothing to do with how much you really, really want the trade to work out.

One of the biggest enemies of good traders is overconfidence. Especially after a nice run of winning trades, a trader can get caught up in the euphoria and believe that he finally has the secret to successful trading under control. While he's checking the real estate listings for that beachfront estate in Maui, BAM! The next trade is a disaster. Does that mean that the trader is a disaster, too? No, it just means that the markets won this time around.

Most day traders work in zero-sum markets, where for every winner, there's a loser. Hence, not everyone can make money every day. The challenge is to maintain an even keel so as not to be distracted by confidence when the trading is going well or by fear when the trading is going poorly. The next trade is a new trade.

If you don't know who you are, Wall Street is an expensive place to find out

The best traders know their limits. They know what gets them excited, what gets them angry, and what they need to watch out for. They haven't necessarily figured it out in front of a screen, either. Instead, they've looked back on their lives and realized how to apply their strengths and weaknesses to trading.

If you are new to trading, consider your own capabilities when designing a trading plan and think carefully about the things that are likely to trip you up. By thinking about those things, you can pay attention and act accordingly.

If you wait to trade with real money to find out your tolerances for risk and stress, you're going to lose a lot of real money first.

Chapter 3

Deciding What to Trade and How to Trade It

*S*o *what* are you going to trade? Stocks, corn, or bitcoins? You have myriad choices, but you have to choose so that you can learn the market, know what changes to expect, and make your trades accordingly. And to avoid the devilment of the wash-sale rule, which can limit the tax deductibility of short-term losses (and which you can read about in Chapter 15), you probably want to make your universe of trading assets to be as broad as possible.

Still, you can't trade everything. A day has only so many hours, and your head can hold only so many ideas at any one time. Furthermore, some trading strategies lend themselves better to certain types of assets than others (see Chapter 8). By finding out more about all the various investment assets available to a day trader, you can make better decisions about what you want to trade and how you want to trade it.

Defining a Good Day-Trading Asset

In academic terms, the universe of investable assets includes just about anything you can buy at one price and sell at another, potentially higher price. Artwork and collectibles, real estate, and private companies, for example, are all considered to be investable assets.

Day traders have a much smaller group of assets to work with. Expecting a quick, one-day profit on price changes in real estate isn't realistic. Online auctions for collectible items take place over days, not minutes. If you're going to day trade, you want to find assets that trade easily, several times a day, in recognized markets. In other words, you want *liquidity*. As an individual trading your own account, you want assets that you can purchase with relatively low capital commitments. And finally, you may want to use *leverage* — borrowed money — to improve your return, so you want to look for assets that can be purchased using other people's money. The following sections outline the characteristics of good assets for day trading.

Looking for liquidity

Liquidity is the ability to buy or sell an asset in large quantity without affecting the price levels. Day traders look for *liquid assets* so they can move in and out of the market quickly without disrupting price levels. Otherwise, they may not be able to buy at a good price or sell when they want.

At the most basic level, financial markets are driven by supply and demand. The more of an asset supplied in the market, the lower the price; the more of an asset that people demand, the higher the price. In a perfect market, the amount of supply and demand is matched so that prices don't change. This situation occurs if a high volume of people are trading such that the supply and demand are constantly matched or if the frequency of trades is very low, which keeps the price from changing.

You may be thinking, wait, don't I want big price changes so that I can make money quickly? Yes, you want price changes in the market, but you don't want to be the one causing them. The less liquid a market is, the more likely your buying and selling are to affect market prices, and the smaller your profit will be.

Volume

Volume is the total amount of a security that trades in a given time period. The greater the volume, the more buyers and sellers are interested in the security and the more easily you can get in there and buy and sell without affecting the price.

Day traders also look at the relationship between volume and price. This important technical indicator is discussed in more detail in Chapter 7. Here's the simple analysis:

✔ High volume with no change in price levels means an equal match between buyers and sellers.

✔ High volume with rising prices means that buyers outnumber sellers, so the price will continue going up.

✔ High volume with falling prices means that sellers outnumber buyers, so the price will keep going down.

Frequency

Another measure of liquidity is *frequency,* or how often a security trades. Some assets, like stock market futures, trade constantly, from the moment the market opens until the very last trade of the day, and then continue into overnight trading. Others, like agricultural commodities, trade only during market hours or only during certain times of the year. Other securities, like stocks, trade frequently, but the volume rises and falls at regular intervals related to such things as *options expiration* (the date at which options on the stock expire).

Much of the market is dominated by *high-frequency traders,* which are pro-prietary computerized systems that enter, execute, or cancel buy and sell orders in the blink of an eye — or less. These traders have thrown a wrench into a few trading days, but they are only partially responsible for the type of frequency being discussed here. That's because high-frequency traders look for securities that already trade frequently to make the programs work better.

Finding the standard deviation — the hard way

Here's the equation you use to calculate standard deviation:

$$\sigma = \sqrt{\frac{1}{N} \sum_{i=1}^{N} \left(x_i - \bar{x} \right)^2}$$

In this equation, N is the number of price quotes, x_i is any one price quote, and the funky x with the line over it is the average of all the prices over time.

To calculate standard deviation for yourself, you calculate the difference between any given price and the average value. So if the average price is $5 and the closing price today is $8, the difference is $3. (More likely, the research service that you use would calculate the difference for you; you can learn more about research services in Chapter 13.)

After you have all the differences between the prices and the average for the time period in question, you find the square of these differences. If the difference for one day's price is $8, then the square is $64. You add up all the squared differences over the period of time that you are looking at and then find the average of them. That number is called the *variance,* or σ^2. Finally, calculate the square root of the variance, and you have the standard deviation.

Homing in on high volatility

The *volatility* of a security is how much the price of an asset varies over a period of time. It tells you how much prices fluctuate and thus how likely you are to be able to take advantage of that. For example, if a security has an average price of $5 but trades anywhere between $1 and $14, it is more volatile than one with an average price of $5 that trades between $4 and $6.

One standard measure of volatility and risk is *standard deviation,* which is how much any given price quote varies from a security's average price. If you are dying to see it, the math is explained in the sidebar "Finding the standard deviation — the hard way," but you can calculate it with most spreadsheet programs and many trading platforms.

The higher the standard deviation, the higher the volatility; the higher the volatility, the more a security's price is going to fluctuate, and the more profit — and loss — opportunities there are for a day trader.

Standard deviation is also a measure of risk that can be used to evaluate your trading performance. That use of the measure is discussed in Chapter 16.

Staying within your budget

You don't necessarily need a lot of money to begin day trading, but you do need a lot of money to buy certain securities. Stocks generally trade in *round lots,* which are orders of at least 100 shares. If you want to buy a stock worth $40 per share, you need $4,000 in your account. Your broker will probably let you borrow half of that money, but you still need to come up with the other $2,000.

Options and futures trade by contract; one contract represents some unit of the underlying security. For example, in the options market, one contract is good for 100 shares of the stock. These contracts also trade in round lots of 100 contracts per order.

No one will stop you from buying a smaller amount than the usual round lot in any given security, but you'll probably pay a high commission and get worse execution for your order. Because the returns on each trade tend to be small anyway, don't take up day trading until you have enough money to trade your target asset effectively. Otherwise, you'll pay too much to your broker without getting much for yourself.

Bonds do not trade in fractional amounts; they trade on a per-bond basis, and each bond has a face value of $1,000. Some trade for more or less than that, depending on how the bond's interest rate differs from the market rate of interest, but the $1,000 figure is a good number to keep in mind when thinking about capital requirements. Many dealers have a minimum order of ten bonds, though, so a minimum order would be $10,000.

Making sure you can use margin

Most day traders make money through a large volume of small profits. One way to increase the profit per trade is to use borrowed money to buy more shares, more contracts, or more bonds. *Margin* is money in your account that you borrow against, and almost all brokers will be happy to arrange a margin loan for you, especially if you're going to use the money to make more trades and generate more commissions for the brokerage firm. In Chapter 9, I discuss how margin is used within an investment strategy. Here, though, you want to think about how margin affects your choice of assets for day trading.

The following section gives you more information on how margin works and what you need to consider when selecting assets to trade, but here's what you need to know now: Most stocks and bonds are marginable (able to be purchased on margin), and the Federal Reserve Board allows traders to borrow up to 50 percent of their value. But not all securities are marginable. Stocks priced below $3 per share, those traded on the OTC Bulletin Board or OTC Link (discussed later in this chapter), and those in newly public companies often cannot be borrowed against or purchased on margin. Your brokerage firm should have a list of securities that are not eligible for margin.

If leverage is going to be part of your day-trading strategy, be sure that the assets you plan to trade are marginable.

Generally, your stock or bond account must hold the greater of $2,000 or 50 percent of the purchase price of securities when you borrow the money. So, for example, if you want to buy $5,000 worth of something on margin, you need to have $2,500 in your account. The price of those securities can go down, but if they go down so much that the account now holds only 25 percent of the value of the loan, you'll get a *margin call*. That means that you have to add cash or securities to your account right then and there. If not, your position will be liquidated.

Excess margin is the amount of money in your account over and above the minimum. For example, if you have $100,000 in your account and need 30 percent as maintenance margin, then you can borrow against an additional $70,000, the amount in excess of the 30 percent used for maintenance.

For derivatives, the margin rules are a bit different. Each contract has its own requirement for the initial margin and maintenance levels that must be kept on account; in the argot of the derivatives markets, margin is also known as a *performance bond*. If you are trading the Chicago Mercantile Exchange's E-mini MSCI Emerging Markets index contracts, for example, your initial margin per contract is $10,000, and your maintenance margin is $8,000. You can find current margin requirements for Chicago Mercantile Exchange and Chicago Board of Trade products at the Chicago Mercantile Exchange's website, www.cmegroup.com.

Margin requirements aren't set by the brokerage firms. Instead, the minimum amount in your account — and thus the maximum amount you can borrow — is set by the Federal Reserve Board under Regulation T. That's because of concerns that if too much borrowing takes place, the borrowers will panic in a financial downturn and drag the market down even further. (Excessive trading on margin was a contributing factor to the stock market crash of 1929, in which the Dow Jones Industrial Average fell 13 percent in one day, and the market did not fully recover until 1954. The financial crisis of 2008 wasn't caused by leverage in the stock market but by excessive borrowing in the real estate market.)

Changing margin rules for pattern day traders

FINRA, the Financial Industry Regulatory Authority that oversees the activities of member brokerage firms (which pretty much includes every brokerage firm in the United States), has rules about margin for day trading accounts to help brokerage firms manage their risks while accommodating the needs of active customers. Their rules complement those of the Federal Reserve Bank.

The FINRA regulations include a category of brokerage customer known as the *pattern day trader*. These are folks who day trade, which FINRA defines as buying, selling or selling short, and then buying the same security on the same day four or more times in five business days. Furthermore, pattern day traders, according to FINRA, make enough day trades that they constitute more than 6 percent of their total trading activity for that same five-day period. Brokerage firms can classify customers as pattern day traders before they make a single trade. For example, if the firm offers you special training or services designed for active traders, it may put you into that category.

Pattern day traders have to meet a different margin requirement. They need to start the trading day with at least $25,000 in cash and securities and maintain that amount throughout the trading day. The reason for these requirements is that margin requirements for other customers are based on the value of the account at the end of the day, but most day traders close out their positions overnight, which means that firms weren't managing their intra-day risk. Having the minimums in place helps protect the broker, but it also limits how much you can borrow if you have less than $25,000 in your day-trading account.

Being a pattern day trader under FINRA offers some advantages, the greatest one being that you can borrow more money during the day. Meet the standards, and you're allowed to borrow four times your excess margin as long as you close your trades out at the close of the market or before. A regular customer can only borrow one times the excess. If you exceed your margin limit, you have five days to deposit more cash or securities in your account.

Obeying your brokerage firm's margin policies

The Fed limits the amount that can be borrowed, and FINRA monitors how member brokerage firms comply. All brokerage firms have to meet those rules, but some set stricter limits for their customers.

The brokerage firms also set the interest rates for margin and the requirements for customers who want to borrow money to trade. The rates can be high; in 2013, brokerage firm Charles Schwab charged an annual rate of 8 percent on margin loans between $25,000 and $49,999.

Day traders have to pay margin interest, even though their loans are of short duration. Because it takes three days for a securities trade to settle, to the accountants, it looks as though you borrowed the money for three full days, not three hours. Some brokerage firms charge you interest for the full three days.

You won't pay the quoted interest rate each day, however; the quoted rate is almost always annualized. Divide it by 365 to find the daily rate. If the annual rate is 8.00 percent, then the daily rate will be 8.00 ÷ 365 = 0.02 percent. Check with your brokerage firm to find out the specifics of the margin interest calculation for day traders so that you understand what you'll be charged before you start to trade.

Trading Types of Securities

In the financial markets, people buy and sell securities every day, but just what are they buying or selling? *Securities* are financial instruments. In the olden days, they were pieces of paper, but now they are electronic entries that represent a legal claim on some type of underlying asset. This asset may be a business, if the security is a stock, or it may be a loan to a government or a corporation, if the security is a bond. In this section, I cover different types of securities that day traders are likely to run across and tell you what you need to jump into the fray.

In practice, *asset* and *security* are synonyms, and *derivative* is considered to be a type of asset or security. But to be precise, these three are not the same:

- ✔ An *asset* is a physical item. Examples include a company, a house, gold bullion, or a loan.

- ✔ A *security* is a contract that gives someone the right of ownership of the asset, such as a share of stock, a bond, a promissory note.

- ✔ A *derivative* is a contract that draws its value from the price of a security. Examples include options and futures.

Stocks

A *stock,* also called an *equity,* is a security that represents a fractional interest in the ownership of a company. Buy one share of Microsoft, and you are an owner of the company, just as Bill Gates is. He may own a much larger share of the total business, but you both have a stake in it. Stockholders elect a board of directors to represent their interests in how the company is managed. Each share is a vote, so good luck getting Bill Gates kicked off Microsoft's board.

A share of stock has *limited liability,* which means that you can lose all of your investment but no more than that. If the company files for bankruptcy, the creditors cannot come after the shareholders for the money that they are owed.

Some companies pay their shareholders a *dividend,* which is a small cash payment made out of firm profits. Because day traders hold stock for really short periods of time, they don't normally collect dividends.

How U.S. stocks trade

Stocks are priced based on a single share, and most brokerage firms charge commissions on a per-share basis. Despite this per-share pricing, stocks are almost always traded in round lots of 100 shares. The supply and demand for a given stock is driven by the company's expected performance.

A stock's price is quoted with a bid and an ask.

- ✔ The *bid* is the price that the broker pays to buy the stock from you if you are selling.

- ✔ The *ask* is the price that the broker charges you if you are the one buying.

You can remember the difference between the bid and the ask this way: The *broker buys* on the *bid.* Let alliteration be your friend!

The difference between the bid and the ask is the *spread,* and that represents the dealer's profit.

Here is an example of a price quote:

MSFT $31.60 $31.61

This quote is for Microsoft (ticker symbol: MSFT). The bid, listed first, is $31.60, and the ask is $31.61. That's the smallest spread you'll ever see! The spread here is so small because Microsoft is a liquid stock, and no big news events are going on that may change the balance of buyers and sellers.

The brokerage firm makes money from the commission *and* from the spread. Many novice day traders focus on the amount of the commission and forget that some brokerage firms can execute the order better than others, thus keeping the spread narrower. You need to consider the total cost of trading when you design a trading strategy and choose a brokerage firm, and brokers must disclose data on trade execution quality if you request it.

I tend to use the words *broker* and *dealer* interchangeably, but there is a difference. A *broker* simply matches buyers and sellers of securities, whereas a *dealer* buys and sells securities out of its own account. Almost all brokerage firms are both brokers and dealers.

Where U.S. stocks trade

U.S. stocks trade mostly on organized *exchanges* such as the New York Stock Exchange and NASDAQ, but they trade more and more on electronic communications networks, some of which are operated by the exchanges themselves.

The old-line exchanges are what you may think about when someone mentions stock exchanges: brick-and-mortar buildings with lots of people running around to execute trades in person. They are still major factors in the market, but they have competition from electronic communication networks, which were created with the theory being that more competition would make markets function even better. It hasn't quite worked out that way. Spreads between bid and ask prices have narrowed, but volatility has increased since they became a factor in the market. On the other hand, volatility creates opportunity for day traders, so that's not necessarily a bad thing.

When you place an order with your brokerage firm, the broker's computer executes that order wherever it can get the best deal. But is that the best deal for you or the best deal for the brokerage firm? It's tough to know the right answer. In general, firms that do more trading and participate in several exchanges and electronic communications networks can get you the best execution. (To find out more about choosing brokerage firms, turn to Chapter 11.)

The financial markets are in a state of flux, with a lot of mergers and acquisitions among the exchanges. By the time you read the information here, things may have changed again, which I think is fascinating. It wasn't so long ago that these exchanges were staid organizations run like private clubs.

The New York Stock Exchange (NYSE)

The New York Stock Exchange is the most famous of all stock exchanges. Most of the largest U.S. corporations trade on it, and they pay a fee for that privilege.

To be listed on the New York Stock Exchange, a company generally needs to have at least 2,200 shareholders excluding insiders, trade at least 100,000 shares a month for the last six months, carry a *market capitalization* (number of shares outstanding multiplied by price per share) of at least $100 million, and post total pre-tax earnings of $10 million over the previous three years.

The New York Stock Exchange is more than 200 years old, but it has been going through some big corporate changes in order to stay relevant. It's a *floor-based exchange.* The trading area is a big open space in the building, known as the *floor.* The floor broker, who works for the member firm, receives the order electronically and then takes it over to the trading post, which is the area on the floor where the stock in question trades. At the trading post, the floor broker executes the order at the best available price.

Although it was once an independent, membership-based organization, the New York Stock Exchange is now thoroughly modern. In 2007, it merged with Euronext, a holding company for five different European securities exchanges. Then NYSE Euronext bought the American Stock Exchange, once a major competitor to the NYSE, and phased it out. The combined company offers stock, bond, and derivates trading in person at the remaining physical exchanges and electronically through Arca, its electronic exchange. Of course, the percentage of trading that has been done by actual people standing on the floor of an actual building has fallen steadily over the years. Most trading is done electronically by small day traders and big institutions alike, with almost 30 percent of trading executed by computer algorithms.

To give you a clue about the importance of computerized trading, the NYSE allows brokerage firms to place their servers on the floor of the exchange — for a fee, of course. For some, the millisecond advantage is worth it.

NASDAQ

NASDAQ used to stand for the National Association of Securities Dealers Automated Quotation System, but now it's just a name, not an acronym, pronounced just like it's spelled. When NASDAQ was founded, it was an electronic communication network (more on those shortly) that handled companies that were too small or too speculative to meet New York Stock

Exchange listing requirements. What happened was that brokers liked using the NASDAQ network, and technology companies on the exchange (Microsoft, Intel, Apple) that were once small and speculative became huge international behemoths.

When a customer places an order, the brokerage firm's computer looks to see whether a matching order is on the network. Sometimes, the order can be executed electronically; in other cases, the brokerage firm's trader needs to call other traders at other firms to see whether the price is still good. A key feature of NASDAQ is its *market makers,* who are employees of member brokerage firms who agree to buy and sell minimum levels of specific stocks in order to ensure that some basic level of trading is taking place.

NASDAQ divides its listed companies into three categories:

- ✓ **The NASDAQ Global Select Market** includes the 1,000 largest companies on the exchange. Companies that make the list have a minimum average market capitalization of $550 million and total earnings of at least $11 million in the prior three fiscal years.

- ✓ **The NASDAQ Global Market** includes companies that are too small for the Global Select Market but that aren't exactly small. To make the Global Market, companies generally need to have a market capitalization of at least $75 million, at least 1.1 million shares outstanding, at least 400 shareholders, and a minimum price per share of $4.

- ✓ **The NASDAQ Capital Market** is for companies that do not qualify for the NASDAQ Global Market. To qualify here, companies need a market capitalization of at least $50 million, at least 1 million shares outstanding, about 300 shareholders, and a minimum price per share of $4.

As a day trader, you'll find that NASDAQ Global Select Market companies are the most liquid. You may also notice changes in trading patterns when a company is close to being moved between categories. An upgrade is a sign of good news to come and increased market interest. A downgrade means that the company most likely isn't doing well and will be of less interest to investors.

The new electronic exchanges

NASDAQ was the first electronic stock exchange, but it's now an institution. Several new exchanges have emerged to compete with the NYSE and NASDAQ. These firms usually started at electronic communications networks but grew enough to become something else. They have created new trading opportunities and reduced costs, but they have also added to the volatility in the market. The following sections discuss the two electronic exchanges in the stock market now.

BATS Exchange

BATS (www.batstrading.com) stands for Better Alternative Trading System. It was founded to improve trade execution times, and it is now the third-largest exchange in the U.S. Several exchange-traded funds are listed directly on BATS. The exchange had tried to offer stock listings, too, beginning with its own IPO, but a trading system failure stopped the IPO and scaled back those ambitions — at least for now.

National Stock Exchange

The National Stock Exchange has its roots in the Cincinnati Stock Exchange, which was founded in 1885. It converted to all-electronic in 1980 and is now owned by the Chicago Board Options Exchange and a group of brokerage firms. It is an electronic communications network that trades all exchange-listed equities, but it does not list securities on its own.

The high-risk over-the-counter exchanges

When the traditional floor-based exchanges were the primary game, a few companies emerged to trade stocks that were not eligible for exchange listing. These businesses are still around, and many traders like them because they can find stocks that have good volatility that are too small to attract the attention of the big guys with their big computers. However, the risk level is a lot higher: Some of these stocks don't trade enough for a day trader, and a few of these stocks are not issued by legitimate companies.

Over-the-Counter Bulletin Board (OTC BB)

The Over-the-Counter Bulletin Board is the market for companies that are reporting their financials to the U.S. Securities and Exchange Commission but that don't qualify for listing in any NASDAQ category. It also includes some foreign issuers that have not received listing in a U.S. market. American Bulletin Board companies have four-letter ticker symbols followed by *.OB*. For example, Sanborn Resources ticker symbol is SANB.OB. Foreign issuers trade with five-letter symbols, four letters followed by an *F*. ACS Motion Control, based in Israel, trades as ACSEF.

Brokerage firms carry quotations on OTC BB stocks through their NASDAQ workstations or other quotation services, enabling them to find current prices and locate buyers and sellers for any orders that they have. Quotes are also posted on the OTC BB website, www.otcbb.com.

In many cases, OTC BB companies are those that used to be on NASDAQ, but the stock prices have lost too much of their value to maintain their listing. A Bulletin Board listing is often a last hurrah before oblivion.

OTC Link

Once upon a time, few electronic networks existed, and they didn't have enough room for many companies to trade on them. Smaller companies did not trade daily. To find current prices, brokerage firms subscribed to a price service that sent out a weekly newsletter listing the prices for those companies. The newsletter was printed on pink paper, so it became known as the *Pink Sheets.* In the more modern era, the newsletter has moved online and changed its name to OTC Link (www.otcmarkets.com).

OTC Link does not have listing requirements for companies. Most of the companies don't qualify for listing on the NASDAQ or OTC BB, usually because they aren't current on their filings with the Securities and Exchange Commission. These companies have four- or five-letter ticker symbols and are sometimes shown with the suffix *.PK* after the ticker. Orders for OTC Link companies are placed through brokerage firms who use the service to find prices and match buyers and sellers.

Not all OTC Link companies are legitimate. Because of the minimal listing requirements, it tends to be the hangout for penny stocks (those trading at less than $1.00 per share), fraudulent companies, and securities that are easily manipulated by boiler-room operators. It can be a tough crowd, and a lot of people get burned.

Dark pools

Don't be put off by the word *dark* — dark pools, also known as dark liquidity, are good for traders. These exchanges allow people to place buy and sell orders that will be executed only if someone takes the other side. Of course, that's how most markets operate, but dark pools don't publish the prices or the sizes of the orders. Traders use them for low-cost execution, not price discovery. The downside is that price listings carry information about where the market is headed.

Bonds

A *bond* is a loan. The bond buyer gives the bond issuer money. The bond issuer promises to pay interest on a regular basis. The regular coupon payments are why bonds are often called *fixed income investments.* Bond issuers repay the money borrowed — the principal — on a predetermined date, known as the *maturity.* Bonds generally have a maturity of more than ten years; shorter-term bonds are usually referred to as *notes,* and bonds that mature within a year of issuance are usually referred to as *bills.* Most bonds in the United States are issued by corporations (corporate bonds) or by the Federal government (Treasury bonds). Some are issued by local governments (municipal bonds).

Over the years, enterprising financiers realized that some investors needed regular payments but others wanted to receive a single sum at a future date. So they separated the *coupons,* the interest payments on a bond, from the principal. The principal payment, known as a *zero-coupon bond,* is sold to one investor, while the coupons, called *strips,* are sold to another investor. The borrower makes the payments just like with a regular bond. (Regular bonds, by the way, are sometimes called *plain vanilla.*)

The borrower who wants to make a series of payments with no lump-sum principal repayment would issue an *amortizing* bond to return principal and interest on a regular basis. If you think about a typical mortgage, the borrower makes a regular payment of both principal and interest. This way, the amount owed gets smaller over time so that the borrower does not have to come up with a large principal repayment at maturity.

Other borrowers prefer to make a single payment at maturity, so they issue *discount bonds.* The purchase price is the principal reduced by the amount of interest that otherwise would be paid.

If a company goes bankrupt, the bondholders get paid before the shareholders do. In some bankruptcies, the bondholders take over the business, leaving the current shareholders with nothing.

How bonds trade

Bonds often trade as single bonds, with a face value of $1,000, although some brokers take on only minimum orders of ten bonds. Bonds do not trade as frequently as stocks do because most bond investors are looking for steady income, so they hold their bonds until maturity. Bonds have less risk than stocks, so they show less price volatility. The value of a bond is mostly determined by the level of interest rates in the economy. As rates go up, bond prices go down; when rates go down, bond prices go up. Bond prices are also affected by how likely the loan is to be repaid. If traders don't think that the bond issuer will pay up, then the bond price will fall.

Generally speaking, only corporate and municipal bonds have repayment risk. The U.S. government could default, but that scenario is unlikely as long as the government can print money. Most international government bonds have similarly low default risk, but some countries *have* defaulted. The most notable was Russia, which refused to print money to repay its debts in the summer of 1998 — a decision that caused huge turmoil in the world's financial markets, including the collapse of a major hedge fund, Long-Term Capital Management.

Investment banks and the federal government sell new bonds directly to investors. After they are issued, bonds are said to trade in the secondary market; some are listed, and some trade over-the-counter, meaning dealers trade them among themselves rather than over an organized exchange.

A bond price quote looks like this:

> 0.125 July 14 n 99:98 99:99

Translation: This bond is a U.S. Treasury note maturing in July 2014 and carrying an interest rate of 0.125 percent. Similar to stocks, the numbers right after the *n* (for *note*) list the bid and ask. The first number is the bid, the price that the dealer pays to buy the bond from you if you are selling. The second number is the ask, the price that the dealer charges you if you're buying. The difference is the spread, and that's the dealer's profit.

Most bonds are not suitable for day traders. Only Treasury bonds, issued by the U.S. government, have enough consistent trading volume to attract a day trader. Because of the capital required to trade and the relatively low liquidity of many types of bonds, many traders prefer to use *futures* to bet on interest rates. I discuss futures in detail later in this chapter.

If you're one of those day traders who wants to buy or sell bonds anyway or if you just want to know more about the market, then read on.

Listed bonds

Some larger corporate bonds are traded on the New York Stock Exchange. Those wanting to buy or sell them place an order through their brokerage firm, which sends an order to the floor broker. The process is almost identical to the trading of listed stocks.

Over-the-counter trading

Most corporate and municipal bonds trade over-the-counter, meaning no organized exchange exists. Instead, brokerage firms use electronic price services to find out where the buyers and sellers are for different issues. Over-the-counter bonds don't trade much. Buyers often give their quality, interest rate, and maturity requirements to their broker, and the broker waits until a suitable bond comes to market.

Treasury dealers

Unlike the corporate and municipal bond market, the Treasury market is one of the most liquid in the world. The best way to buy a new Treasury bond is directly from the government because no commission is involved. You can get more information from the Treasury Department's website, www. treasurydirect.gov; it has information on all kinds of government bonds for all kinds of purchasers.

After the bonds are issued, they trade on a secondary market of Treasury dealers. These are large brokerage firms registered with the government who agree to buy and sell bonds and maintain a stable market for the bonds.

If your brokerage firm is not a Treasury dealer, it has a relationship with one that it can send your order to.

Treasury dealers do quite a bit of day trading in Treasury bonds for the firm's own account. After all, the market is liquid enough that day trading is possible. Few individual day traders work the Treasury market, though, because it requires a great deal of capital and leverage to make a high return.

Exchange-traded funds (ETFs)

Exchange-traded funds (or ETFs) are a cross between mutual funds and stocks, and they offer a great way for day traders to get exposure to market segments that may otherwise be difficult to trade. The category is sometimes called *exchange-traded products* because some of the funds are structured more as a trading strategy than as mutual funds. A money-management firm buys a group of assets — stocks, bonds, or others — and then lists shares that trade on the market. In most cases, the purchased assets are designed to mimic the performance of an index, and investors know what those assets are before they purchase shares in the fund. The big advantage for day traders is that an ETF can be bought or sold at any time during the trading day, long or short, with cash or on margin, through a regular brokerage account. This flexibility is great for day traders.

Although an ETF looks a little bit like an index mutual fund or a market index futures contract, it has a very different structure. ETFs have two types of shares, creation units and retail shares:

- **Creation units:** These shares are held by authorized participants, which are different trading and brokerage firms that agree to commit cash to the fund. Creation unit holders can exchange their shares for the actual securities held in the fund, or they can add the appropriate securities to the fund in order to make new creation units. They do this to keep the value of the ETF in line with the underlying market index. So if the price of an ETF falls below the value of the securities in it, the authorized participants will trade in their creation units for the securities and then sell them on the open market. If the price of an ETF rises above the value of the securities, then the authorized participants will buy up the securities and exchange them for more creation units that they can sell at a nice profit.

- **Retail shares:** These ETF shares are listed on the exchange to be bought and sold by regular investors and traders. If you day trade ETFs, you'll be working with the retail shares.

Most of the time, the price of both the creation units and the retail shares are right in line with the price of the securities. On occasion, though, the value of the ETF and its investments will diverge. For example, on May 6, 2010, the U.S. stock market had a major break. Late in the trading day, the Dow Jones Industrial Average fell almost 1,000 points and then recovered almost right away. The cause was a single large sale of futures contracts, but it did a lot of disruption. Stock prices fell and then rebounded so quickly that ETF pricing couldn't keep up. ETF traders had a difficult time determining when to buy and when to sell because fund valuations were just wrong. It added more uncertainty to an already rough afternoon.

Traditional ETFs are available on the big market indexes, like the Standard & Poor's 500 and the Dow Jones Industrial Average. They are also available in a variety of domestic bond indexes, international stock indexes, foreign currencies, and commodities. Because traders are often interested in a market segment that doesn't have an index on it, some ETF companies develop their own niche indexes and issue ETFs based on them. Hence, you can find ETFs for such markets as green energy and Islamic investing. The liquidity in the securities in the underlying index may be low, though, so these funds may be more volatile in trading — and may even have arbitrage opportunities.

Strategy ETFs are funds that are based on an investing strategy rather than an underlying index. They can be dangerous for long-term investors who do not know what they are buying, but hey, this book is for traders! Traders often find great opportunities in strategy ETFs. For example, an inverse ETF is designed to move the opposite of the underlying index, and a leveraged ETF is designed to move in greater magnitude than the index. They give you a bigger toolbox to use to take on the markets.

You can learn more about the thousands of different ETFs on the market at www.morningstar.com/Cover/ETFs.aspx.

How U.S. exchange-traded funds trade

For day traders, the advantage of exchange traded funds is that they can be bought and sold just like stocks, discussed earlier in this chapter. Customers place orders, usually in round lots, through their brokerage firms. The price quotes come in decimals and include a spread for the dealer.

Where U.S. exchange-traded funds trade

The firm that sets up the exchange-traded fund gets to choose the market where it trades, as long as the fund meets the exchange's requirements for size, liquidity, and financial reporting. Exchange-traded funds trade anywhere that listed stocks trade.

Cashing In with Currency, the Big Kahuna

Cash is king, as they say. It's money that's readily available in your day-trading account to buy more securities. For the most part, the interest rate on cash is very low, but if you close out your positions every night, you'll always have a cash balance in your brokerage account. The firm will probably pay you a little interest on it, so it will contribute to your total return, but not by much.

But one type of cash investment can be really exciting for a day trader, and that's currency. Every day, trillions (yes, that's trillions with a *t*) of dollars of currency are exchanged between governments, banks, travelers, businesses, and speculators. With every trade and every blip in exchange rates, you have new opportunities to make money. Currency is a bigger, more liquid market than the U.S. stock and bond markets combined. It's often referred to as the *forex* market, short for *foreign exchange*. Foreign currency may be an attractive place to store some of your trading cash, and it can be a great asset to day trade.

Here's another neat thing about the currency market: Some types of currency trades are tax free. (Taxes are covered in more detail in Chapter 15.) These trades are usually longer-term, involving the currency itself, not day trades and not trades in the futures or forward market. But still — tax free! In other words, don't get suckered by ads for currency trading firms that promise tax-free income until you read the fine print.

How currency trades

The exchange rate is the price of money. It tells you how many dollars it takes to buy yen, pounds, or euros. The price that people are willing to pay for a currency depends on the investment opportunities, business opportunities, and perceived safety in each nation. If American businesses see great opportunities in Thailand, for example, they have to trade their dollars for baht in order to pay rent, buy supplies, and hire workers there. This situation increases the demand for baht relative to the dollar and causes the baht to go up in price relative to the dollar.

Exchange rates are quoted on a bid-ask basis, just as bonds and stocks are. A quote may look like this:

    USDJPY=X 97.3150 97.5250

This is the exchange rate for converting the U.S. dollar into Japanese yen. The bid price of 97.3150 is the amount of yen that a dealer would give you if you wanted to sell a dollar and buy yen. The ask price of 97.5250 is the amount of yen the dealer would charge you if you wanted to buy a dollar and sell yen. The difference is the dealer's profit, and naturally, you'll be charged a commission, too.

Note that with currency, you're a buyer and a seller at the same time, which can increase the profit opportunities, but it can also increase your risk.

Day traders can trade currencies directly at current exchange rates, which is known as *trading in the spot market.* When you exchange money to go on vacation in a foreign land, you are exchanging on the spot, and you are allowed to do it as a trader or as an investor. Day traders can also use currency exchange-traded funds (discussed earlier in this chapter) or currency futures (discussed later in this chapter) to profit from the changing prices of money.

Where currency trades

Spot currency — the real-time value of money — does not trade on an organized exchange. Instead, banks, brokerage firms, hedge funds, and currency dealers buy and sell amongst themselves all day, every day.

Day traders can open dedicated forex accounts through their brokers or currency dealers and then trade as they see opportunities during the day.

If you are interested in trading currencies, be sure to check out the fees involved. Some banks and brokerages are really set up to do forex trades for businesses and travelers, so the fees will be too high for you to have a decent profit potential. You can learn more about different types of accounts that day traders may have in Chapter 11.

Considering Commodities and How They Trade

Commodities are basic, interchangeable goods sold in bulk and used to make other goods. Examples include oil, gold, wheat, and lumber. Commodities are popular with investors as a hedge against inflation and uncertainty. Stock prices can go to zero, but people still need to eat! While commodity prices usually tend to increase at the same rate as in the overall economy, meaning they maintain their real (inflation-adjusted) value, they can also be susceptible to short-term changes in supply and demand. A cold winter increases demand for oil, a dry summer reduces production of wheat, and a civil war could disrupt access to platinum mines.

Day traders aren't going to buy commodities outright. If you really want to haul bushels of grain around all day, you can do that without taking on the risks of day trading (you'd get more exercise, too). Instead, day traders who want to play with commodities can look to other investments. The most popular way is to buy futures contracts, which change in price with the underlying commodity (discussed later in this chapter). Increasingly, many people trade commodities through exchange-traded funds that are based on the value of an underlying basket of commodities.

Commodity prices affect the broad economy, not just the prices of commodities contracts on the futures exchanges. If you day trade stocks in particular, you may find that changes in the price of oil or agricultural commodities affect many of the companies that you are involved with as well as the broader stock market indexes.

Dealing in Derivatives

Derivatives are financial contracts that draw their value from the value of an underlying asset, security, or index. For example, an S&P 500 futures contract gives the buyer a cash payment based on the price of the S&P 500 index on the day that the contract expires. The contract's value thus depends on where the index is trading. You're not trading the index itself; instead, you're trading a contract with a value derived from the price of the index. The index value changes all the time, so day traders have lots of opportunities to buy and sell.

Many day traders choose derivatives because these products give traders access to much of the economic universe, including stocks, bonds, commodities, and currencies. Furthermore, derivatives may have more favorable tax treatment for day traders than many other assets; more than one new day trader playing the stock market has been burned by the so-called *wash-sale rule,* which limits the deductibility of short-term losses. (I discuss this rule in Chapter 15.) Futures aren't subject to wash-sale rules. Read on to find out more and see if they are right for you!

Getting to know types of derivatives

Day traders are likely to come across three types of derivatives: options, futures, and warrants. Options and futures trade on dedicated derivatives exchanges, whereas warrants trade on stock exchanges.

What about bitcoins?

Bitcoins are a virtual currency that is created through a computer-programming mining process. They can then be exchanged for goods or traded for dollars, yen, or euros. Bitcoins have a novelty factor (some tech conferences accept bitcoins as payment for registration or t-shirts), and some people think that they will be the global currency of the future. Who knows? There is a market for trading them, some people have made money, and if you're game, it could be the market for you. Just be sure to trade them the same way you would trade anything. Have a plan, stick to the plan, and manage your risk. You can get more information at https://bitcoinfoundation.org.

Options

An *option* is a contract that gives the holder the right, but not the obligation, to buy or sell the underlying asset at an agreed-upon price at an agreed-upon date in the future. An option that gives you the right to buy is a *call,* and one that gives you the right to sell is a *put.* A call is most valuable if the stock price is going up, whereas a put has more value if the stock price is going down.

Here's one way to remember the difference: You *call up* your friend to *put down* your enemy.

For example, a MSFT 2013 Aug 26.00 call gives you the right to buy Microsoft at $26.00 per share at the expiration date on the third Friday in August 2013. (Did you know that traders refer to Microsoft as "Mr. Softy"? Clever, huh?) If Microsoft is trading above $26.00, you can exercise the option and make a quick profit. If it is selling below $26.00, you could by the stock cheaper in the open market, so the option would be worthless.

You can find great information on options, including online tutorials, at the Chicago Board Options Exchange website, www.cboe.com.

Futures

A *futures* contract gives you the obligation to buy a set quantity of the underlying asset at a set price and a set future date. Futures started in the agricultural industry because they allowed farmers and food processors to lock in their prices early in the growing season, reducing the amount of uncertainty in their businesses. Futures have now been applied to many different assets, ranging from pork bellies (which really do trade — they are used to make bacon) to currency values. A simple example is a lock in a home mortgage rate; the borrower knows the rate that will be applied before the sale is closed and the loan is finalized. Day traders use futures to trade commodities without having to handle the actual assets.

Most futures contracts are closed out with cash before the settlement date. Financial contracts — futures on currencies, interest rates, or market index values — can only be closed out with cash. Commodity contracts may be settled with the physical items, but almost all are settled with cash. No one hauls a side of beef onto the floor of the Chicago Board of Trade!

Warrants

A *warrant* is similar to an option, but it's issued by the company rather than sold on an organized exchange. (After they are issued, warrants trade similarly to stocks.) A warrant gives the holder the right to buy more stock in the company at an agreed-upon price in the future.

A cousin of the warrant is the *convertible bond,* which is debt issued by the company. The company pays interest on the bond, and the bondholder has the right to exchange it for stock, depending on where interest rates and the stock price are. Convertibles trade on the stock exchanges.

Buying and selling derivatives

Derivatives trade a little differently than other types of securities because they are based on promises. When someone buys an option on a stock, they aren't trading the stock with someone right now; they're buying the right to buy or sell it in the future. That means that the option buyer needs to know that the person on the other side is going to pay up. Because of that, the derivatives exchanges have systems in place to make sure that those who buy and sell the contracts will be able to perform when they have to. Requirements for trading derivatives are different than in other markets.

How derivatives trade

I talk about marginability earlier in this chapter, but the word *margin* is used differently when discussing derivatives, in part because derivatives are already leveraged. You aren't buying the asset, just exposure to the price change, so you can get a lot of bang for your buck. (The risks and rewards of leverage are covered in detail in Chapter 9.)

Margin in the derivatives market is the money you have to put up to ensure that you'll perform on the contract when it comes time to execute it. In the stock market, margin is collateral against a loan from the brokerage firm. In the derivatives markets, margin is collateral against the amount you may have to pay up on the contract. The more likely it is that you will have to pay the party who bought or sold the contract, the more margin money you have to put up. Some exchanges prefer to use the term *performance bond* instead of *margin.*

To buy a derivative, you put up the margin with the exchange's clearing house. That way, the exchange knows that you have the money to make good on your side of the deal — if, say, a call option that you sell is executed or you lose money on a currency forward that you buy. Your brokerage firm arranges for the deposit.

At the end of each day, derivatives contracts are *marked-to-market,* meaning that they are revalued. Profits are credited to the trader's margin account, and losses are deducted. If the margin falls below the necessary amount, the trader gets a call and has to deposit more money.

By definition, day traders close out at the end of every day, so their options are not marked-to-market. The contracts are someone else's problem, and the profits or losses on the trade go straight to the margin account, ready for the next day's trading.

Where derivatives trade

In the olden days, derivative trading involved *open outcry* on physical exchanges. Traders on the floor received orders and executed them among themselves, shouting and using hand signals to indicate what they wanted to do. As I write this, vestiges of floor trading remain on some derivatives exchanges, but there are fewer and fewer of them.

Almost all traders work "upstairs," as they say on the exchanges, trading electronically. Some are employees of large commodities brokerage firms, and others are independent. Employed and independent traders alike may work by executing someone else's orders for a fee, or they may work for proprietary accounts.

All the derivatives exchanges offer electronic trading services, even if they still have trading floors. As electronic trading has become more popular, it has chased many experienced floor traders into retirement because they can't all make the transition, and it has caused much restructuring and consolidation among the exchanges.

Chicago Board Options Exchange (CBOE)

The Chicago Board Options Exchange, often known by the acronym CBOE (pronounced *see-bo*), is the largest options market in the United States. This is where orders for stock options are traded. Brokerage firms use floor brokers in the trading pits or the CBOE's electronic trading system to handle customer orders. You can find out more at its website, www.cboe.com.

The CME Group

The CME Group (www.cmegroup.com) is made up of the Chicago Board of Trade (CBOT), the Chicago Mercantile Exchange (CME, also called the Merc), and the New York Mercantile Exchange (NYMEX). The three exchanges merged in 2008, although people often refer to each by its former name. Historically, the Board of Trade specialized in such agricultural commodities as corn, wheat, rice, oats, and soybeans, while the Merc offered contracts in non-grain agricultural products (like milk, butter, cattle, pork bellies, and fertilizer) and in foreign exchange, interest rates, and Standard & Poor's and NASDAQ indexes. Fuels and metals traded at the New York Mercantile Exchange.

The combined CME Group offers a suite of products, known as their *E-mini* contracts, for smaller traders. These products allow day traders to play in different agricultural and financial markets without as much margin as would be required for full-sized CME contracts. The E-minis are all traded electronically, too. Currently, E-minis are available on wheat, corn, and soybeans, as well as on stock market indexes in the United States and overseas.

Intercontinental Exchange (ICE)

The Intercontinental Exchange (www.theice.com) is a relatively new company that has acquired commodity and futures exchanges in North America and Europe. In 2008, it acquired the New York Board of Trade, which offers a range of agricultural and financial contracts, especially on coffee, cotton, and currency exchange rates. Orders are filled in the trading pits or through an electronic trading system. Although the ICE doesn't have contracts designed specifically for smaller traders, many day traders who like commodities and who have enough capital to manage the margin trade there.

International Securities Exchange (ISE)

The International Securities Exchange (www.ise.com) is the U.S. subsidiary of Eurex, a German derivatives trading firm. It handles trades in equity and foreign-exchange options, including a series of mini options for small traders. These minis are options on only 10 shares of the underlying, as opposed to a standard option, which is on 100 shares.

Chapter 4

Defining Trading: Risk, Reward, and Timing

In This Chapter

▶ Taking on risk and getting a return

▶ Investing for the long haul versus trading for the day

▶ Keeping the risks in mind

Day trading isn't investing, nor is it gambling — at least not if done right. But the lines between the three can be thin. By knowing where the lines are, you'll be in a better position to follow your trading strategy and make more money. And if you can avoid the trap of gambling, you'll be better able to preserve your trading capital.

The difference between investing and gambling is the *risk and return trade-off*. In investing, the odds are generally in your favor, but that doesn't mean you're going to make money. In gambling, the odds are against you. And unlike in the finer establishments in Las Vegas, if you end up gambling as a day trader, no one is going to bring you free drinks or tickets to some extravagant show to help ease the pain of failing. A lot comes down to personality; if you're on a casino's "do not admit" list, you probably aren't a great candidate for day trading.

Day trading is starting to look more like gambling than it has in years past, because high-frequency traders are taking more of the arbitrage and scalping opportunities. Be sure you're comfortable with the risk before you start to trade.

This chapter starts off with a lot of gory details about risk and return. My goal is to help you understand how the securities markets price risk and reward those who are willing to take it. Then I explain the differences in risk and reward for investors, traders, and gamblers to give you better information to help you plan your day trading.

Understanding Risk and Return

Investors, traders, and gamblers have this in common: They put their money at risk, and they expect to get a return. Ideally, that return comes in the form of cold, hard cash, but if they're not careful, they could get nothing — or worse, end up owing money. Traders should risk no more than they can afford to lose.

Trading is a business: The more you know about the potential risks and the sources of your potential return, the better off you'll be. Your risk is that you won't get the return you expect, and your reward is that you get fair compensation for the risk you take.

What is risk, anyway?

Risk is the measurable likelihood of loss. The riskier something is, the more frequently a loss will occur, and the larger that loss is likely to be. Playing in traffic is riskier than driving in traffic, and skydiving is riskier than gardening. This doesn't mean that you can't have losses in a low-risk activity or big gains in a high-risk one. It just means that with the low-risk game, losses are less likely to happen, and when they do, they're likely to be small.

What's the difference between risk and uncertainty? Risk involves the *known* likelihood of something good or bad happening so that it can be priced. What's the likelihood of your living to be 100? Or of getting into a car accident tonight? Your insurance company knows, and it figures your rates accordingly. What's the likelihood of aliens from outer space arriving and taking over the Earth? Who knows! It could happen, but that event is uncertain, not risky — at least until it happens.

The ability to measure risk makes modern business possible. Until mathematicians were able to use statistics to quantify human activities, people assumed that bad things were simply the result of bad luck or the wrath of the gods. But when people understand probability, they can apply and use that to assess the likelihood of an event happening and determine the commensurate compensation for taking the risk. If a sailor agreed to join a voyage of exploration, what was the probability that he would return home alive? And what would be fair compensation to him for that risk? What was the probability of a silo of grain going up in flames? And how much should the farmer charge the grain buyers for the risk that he was taking, and how much should someone else charge to insure the farmer against that fire?

Considering the probability of a loss

Whenever you take risk, you take on the probability of loss. If you know what that probability is, you can determine whether the terms you're being offered are fair and whether you have a reasonable expectation for the size of the loss.

Say that you're presented with this opportunity: You put up $10. You have an 80 percent chance of getting back $11 and a 20 percent chance of losing everything. Should you take it? To find out, you multiply the expected return by the likelihood and add them together: (80% × $11) + (20% × $0) = $8.80. Your expected return of $8.80 is less than the $10 cost of this contract, so you should pass on it.

Now suppose you're offered this opportunity: You put up $10. You have a 90 percent chance of getting back $11 and a 10 percent chance of getting back $6. Your expected return is (90% × $11) + (10% × $6) = $10.50. This contract would be in your favor, so you should take it.

Here's a third proposition: You put up $10. You have a 90 percent chance of getting back $13.89 and a 10 percent chance of losing $20 — even more than you put up. Your expected return is (90% × 13.89) + (10% × –$20) = $10.50. You end up with the same expected return as the preceding proposition, but do you like it as much? Many people would not like that deal because they are looking at the dollar value of the loss rather than the risk. People who overreact to the risk of loss without considering the facts on hand are probably not going to be good traders.

When thinking about loss, most people tend to put too much weight on the absolute dollar amount that they can lose, rather than thinking about the likelihood of losing it. The problem is that the markets don't trade on your personal preferences. This is one of the psychological hurdles of trading that those who are successful can overcome. Can you? (You can find some tips on this in Chapter 8.)

Working with limited liability (usually)

Securities markets rely on the concept of *limited liability*. That is, you cannot lose any more money than you invested in the first place. If you buy a stock, that stock can go down to zero, but it can't go any lower. If the company goes bankrupt, no one can come to you and ask you to cover the bills. On the other hand, the stock price can go up infinitely, so the possible return for your risk is huge. (Microsoft has grown more than 500 fold since it came public, which isn't quite infinity, but I sure wish I had taken that proposition.)

Although most day-trading strategies have the same limited liability — that is, you can lose what you trade and no more — some strategies have *unlimited liability.* If you sell a stock short (borrow shares and then sell them in hopes that the stock goes down in price, allowing you to repay the loan with cheaper shares, a strategy discussed in Chapter 9), and if the stock goes up drastically, you have to repay the loan with those highly valued shares! Most likely, you're going to close out your position before that happens, but even if you close out your positions every night like a good day trader should, some strategies have the potential to cost you more money than you have in your trading account.

To protect themselves and to protect you against losing more money than you have, brokerage firms and options exchanges require you to keep enough funds in your account to cover shortfalls (known as *margin,* discussed in Chapter 3). You have to be approved before you can trade in certain securities. For example, anyone trading options has to fill out an agreement that the brokerage firm must first approve and then keep on file.

Playing the zero-sum game

Many day trading strategies are *zero-sum games,* meaning that for every winner on a trade, there is a loser. It's especially true in options markets. Of course, the person on the other side of the trade may not mind being a loser; she may have entered into a trade to *hedge* (protect against a decline in) another investment and is happy to have a small loss instead of a much larger one.

The problem for you as a day trader is that a zero-sum game has little wiggle room. Every trade you make is going to win or lose, and your losses may exactly offset your winners. Beating the odds is even tougher when so many traders are using computer algorithms. Backtesting and tracking (see Chapter 16) are important for assessing your changing risk.

Finding the probability of not getting the return you expect

In addition to absolute measures of risk and liability, you also need to consider *volatility.* That's how much a security's price may go up or down in a given time period.

The math for measuring volatility is based on standard deviation (discussed in Chapters 3 and 16). A standard deviation calculation starts with the average return over a given time period. That average is the *expected* return — the return that, on average, you'll get if you stick with your trading strategy. But any given week, month, or year, the return may be very different from what you expect. The more likely you are to get what you expect, the less risk you take in the form of volatility.

Standard deviation shows up many times in trading, and you can find a detailed explanation of it in Chapter 16. The key thing to know is this: The higher the standard deviation of the underlying securities, the more risk you take with your trade. However, the same volatility creates trading opportunities for day traders to exploit. A security with a low standard deviation isn't going to offer you many chances to make money over the course of a day.

Standard deviation is used to calculate another statistic: beta. *Beta* tells you how risky a security is relative to the risk of the market itself. If you buy a stock with a beta of more than 1, that stock is expected to go up in price by a larger percentage than the market when the market is up, and it's expected to go down by a larger percentage than the market when the market is down.

High-beta stocks and options on high-beta stocks are riskier than low-beta stocks, but they offer a greater potential for return.

The word *beta* comes from the *capital assets pricing model,* an academic theory that says that the return on an investment is a function of the risk-free rate of return (discussed in the next section), the extra risk of investing in the market as a whole, and then the volatility — beta — of the security relative to the market. Under the capital assets pricing model, no other sources of risk and return exist. Any other sources would be called *alpha,* but in theory, alpha doesn't exist. Not everyone agrees with that, but the terms *alpha* and *beta* have stuck.

Getting rewarded for the risk you take

When you take risk, you expect to get a return. That's fair enough, right? That return comes in a few different forms related to the risk taken. Although you may not really care how you get your return as long as you get it, thinking about the breakdown of returns can help you think about your trading strategy and how it works for you.

Opportunity cost

The *opportunity cost* of your money is the return you could get doing something else. Is your choice day trading or staying at your current job? Your opportunity cost is your current salary and benefits. You'd give up that money if you quit to day trade. Is the opportunity cost low enough that it's worth your while? It may be. Just because taking advantage of an opportunity carries a cost doesn't mean that the opportunity isn't worth it.

When you trade, you want to cover your opportunity cost. Your cost will be different than someone else's, but if you know what that cost is up front, you'll have a better idea of whether your return is worth your risk.

Here's another way to think about opportunity cost. When you make one trade, you give up the opportunity to use that money for another trade. That means you only want to trade if you know that the trade is going to work out, more likely than not. That's why you need to plan your trades (see Chapter 2) and *backtest* (run a simulation using your strategy and historic securities prices) and evaluate your performance (see Chapter 16). By doing these things, you know that you are trading for the right reasons and not just out of boredom.

Risk-free rate of return and the time value of money

The value of money changes over time. In most cases, this change is the result of *inflation,* which is the general increase in price levels in an economy. But the value of money also changes because you give up the use of money for some period of time. That's why any investment or trading opportunity should include compensation for the *time value of your money.*

In day trading, your returns from the time value of money are small, because you only hold positions for a short period of time and close them out over-night. Still, there's some time component to the money you make. That small-est return is known as the *risk-free rate of return.* That's what you demand for giving up the use of your money, even if you know with certainty that you'll get your money back. In practice, investors think of the risk-free rate of return as the rate on U.S. government treasury bills, which are bonds that mature in less than one year. This rate is widely quoted in *The Wall Street Journal* and electronic price-quote systems.

If you cannot generate a return that's at least equal to the risk-free rate of return, you shouldn't be trading because your return wouldn't be appropriate to the risk you're taking.

Risk-return tradeoff

Economists say that there's no such thing as a free lunch. Whatever return you get, you get because you took some risk and gave up another oppor-tunity for your time and money. In that sense, there's no secret to making money. It's all about work and risk.

This concept is known as the *risk-reward tradeoff.* The greater the potential reward, the greater the amount of risk you're expected to take and thus the greater potential you have for loss. But if you understand the risks you're taking, you may well find that they're worth it. That's why you have to think about the risks and rewards up front.

Market efficiency in the real world

The reason a balance exists between risk and reward is that markets are reasonably efficient. This efficiency means that prices reflect all known information about the companies and the economy and that all participants understand the relative tradeoffs available to them. Otherwise, you'd have opportunities to make a riskless profit, and that just won't do, according to the average economist. "You can't pluck nickels out of thin air," they like to say. In an efficient market, if an opportunity exists to make money without risk, someone would have taken advantage of it already.

Here's how market efficiency works: You have information that says that Company A is going to announce good earnings tomorrow, so you buy the stock. Your increased demand causes the price to go up, and pretty soon, the stock price is where it should be, given that the company is doing well. The information advantage is rapidly eliminated. In most cases, everyone gets the news — or hears the rumor — of the good earnings at the same time, so the price adjustment happens quickly.

Wouldn't it be great to get the news of a good earnings report before everyone else and make a quick trading profit? Yep. At least until the Feds show up and haul you off to prison — talk about your opportunity costs. Trading on *material inside information* (information that is not generally known that would affect the price of the security) is illegal. And yes, the Securities and Exchange Commission and the exchanges monitor trading to see whether trading patterns suggest illegal trading based on inside information because they want all investors and traders to feel confident that the investment business is fair. Be very wary of tips that seem too good to be true.

The markets may be more or less efficient, but that doesn't mean they work by magic. Price changes happen because people act on news, and the people who act the fastest are day traders. In the example, notice that it was the activity of traders that caused the price of Company A stock to go up to reflect the expected good earnings report.

In economic terms, *arbitrage* is a riskless profit. A hard-core believer in academic theory would say that arbitrage opportunities don't exist. In practice, though, they do. Here's how arbitrage works: Although Company A is expected to have a good earnings announcement tomorrow, you notice that the stock price has gone up faster than the price of a call option on Company A, even though premium should reflect the stock price. So you sell Company A (borrowing shares and selling it short if you have to) and then use the proceeds to buy the option. When the option price goes up to reflect the stock price, you can sell the option (that is, close out your short position) and lock in a riskless profit — at least, before your trading costs are considered. Chapter 10 discusses arbitrage in more detail.

The oldest economics joke ever told

After you become wise to the ways of risk and return, this joke should make sense to you:

Two economists are walking down the street. One sees a $20 bill on the sidewalk and stops to pick it up. "Don't bother," says the other.

"If it were real, someone would have taken it already."

"Don't be so sure," says the first economist. He picks it up, sees that it is real, then turns to his friend and says, "How about if I buy you a free lunch?"

Market efficiency isn't perfect. It can take a while for people to make a logical decision about what an asset is worth, and until that happens, trading can be irrational and inefficient. Whether it's Japanese stocks, Internet stocks, condominiums in Florida, or gold, the markets have pockets of craziness that defy rhyme and reason. In the short term, a wave of panic or euphoria can overtake the market during a single trading day, pushing prices into inefficient territory. On days like that, your ability to keep calm and steer into the trend, rather than getting swept up into an uncontrollable craze, will help you have more winning trades.

Bubbles and panics happen, and they happen more often than academic economists like to admit. However, most days, trading is efficient. Your edge comes from knowing the markets, having good risk management, and being able to walk away. Don't count on crazy price action every day.

Differentiating Trading, Investing, and Gambling

Day trading is a cousin to both investing and gambling, but it is not the same as either. Day trading involves quick reactions to the markets, not a long-term consideration of all the factors that can drive an investment. It works with odds in your favor, or at least that are even, rather than with odds that are against you.

Still, the three activities overlap. Many day traders also invest, and some came to trading after years of watching the markets as an investor. In addition, more than one day trader claims that good poker skills are useful for understanding market psychology, and many day traders can point to a winning trade that was made for no particular reason at all. To help you keep straight the differences between day trading, investing, and gambling, this section explains which is which so that you can better understand what you're doing when you day trade. After all, you can increase your chances of success if you stick to the business at hand.

Investing is slow and steady

Investing is the process of putting money at risk in order to get a return. It's the raw material of capitalism. It's the way that businesses get started, roads get built, and explorations get financed. It's how our economy matches people who have more money than they need, at least during part of their lives, with people who need it in order to grow society's capabilities.

Investing is heady stuff. And it's very much focused on the long term. Good investors do a lot of research before committing their money because they know that it will take a long time to see a payoff. That's okay with them. Investors often invest in things that are out of favor, because they know that, with time, others will recognize the value and respond in kind.

One of the best investors of all time is Warren Buffett, chief executive officer of Berkshire Hathaway. His annual letters to shareholders offer great insight. You can read them at www.berkshirehathaway.com/letters/letters.html.

What's the difference between investing and saving? When you save, you take no risk. Your compensation is low; it's just enough to cover the time value of money. Generally, the return on savings equals inflation and no more. In fact, a lot of banks pay a lot less than the inflation rate on a federally insured savings account, meaning that you're paying the bank to use your money.

In contrast to investing, day trading moves fast. Day traders react only to what's on the screen. There's no time to do research, and the market is always right when you're day trading. You don't have two months or two years to wait for the fundamentals to work out and the rest of Wall Street to see how smart you were. You have today. And if you can't live with that, you shouldn't be day trading.

Trading works fast

Trading is the act of buying and selling securities. All investors trade, because they need to buy and sell their investments. But to investors, trading is a rare transaction, and they get more value from finding a good opportunity, buying it cheap, and selling it at a much higher price sometime in the future. But traders are not investors.

Traders look to take advantage of short-term price discrepancies in the market. In general, they don't take a lot of risk on each trade, so they don't get a lot of return on each trade, either. Traders act quickly. They look at what the market is telling them and then respond. They know that many of their trades won't work out, but as long as more than half work, they'll be okay. They don't do a lot of in-depth research on the securities they trade, but they know the normal price and volume patterns well enough that they can recognize potential profit opportunities.

Trading keeps markets efficient because it creates the short-term supply and demand that eliminates small price discrepancies. It also creates a lot of stress for traders, who must react in the here and now. Traders give up the luxury of time in exchange for a quick profit.

Speculation is related to trading in that it often involves short-term transactions. Speculators take risks, assuming a much greater return than may be expected, and a lot of what-ifs may have to be satisfied for the transaction to pay off. Many speculators hedge their risks with other securities, such as options or futures.

Gambling is nothing more than luck

A *gambler* puts up money in the hopes of a payoff if a random event occurs. The odds are always against the gambler and in favor of the house, but people like to gamble because they like to hope that, if they hit it lucky, their return will be as large as their loss is likely.

Some gamblers believe that the odds can be beaten, but they are wrong. (Certain card games are more games of skill than gambling, assuming you can find a casino that plays under standard rules. Yeah, you can count cards when playing blackjack with your friends, but doing so is a lot harder in a professionally run casino.) They get excited about the potential for a big win and get caught up in the glamour of the casino, and soon the odds go to work and drain away their stakes.

There is such a thing as a *fair lottery,* which takes place when the expected payoff is higher than the odds of playing. You won't find it at most casinos, although sometimes the odds in a sports book or horse race favor the bettor, at least in the short term. A more common example takes place in lotteries when the jackpots roll over to astronomical amounts. For example, in May 2013, the multi-state Powerball lottery had a jackpot of $590 million, but the odds of winning were 1 in 175 million. This means that a $1.00 ticket had an expected value of $3.37, making it a fair proposition. (That $590 million was a record that has not been beaten.)

Trading is not gambling, but traders who are not paying attention to their strategy and its performance can cross over into gambling. They can view the blips on their computer screen as a game. They can start making trades without any regard for the risk and return characteristics. They can start believing that how they do things affects the trade. And pretty soon, they are using the securities market as a giant casino, using trading techniques that have odds as bad as any slot machine.

Managing the Risks of Day Trading

When you know more about the risks, returns, and related activities of day trading, you can think more about how you're going to run your day-trading business. Before you flip through the book to find out how to get started, consider two more kinds of risk that you need to think about:

✔ Business risk
✔ Personal risk

You need to understand and manage both in order to better manage the risks of the trading day.

It's your business

Business risk is the uncertainty of the timing of your cash flow. Not every month of trading is going to be great, but your bills will come due no matter what. You'll have to pay for subscriptions while keeping the lights turned on and the computer connected to the Internet. Taxes come due four times a year, and keyboards hold a mysterious attraction for carbonated beverages, causing them to short out at the most inopportune times.

Keep track of your business expenses and keep them as low as is reasonable. You should invest in your business, obviously, but only to the extent that you can pay your bills even if you have an off month in the market.

Regardless of what happens to your trading account, you need cash on hand to pay your bills or you'll be out of business. The best way to protect yourself is to start out with a cash cushion just for covering your operating expenses. Keep this cushion separate from your trading funds. Replenish it during good months. Walk away from trading if it goes down to zero.

It's your life

The *personal risk* of trading is that it becomes an obsession that crowds out everything else in your life. Trading is a stressful business, and the difference between those who succeed and those who fail is often psychological. You need to be on when you are trading and then, at the end of the trading day, close out the emotions the same way that you close out your positions. It's not easy, so you need to have ways to manage your mood. Figure those out before you start trading, and you'll be ahead of the game.

In fact, the personal risk is so great that I devote an entire chapter to managing it — Chapter 14. Go there if anything you have read in this chapter alarms you.

Chapter 5

Regulation and the Modern Trader

. . . .

In This Chapter

▶ Identifying the regulators

▶ Considering basic brokerage requirements

▶ Avoiding insider trading tips

▶ Protecting the markets in crisis situations

▶ Following procedure when you take on partners

. . . .

*T*he financial markets are wild and woolly playgrounds for capitalism at its best. Every moment of the trading day, the actions of buyers and sellers determine what the price of a stock, commodity, or currency should be at that moment, given the supply, the demand, and the information out there. It's beautiful.

One reason the markets work well most of the time is that they are regulated. That may seem like an oxymoron: Isn't capitalism all about free trade, unfettered by any rules from nannying bureaucrats? Ah, but for capitalism to work, people on both sides of a trade need to know that the terms will be enforced. They need to know that the money in their accounts is there and is safe from theft. And they need to know that no one has an unfair advantage. *Regulation* creates the trust that makes markets function.

As a day trader, you may not be managing money for other investors, and you may not answer to an employer, but that doesn't mean you don't have rules to follow. Day traders have to comply with applicable securities laws and exchange regulations, some of which specifically address those who make lots of short-term trades. Likewise, brokers and advisors who deal with day traders have regulations that they need to follow. Understanding all these different rules and regulations can help you make better decisions about whom to deal with. In this chapter, you find out who does the regulating, what they look at, and how they affect you.

Looking Back on the Road to Regulations

With the advent of the telegraph, traders were able to receive daily price quotes. Many cities had *bucket shops,* storefront businesses where traders bet on changes in stock and commodity prices. These traders weren't buying the security itself, even for a few minutes; instead they were placing bets against others. These schemes were highly prone to manipulation and fraud, and they were wiped out after the stock market crash of 1929.

After the 1929 crash, small investors began trading off the ticker tape, which was a printout of price changes sent by telegraph, or wire. In most cases, traders made these transactions by going down to their brokerage firm's office, sitting in a conference room, and placing orders based on the changes they saw come across the tape. Really serious traders got wires installed in their own offices, but the costs were prohibitive for most individual investors. In any event, traders still had to place their orders through a broker. Because they didn't have direct access to the market, they couldn't count on timely execution.

Another reason there was so little day trading back then is that all brokerage firms charged the same commissions until 1975. That year, the Securities and Exchange Commission ruled that this practice amounted to price fixing. After this ruling, brokers could compete on their commissions. Some brokerage firms, such as Charles Schwab, began to allow customers to trade stock at discount commission rates, which made active trading more profitable. Some brokerage firms don't even charge commissions anymore (but don't worry; they get money from you in other ways).

The system of trading off the ticker tape more or less persisted until the stock market crash of 1987. Brokerage firms and market makers were flooded with orders, so they took care of their biggest customers first and pushed the smallest trades to the bottom of the pile. After the crash, the exchanges and the Securities and Exchange Commission called for several changes designed to reduce the chances of another crash and improve execution if one were to happen. One of those changes was the Small Order Entry System, often known as SOES, which gave orders of 1,000 shares or less priority over larger orders.

Then, in the 1990s, Internet access became widely available, and several electronic communications networks started giving small traders direct access to price quotes and trading activities. This meant that traders could place orders on the same footing as the brokers they once had to work through. In fact, thanks to the SOES, the small traders had an advantage: They could place orders and then sell the stock to the larger firms, locking in a nice profit. Day trading looked like a pretty good way to make a living.

SOES coincided with the rise of the commercial Internet, making the late 1990s a golden era for day traders, at least in the popular imagination. More and more discount brokerage firms offered Internet trading while Internet stocks became wildly popular. No one needed SOES to make profits when Pets.com and Webvan were going up in price day after day, at least for a while. (Remember that? No? Well, it was fun while it lasted.)

Then market for tech stocks cratered in 2000, in part because so many of the companies cratered, too. For much of the next decade, the markets were mostly quiet while new products were introduced that appealed to day traders, including exchange-traded funds and miniature commodities contracts (both of which are discussed in Chapter 3).

And then things got crazy. In 2008, brokerage firms failed, and the financial markets came darn near close to collapse. All that volatility was a lot of fun for those traders who could handle it. The brokerage firms developed larger and more sophisticated trading programs that seemed to work well until a single large order on the afternoon of May 6, 2010, caused everything to go haywire. That so-called "flash crash" exposed the risks created by high-frequency trading programs; at first, no one wanted to blame technology and instead tried to place the blame on traders whose fingers were too big to punch the numbers on their order-entry machines.

The financial system received generous government bailouts in the fall of 2008 in the hopes of staving off another depression. The exchanges and the federal government created new regulations in the major institutions, although little has changed for day traders — at least so far.

So what are the regulations that affect day traders? Well, keep reading!

Reviewing the Regulators

In the United States, financial markets receive general regulatory oversight from two government bodies: the Securities and Exchange Commission (SEC) and the Commodity Futures Trading Commission (CFTC). Both have similar goals: to ensure that investors and traders have adequate information to make decisions and to prevent fraud and abuse.

Neither body has complete authority over the markets, though. Instead, much of the responsibility for proper behavior has been given to self-regulatory organizations that brokerage firms join, and to the exchanges themselves. It's not straightforward, but the overlap between these organizations seems to ensure that problems are identified early on and that the interests of companies, brokers, and investment managers are fairly represented.

Stock and corporate bond market regulation

The stock and corporate bond markets are the most prominent. Regulators are active and visible because these markets have a relatively large number of relatively small issuers. In the currency market, by contrast, the only issuers are governments, and there are a lot fewer of them than there are public companies. When one of these companies turns out to have fraudulent numbers, the headlines erupt, and suddenly everyone cares about what the SEC is up to. That's just the first layer in regulating this market.

Given the rate at which exchanges are merging and organizations are rearranging themselves, the following list may well have changed by the time you read it. But even if the organizations go away, the regulations won't.

The U.S. Securities and Exchange Commission (SEC)

The SEC (www.sec.gov) is a government agency that ensures that markets work efficiently. The Commission has five commissioners, appointed by the President and confirmed by Congress, who serve staggered five-year terms. This structure is designed to keep the SEC nonpartisan. One of the commissioners is designated as the chair.

The SEC has three functions:

✔ To ensure that any companies that have securities listed on exchanges in the United States report their financial information accurately and on time so that investors can determine whether investing in the company makes sense for them

✔ To provide oversight to the markets by ensuring that the exchanges and self-regulatory organizations have sufficient regulations in place and that those regulations are enforced

✔ To regulate mutual funds, investment advisors, and others who make decisions for other people's money

In addition to its standard regulations, which brokerage firms know by heart, the SEC occasionally passes temporary regulations in times of market stress that may affect day traders. For example, during the 2008 financial crisis, the SEC placed restrictions on short-selling the stock of different financial companies.

The Financial Industry Regulatory Authority (FINRA)

FINRA (www.finra.org) was formed in 2007 by the merger of the New York Stock Exchange's regulatory department and the National Association of Securities Dealers. It represents and regulates all stock and bond brokerage firms and their employees. More than 4,245 firms are members, with 630,150 employees registered to sell securities. FINRA administers background checks and licensing exams, regulates securities trading and monitors how firms comply, and provides information for investors so that they are better informed about the investing process.

FINRA also requires brokers to know who their customers are and whether an investment strategy is suitable for them, the so-called *know your customer rule*. I discuss suitability later in this chapter, but for now, know that that's a FINRA function.

A good first stop for a day trader is FINRA's BrokerCheck service, which you can find at `www.finra.org/Investors/ToolsCalculators/BrokerCheck`. BrokerCheck allows you to look up brokerage firms and individual brokers to see whether they're in good standing. If any complaints have been filed, you can see what they are and decide for yourself how you feel about them. This great information can help you head off problems with sales people or brokerage firms early on. BrokerCheck has helped me a time or two when I've been looking into potential business partners.

FINRA's predecessor, the National Association of Securities Dealers, started as a self-regulatory organization, but in the late 1960s, it saw that member firms needed a better way to trade over-the-counter securities (securities that don't trade on an organized exchange like the New York Stock Exchange). In 1971, it formed its own electronic communication network, the National Association of Securities Dealers Automated Quotation system, or NASDAQ, pronounced as one word: NAZ-dack. In 2000, the NASD divested NASDAQ, which is now known only by that name, and returned to its self-regulatory organization roots. Although the two are now separate, brokerage firms that trade securities on NASDAQ must be members of FINRA.

The exchanges

Although the New York Stock Exchange and NASDAQ got out of the brokerage oversight business when they formed FINRA, they are both involved in regulation. In particular, these and the smaller exchanges work to ensure that companies with securities traded on the exchange meet the criteria set for their listings. These criteria include timely financial reporting with the SEC and minimum numbers of shares that are actually traded. (Chapter 3 has a description of the different exchanges and their listing requirements.)

The exchanges also monitor how securities are traded in order to look for patterns that may point to market manipulation or insider trading. Each exchange works with the brokerage firms that are allowed to trade on its exchange to make sure that the brokers know who their customers are and that the brokers have systems in place to make certain that their customers play by the rules.

The Federal Reserve System

The Federal Reserve System, known as the Fed to friend and foe alike, is the central bank of the United States, and one of its roles is to ensure the integrity of the country's financial system. Although most Federal Reserve regulation is aimed at commercial banks, the Fed gets involved in securities markets in times of crisis to ensure that the markets continue to function. In the 2008 financial crisis, this involvement included arranging the mergers of failing brokerage firms as well as buying troubled assets from different banks, brokerage firms, and insurance companies.

The Securities Investor Protection Corporation

The Securities Investor Protection Corporation (SIPC) was founded in 1970 to protect brokerage accounts from losses in the event of the firm's bankruptcy. If your firm goes under (and several have over the years, including some that were once household names), you'll be able to get your cash and securities back.

The SIPC doesn't insure against fraud, however. If you're dealing with a firm or a salesperson who rips you off, you have to get redress through the courts and the Securities and Exchange Commission. You want to find a brokerage firm that is an SIPC member, but your due diligence can't stop there. For example, you should check your broker through FINRA's BrokerCheck, discussed in the earlier section "The Financial Industry Regulatory Authority (FINRA)."

Likewise, almost all disputes that clients have with brokerage firms go to arbitration, not the courts, and many people believe that the arbitration process is biased in favor of the brokers. You have recourse, but you may not have as much as you would like.

Treasury bond market regulation

Treasury bonds are a slightly different animal than corporate bonds. They are issued by the U.S. government, so the Treasury Department's Bureau of the Public Debt (www.treasurydirect.gov) handles regulation, with the SEC providing additional oversight. The firms that trade Treasury bonds are FINRA members, so those rules apply, too.

Derivatives market regulation

The derivatives markets, where options and futures are traded, don't deal in stocks and bonds directly. Instead, they link buyers and sellers of contracts where the value is linked to the value of an underlying security. Derivatives are popular with day traders, because they give these traders a way to get exposure to interest rates and market index performance with less capital than would be required to buy Treasury bonds or large groups of stocks directly.

Derivatives markets have their own regulatory bodies, but they match the format and hierarchy of stock and bond market regulation. The organizations may not be household names, but their functions are familiar.

Commodity Futures Trading Commission (CFTC)

The CFTC (www.cftc.gov) is a government agency founded in 1974 to oversee market activities in agricultural and financial commodities. The government realized that these markets needed some regulation but were sufficiently different from traditional stock exchanges that the SEC might not be the best agency to handle it. The CFTC is structured similarly to the SEC, with five commissioners holding staggered five-year terms, appointed by the President and confirmed by Congress. One of the commissioners is designated as the chair. This structure is designed to keep the CFTC nonpartisan.

For decades, futures trading was regulated by the U.S. Department of Agriculture because it involved nothing but agricultural commodities like grain, pork bellies, and coffee. As traders demanded such new products as futures on interest rates and currencies, it became clear that a new regulatory body was needed, and that was the CFTC.

The CFTC has two main functions:

✔ To ensure that the markets are liquid and that both parties on an options or futures transaction are able to clear (that is, to meet their contractual obligations)

✔ To provide oversight to the markets by ensuring that the exchanges and self-regulatory organizations have sufficient regulations in place and that those regulations are enforced

National Futures Association (NFA)

The NFA (www.nfa.futures.org) regulates 4,200 firms with 55,000 employees who work on the different futures exchanges. It administers background checks and licensing exams, regulates futures trading and monitors how firms comply, and provides information for investors so that they're better informed about futures trading and how it differs from more traditional investments.

Firms that handle futures are known as *futures commission merchants,* or FCMs, rather than *brokers.* You can find information on FCMs and their employees through the NFA's Background Affiliation Status Information

Center, which has the clever acronym BASIC. You can access it at `www.nfa.futures.org/basicnet` or through the NFA's home page. BASIC allows you to look up futures firms and employees to see whether they are registered and whether any complaints have been filed against them. If any complaints have been filed, you can see how the problem was resolved. (Consider BASIC the futures equivalent of the legendary permanent record that your elementary school teachers said would follow you for the rest of your life.)

The Securities and Exchange Commission and the National Association of Securities Dealers regulate trading in options on stocks, but the Commodity Futures Trading Commission and the National Futures Association regulate trading on options on futures. As the lines between derivative products get blurrier, you may find a lot of overlap between these different organizations, and many experts in the industry predict that the SEC and CFTC will merge at some point. Because researching firms and people through several self-regulatory organizations is possible, you may as well take the time to do it. Don't be alarmed if someone is listed one place and not the other, but do be alarmed if a firm or person isn't listed anywhere.

The exchanges

Unlike the stock exchanges, the derivatives exchanges haven't merged their regulatory functions. Thus the Chicago Board Options Exchange (CBOE), the CME Group, InterncontinentalExchange, and other derivatives exchanges have their own regulatory groups that ensure that their traders comply with exchange rules and rules of other organizations, especially the CFTC. They also develop new types of trading contracts that satisfy market demands while complying with applicable laws. (Chapter 3 describes the different exchanges and what they do.)

To look for patterns that may point to market manipulation or insider trading, the exchanges also monitor how derivatives are traded. Each works with the futures commission merchants that are allowed to trade on its exchange to ensure that the FCMs know who their customers are and have systems in place to make sure these customers trade well, if not profitably.

On occasion, the exchanges cooperate with regulators of stock and bond markets, especially if the suspicion of fraud or market manipulation exists. After all, insider trading in options is just as illegal as insider trading in stocks!

Foreign exchange (forex) regulation

Because it is the largest, most liquid market in the world, many day traders are taking up trading in foreign exchange, also known as *forex*. But here's the tricky thing: These markets are not well regulated. There's nothing to stop someone from exchanging U.S. dollars for Canadian dollars; tourists do it every day, often at a hotel desk or retail shop. There's no paperwork, no hassle — and no oversight.

Oversight isn't necessary for a simple exchange of bucks to loonies, like when someone at a convenience store buys a tube of Smarties (no, not the dry tablets wrapped in cellophane but rather a fine chocolate candy not available in the States, so if you cross the border, please pick some up for me!). Unfortunately, this situation has allowed some firms to misrepresent forex trading to day traders as regulated when it is not, which has allowed some day traders to get badly burned. Forewarned is forearmed, as the cliché goes.

Some online forex brokers are located outside of the United States, so they are allowed to offer customers more leverage. Increasing leverage can increase return, but it also adds risk. And some jurisdictions have better protections for investors than others. Check to see where a firm is based and what laws apply so that you're protected.

Options and futures on currency

Most currency is traded in the *spot:* Traders exchange one currency for another at the current exchange rate. The spot market is not regulated. But many day traders prefer to pick up exposure to currency using options and futures, to bet on where exchange rates may go and to hedge the risks of unexpected changes. Options and futures on currency are regulated as derivatives, through the CFTC, the NFA, and the relevant futures exchanges. In some cases, though, FCMs get customer referrals from foreign exchange firms that are not themselves registered, which can make it unclear whether customers understand what they are getting into.

If you are participating in an unregulated market like forex, you can protect yourself by doing your research so that you know what the risks and rewards are. For that matter, every market has a few unscrupulous individuals, so you're always better off if you find your own facts rather than rely on someone else. The exchanges and self-regulatory organizations all have great websites with lots of information, and you can see a directory of them in this book's appendix.

Banks and oversight

Banks are responsible for most foreign exchange trading, and banks are heavily regulated. Therefore the Federal Reserve Banks and the U.S. Treasury Department pay attention to forex markets, looking for evidence of manipulation and money laundering (discussed later in the chapter). This oversight keeps the market from being a total free-for-all, even though anyone is allowed to trade currency.

Bank oversight isn't enough to protect you from the outlandish claims made by crooked forex trading firms, but it does ensure that your contracts are fulfilled.

Working with Brokers' Rules

No matter who regulates them, brokers and futures commission merchants have to know who their customers are and what they are up to. That leads to some basic regulations about suitability, pattern day trading, and money laundering — and extra paperwork for you. Don't get too annoyed by all the paperwork you have to fill out to open an account, because your brokerage firm has to do even more.

Gauging suitability

Brokerage firms and FCMs have to make sure that customer activities are appropriate. The firms need to know their customers and be sure that any recommendations are suitable. When it comes to day trading, firms need to be sure that customers are dealing with *risk capital* — money that they can afford to lose. They also need to be sure that the customers understand the risks that they are taking. Depending on the firm and what you're trying to do, you may have to submit financial statements, sign a stack of disclosures, and verify that you have received different guides to trading.

Your financial situation is no one's business but your own — except of course that the various regulators want to make sure that firm employees aren't talking customers into taking risks that they shouldn't be taking. That's why the brokerage firm wants to know who you are and what money you're using for your trading. Sure, you can lie about it. You can tell the broker you don't need the $25,000 you're putting in your account, even if that's the money paying for your kidney dialysis. But if you lose it, you can't say you didn't know about the risks involved.

Money laundering: Al Capone or Watergate?

Although some believe that the term *money laundry* dates back to Al Capone's attempts to evade taxes by owning laundries — businesses that had a large amount of small cash transactions — the Federal Reserve Board says that the term didn't come into use until the Watergate scandal, when Nixon's campaign staff had to hide the money used to pay the people who broke into his opponent's psychiatrist's office.

Making sure the money is legit

Money laundering is the process of creating a provenance for money acquired from illegal activities. Your average drug dealer, Mafia hit man, or corrupt politician doesn't accept credit cards, but he really doesn't want to keep lots of cash in his house, either. How can he collect interest on his money if it's locked in a safe in his closet? And besides, his friends are an unsavory sort; he can't trust them to stay away from his cache. If this criminal fellow takes all that cash to the bank, those pesky bankers will start asking a lot of questions, because they know that most people pursuing legitimate business activities get paid through checks or electronic direct deposit.

Hence, the felon with funds looks for a way to make it appear that the money is legitimate. All sorts of ways to launder money exist, ranging from making lots of small cash deposits to engaging in complicated series of financial trades and money transfers, especially between countries, that become difficult for investigators to trace. Sometimes these transactions look a lot like day trading, which is why legitimate brokerage firms opening day-trade accounts pay attention to who their customers are.

Fighting money laundering took on urgency after the September 11, 2001, attacks, because it was clear that someone somewhere had given some bad people a lot of cash to fund the preparation and execution of their deadly mission. The U.S. and several other nations increased their oversight of financial activities during the aftermath of the strikes on the World Trade Center and Pentagon. That's why a key piece of paperwork from your broker will be the anti-money laundering disclosure. The U.S. Treasury Department's Financial Crimes Enforcement Network (www.fincen.gov), which investigates money laundering, requires financial institutions to have enforcement procedures in place to verify that new investments were not made from ill-gotten funds.

In order for your brokerage firm to verify that it knows who its customers are and where their money came from, you'll probably have to provide the following information when you open a brokerage account:

✔ Your name

✔ Your date of birth

✔ Your street address

✔ Your place of business

✔ Your Social Security number or Taxpayer Identification Number

✔ Your driver's license and passport

✔ Copies of your financial statements

Following special rules for pattern day traders

Here's the problem for regulators: Many day traders lose money, and those losses can be magnified by the use of *leverage strategies* (trading with borrowed money, meaning that you can lose more money than you have in the quest for large profits, discussed in great detail in Chapter 9). If the customer who lost the money can't pay up, then the broker is on the hook. If too many customers lose money beyond what the broker can absorb, then the losses ripple through the financial system, and that's not good.

FINRA has a long list of rules that its member firms have to meet to stay in business. One, still known as NASD Rule 2520 despite the merger of the NASD that created FINRA, deals specifically with day traders. This rule sets the minimum account size and margin requirements for those who fit the definition of day traders, and I'll give you a hint: The requirements are stricter than for other types of accounts to reflect the greater risk, although they give some flexibility on maintenance margin.

FINRA defines day trading as the buying or selling of the same security on the same day in a margin account (that is, using borrowed money). Execute four or more of those day trades within five business days, and you are a *pattern day trader*, unless those four or more trades were 6 percent or less of all the trades you made over those five days.

The National Futures Association does not have a definition of day trading, because futures trades by their very nature are short term.

Here's why NASD Rule 2520 matters: If you are a pattern day trader, you can have a margin of 25 percent in your account, which means you can borrow 75 percent of the cost of the securities that you're trading. Most customers are only allowed to borrow 50 percent. The reason for the higher amount? Pattern day traders almost always close out their positions overnight, so the firm has less risk of having the loan outstanding. However, you have to have a margin account if you are a pattern day trader. That is, you have to sign an agreement saying that you understand the risks of borrowing money, including that you may have to repay more than is in your account and that your broker can sell securities out from under you to ensure you pay what is owed.

Under Rule 2520, you have to have at least $25,000 in your brokerage account at the start of the trading day. If you have losses that take your account below that, you have to come up with more money before your broker allows you to continue day trading. If you don't make the deposits necessary to bring your account up to at least $25,000 and at least 25 percent of the amount of money you've borrowed within five business days, you have to trade on a cash basis (no borrowing), assuming the firm will even let you trade.

Don't bother trying to plead your case, because the broker has to comply with the law. Firms pay a price if they let customers slide. In 2010, FINRA fined brokerage firm Scottrade $200,000 for allowing customers who met the definition of pattern day traders to trade without maintaining $25,000 in their accounts. The firm sent customers warnings but allowed them to trade in violation of the rule — a decision that wasn't cool with the regulators.

The rules set by FINRA and other self-regulatory organizations are minimum requirements. Brokerage firms are free to set higher limits for account size and borrowing, and many do in order to manage their own risks better.

Reporting taxes

On top of the identity paperwork, you have forms to fill out for tax reporting. IRS Form W9 keeps your taxpayer information on record. Then, after the end of the year, the brokerage firm sends you form 1099B listing how much money you made in your account, breaking it out between income and capital gains on stocks, bonds, options, and futures. You use that to ensure that the taxman gets his cut. Tax issues are covered in Chapter 15, but for now, just keep in mind that your federal, state, and local taxing authorities are paying attention to how well your trading does.

Watching Out for Insider Trading

The regulations about suitability and money laundering are very clear. You get a bunch of forms, you read them, you sign them, you present documentation, and everyone is happy. The rules that keep the markets functioning are clear and easy to follow.

But another set of rules also keeps markets functioning — namely, that no one has an unfair information advantage. If you knew ahead of time about big merger announcements, interest-rate decisions by the Federal Reserve, or a new sugar substitute that would eliminate demand for corn syrup, you could make a lot of money in the stock market, trading options on interest-rate futures or playing in the grain futures market. In doing so, however, you'd have an unfair advantage. If everyone believed that such unfair advantages were common, then they would be unwilling to participate in the capital markets, and that would harm the economy.

Insider trading is not well defined. Insider information includes any nonpublic information that a reasonable person would consider when deciding whether to buy or sell a security, and that's a pretty vague standard — especially because the whole purpose of research is to combine bits of immaterial information together to make investment decisions.

Day traders, who buy and sell so quickly, can be susceptible to hot tips. They may be participating in message boards or chat services where hot rumors can get the blood flowing on a dull day. If these hot tips are actually inside information, though, the trader can become liable. If you get great information from someone who is in a position to know — an officer, a director, a lawyer, an investment banker — and you act on this information in your trades or share it with someone who then acts on it, you may be looking at stiff penalties. Civil penalties are usually three times your profits, but the government may decide that your trading was part of a criminal enterprise, making the potential penalties much greater.

Insider trading is difficult to prove, so federal regulators use other tools to punish those it suspects of making improper profits. Martha Stewart wasn't sent to prison on insider trading charges; she was charged with obstructing justice by lying to investigators about what happened.

Whenever a big announcement is made, such as a merger, the exchanges go back and review trading for the past several days to see whether any unusual activities occurred in relevant securities and derivatives. Then they start tracing that activity back to the traders involved through the brokerage firms to see whether the activity was coincidence or part of a pattern.

By the way, most tips turn out to be groundless, or at least not as interesting to the market as it seems like they will be. Real insider information is hard to get, but starting a rumor is easy-peasy.

The bottom line is this: You may never come across inside information. But if a tip seems too good to be true, it probably is, so be careful.

Preparing for Rule Changes in Crisis Conditions

Many regulators sit on the sidelines, watching the markets with little interaction until a big crisis hits. When that happens, they rush in to calm the markets, often by setting up new and temporary rules until everyone is calm and normal market activities can resume.

Three main types of rules apply only in a crisis. They're circuit breakers, short-selling restrictions, and broken trades.

Circuit breakers are temporary halts on trading that apply when the market has excessive volatility, at least in the eye of the New York Stock Exchange. (Traders love volatility, but the NYSE isn't so keen.) Here's how circuit breakers work:

✔ **If the Dow Jones Industrial Average falls by 10 percent** before 2 p.m. New York time, trading stops for one hour. If it falls that much between 2 p.m. and 2:30 p.m., trading stops for a half hour. If it falls that much after 2:30 p.m., trading continues until the bell rings at 4 p.m. or until it hits the 20 percent mark, at which point it's done for the day.

✔ **If the Dow Jones Industrial Average falls by 20 percent** before 1 p.m. New York time, trading stops for two hours. If it falls that much between 1 p.m. and 2 p.m., trading stops for one hour. If it falls that much after 2 p.m., trading closes for the day.

✔ **If the Dow Jones Industrial Average falls by 30 percent,** trading ends for the day, although it most likely would have been shut down already due to the 20 percent rule.

The other exchanges don't have to follow the New York Stock Exchange rules, but they often do. In addition, the NYSE has the right to halt trading in any one security if it falls by more than 10 percent in a five-minute period.

Short-selling restrictions can be put into place if the regulatory authorities believe that action in one industry is dragging down the entire market. In the fall of 2008, short-selling was temporarily banned on financial services stocks.

Finally, if the market really goes haywire, the exchanges have the right to *break trades,* cancelling the buy and sell orders that looked too good to be true. When the Flash Crash of 2010 hit, many traders were thrilled to find that they could buy shares in illustrious and profitable corporations for a fraction of their usual share price. They weren't so thrilled when the exchanges cancelled those trades.

The Securities and Exchange Commission allows stock exchanges to break trades whenever prices in the system are "clearly erroneous," especially if a computer malfunction is involved. Some traders allege that trades are broken even if the prices are not clearly erroneous, denying them a sure-thing profit. The guidelines allow exchanges to consider breaking a trade whenever prices vary by 10 percent for stocks priced under $25, 5 percent for stocks priced between $25 and $50, and 3 percent of stocks priced over $50. Also, the review process should begin within 30 minutes of the trade.

If you see a fabulous bargain, go ahead and make the trade, but know that it may be cancelled if that great price was due to an error.

Taking on Partners

After your day trading proves to be wildly successful, you may want to take on partners to give you more trading capital and a slightly more regular income from the management fees. You can take on partners, but it's a lot of work, and once again, you must follow certain rules and procedures.

If you're trading options and futures and are operating a commodity pool or working as a commodity trading advisor, you need to register with the National Futures Association. If you're trading stocks and bonds, you have to register with the Securities and Exchange Commission unless you meet the exemption tests that let you operate as a hedge fund instead.

Registration is not a do-it-yourself project. For that matter, neither is ensuring that you are exempt from registration even though you have partners. An error or omission may have tremendous repercussions down the line, including fines or jail time. If you want to take on partners for your trading business, spend the money for qualified legal advice. Doing so protects you and shows prospective customers that you're serious about your business.

To qualify as a hedge fund, which is a private investment partnership that does not qualify for registration under the Investment Company Act of 1940, you have to deal only with *accredited investors* (those with at least $1 million in net worth or an annual income of $200,000) or *qualified purchasers* (those with $5 million in investable assets). The idea is that these people understand the risks they're taking and have enough money to lose. Hedge funds do not have to register with the SEC, but they may have to register with the NFA.

Whether or not you need to register, prospective investors will want to see proof that you know what you're doing and know how to handle their money. That step is beyond the scope of this book, but it's something for a successful day trader to consider.

Part II
Exploring Popular Day-Trading Strategies

Pitchfork pattern

Point 2

Point 3

Point 1

Head and shoulders pattern

Head

Left
Shoulder

Right
Shoulder

Cup and handle pattern

Handle

Cup

In this part...

- Find out how the best traders use research and tested strategies to help them determine when to buy and when to sell.

- Dig into money management, which is the key to successful trading. It helps you keep some powder dry for the next opportunity — and there will be a next opportunity, if you stay in the game.

- Get familiar with common strategies, including basic technical patterns, arbitrage, short selling, and leverage.

- Look here for an overview of the online brokers that specialize in traders.

Chapter 6

Managing Your Money and Positions

*Y*ou can't trade if you don't have money. Sure, your brokerage firm will loan you some funds, but only if you have some of your own funds to stake as margin. You have to keep some powder dry.

So how much of your money should you put on the line each time you trade? Risk too much, and you can be put out of business when you lose your capital. Risk too little, and you can be put out of business because you can't make enough money to cover your costs and time.

Over time, many academic theorists and experienced traders have developed different systems of money management designed to help traders, investors, and even gamblers manage their money in such a way as to maximize return while protecting capital. In this chapter, I explain how some of the better-known systems work so that you can figure out how to best apply them to your own trading. Doing so can help you protect your trading funds and figure out what size trades to enter so that you can stay trading as long as you like.

Note: Some of the material in this chapter is related to *leverage,* which is borrowing money to trade. Because leverage can dramatically increase the money that you have available to trade, as well as the risk and return profile of the trades that you make, it affects how you manage your money. Flip to Chapter 9 for more information on leverage and why you may want to use it.

Setting Your Earnings Expectations

Return is a function of risk. If you want a guaranteed return, go down to your bank and open a federally insured deposit account. The returns will be almost comically low, but you'll have no risk. If you want anything higher than what your bank is quoting, well, you have to take on at least a little bit of risk. When you take on risk, you increase both your likelihood of return and your likelihood of loss.

Successful day traders lose money all the time, but they're able to keep trading. If you're looking at a trade with even a 0.5 percent chance of 100 percent loss, the odds indicate that you would lose everything over the course of 200 trades — but only if you put all your money into each trade. If you put only some of your money in that trade, then you'll never lose everything in it. Sure, you won't get all of the upside potential, but you'll be able to hit the potential high return more often because you can make that trade more often.

The key term in investing is *diversification:* If your money is spread out among different assets, your long-return return will be higher for less total risk than if you commit to only one asset.

Trading isn't investing, but the power of diversification holds. If you divide your money among a few different trades or always keep some cash on hand in your account for the next trade, you'll almost definitely make more money in the long run than if you put all your money on one idea. Sure, risking everything on one idea may work a few times, but are you that lucky? If you're smart about your money management, you don't need luck.

Finding your expected return

Before you can figure out how to manage your money, you need to figure out how much money you can expect to make. This amount is your *expected return,* although some traders prefer the word *expectancy.* You start by laying out your trading system and testing it (described in Chapter 16). You're looking for four numbers:

- How many of your trades are losers?
- What's the typical percentage loss on a losing trade?
- How many of your trades are winners?
- What's the typical percentage gain on a winning trade?

Say that you determine that a certain trade loses 40 percent of the time, and it loses 1 percent. Sixty percent of the time, the trade wins, and winning trades are up 1.5 percent. With these numbers, you can calculate your per-trade expected return, like this:

% of losing trades × loss on losing trades + % of winning trades × gain on winning trades = expected return

Which in this example works out to be

0.40 × –0.01 + 0.60 × 0.015 = –0.004 + 0.009 = 0.005, which is the same as 0.5%.

On average, then, you would expect to earn 0.5 percent on every trade you make. Make enough trades with enough money, and it adds up.

You are more likely to make more money if you have a high expectation of winning trades and if those winners are expected to perform well. As long as probability of loss exists, you stand to lose money.

Determining your probability of ruin

Expected return is the happy number. It's how much money you can expect to make if you stay in the trading game. But it has a counterpart that, while not so happy, is at least as important: the *probability of ruin*.

Yes, ruin.

As long as some probability of loss exists, no matter how small, there is some probability that you can lose everything when you're trading. How much you can lose depends on how large each trade is relative to your account, the likelihood of each trade having a loss, and the size of the losses as they occur. (Don't think it can happen? That's what the top executives at AIG, Bear Stearns, Lehman Brothers, and Washington Mutual said.)

Many traders who have winning trading strategies find themselves shut down because a few bad trades ruined them. Every trader has some losses, but these losses don't have to end your trading career if you know the probability of ruin and how to use it. The equation you use to calculate the probability of ruin (*R*) is

$$R = \left[\frac{1-A}{1+A}\right]^{C}$$

In this equation, *A* is the advantage on each trade. That's the difference between the percentage of winning trades and the percentage of losing trades.

In the expected return example discussed earlier, trades win 60 percent of the time and lose everything 40 percent of the time. In that case, the trader's advantage would be

60% − 40% = 20%

And c is the number of trades in an account. Assume that you're dividing the account into ten equal parts, with the plan of making ten trades today. The probability of ruin today is 1.7 percent, as shown in this equation:

$$1.7\% = \left[\frac{1 - 0.20}{1 + 0.20}\right]^{10}$$

Now 1.7 percent isn't a high likelihood of ruin, but it's not zero, either. It can happen. If your advantage is smaller, if the expected loss is larger, or if the number of trades is fewer, then the likelihood becomes even higher.

Figure 6-1 shows you the relationship between the trader's advantage, number of trades, and the corresponding probability of ruin, rounded to the nearest percentage.

Probability of Ruin

Trader's Advantage	Number of Trades									
	1	2	3	4	5	6	7	8	9	10
2%	96%	92%	89%	85%	82%	79%	76%	73%	70%	67%
4%	92%	85%	79%	73%	67%	62%	57%	53%	49%	45%
6%	89%	79%	70%	62%	55%	49%	43%	38%	34%	30%
8%	85%	73%	62%	53%	45%	38%	33%	28%	24%	20%
10%	82%	67%	55%	45%	37%	30%	25%	20%	16%	13%
12%	79%	62%	49%	38%	30%	24%	18%	15%	1%	9%
14%	75%	57%	43%	32%	24%	18%	14%	10%	8%	6%
16%	72%	52%	38%	27%	20%	14%	10%	8%	5%	4%
18%	69%	48%	34%	23%	16%	1%	8%	5%	4%	3%
20%	67%	44%	30%	20%	13%	9%	6%	4%	3%	2%

Figure 6-1: Adding trader's advantage to the mix.

The bigger the edge and the more trades you can make, the lower your probability of ruin. Now, this model is a simplification in that it assumes that a losing trade goes to zero, and that's not always the case. In fact, if you use stops (automatic buy and sell orders, described in Chapter 2), you should never have a 100 percent loss. But you can see steady erosion in your account that will make it harder for you to make money. Hence, probability of ruin is a useful calculation that shows whether you'll lose money in the long run.

The more trades you can make with your account, the lower your probability of ruin. That's why money management is a key part of risk management.

Gaining Advantage with a Money-Management Plan

As long as there's some chance of losing all your money, you want to avoid betting it all on any one trade. But as long as there's a chance of making money, you want to have enough exposure to a winning trade so that you can post good profits. How do you figure out how much money to risk?

Later in this chapter, I describe some of the different money-management systems that traders use to figure out how much money to risk per trade. But first, I want to explain the logic behind a money-management system so that you understand why you need one. That way, you can better manage your funds and improve the dollar returns to your trading.

Minimizing damage while increasing opportunity

Expected return gives you an idea of how much you can get from a trade on average, but it doesn't tell you how much that return may vary from trade to trade. The average of 9, 10, and 11 is 10; the average of –90, 10, and 110 is also 10. The first number series is a lot narrower than the second. The wider the range of returns that a strategy has, the more *volatile* it is.

Measuring volatility

You can measure volatility in several ways. One common measurement is *standard deviation,* which tells you how much your actual return is likely to differ from what you expect to get. The higher the standard deviation, the more volatile, and riskier, the strategy.

In the derivatives markets, volatility is measured by a group of numbers known as the *Greeks:* delta, gamma, vega, and theta. These numbers are based on calculus, but don't worry if you forgot it or never took it!

✔ **Delta** is a ratio that tells you how much the option or future changes in price when

the underlying security or market index changes in price. Delta changes over time.

✔ **Gamma** is the rate of change on delta. A derivative's delta will be higher when it is close to the expiration date, for example, than when the expiration date is further away.

✔ **Vega** is the amount that the derivative would change in price if the implied volatility of the underlying security shifted by 1 percent.

✔ **Theta** is the amount that a derivative's price declines as it gets closer to the day of expiration.

Day traders seek more volatile securities because they offer more opportunities to make money during any given day. For this reason, they need to have ways to minimize the damage that may occur while being able to capitalize on the upward swings. Money management can help with that.

Staying in the market longer

You have only a limited amount of money to trade. Whether it's $1,000 or $1,000,000, once the money's gone, you're out. The problem is that you can have a long string of losing trades before the markets go in a direction that favors you and your system.

Say you trade 100 percent of your account. If you have one trade that goes down 100 percent, then you have nothing. If you divide your account into ten parts, then you can have ten total losers before you're out. If you start with ten equal parts and double each time you lose, you can be out after four losing trades.

On the other hand, if you divide your account into 100 portions, then you can endure 100 losing trades. If you trade fractions of your account, then you can keep going indefinitely, or at least until you get down to a level that's too low to place a minimum order. (That's the philosophy behind the Kelly Criterion, described later in this chapter.) Money management can keep you in the game longer, and that gives you more opportunities to place winning trades.

The riskier your trading strategy, the more thought you need to put into money management. Otherwise, you can find yourself out of the market in no time.

Getting out before you lose everything

A money-management system works best if the trader using it knows when to close out a position. You have to have a trading plan and know when you're willing to get out: at the recent high? A few ticks below the most recent high? A few ticks up from where you entered? A few ticks below where you entered, to limit your losses?

Sometimes the market will go nuts, and you won't be able to get out as quickly as you'd like. In these situations, those tiny chances of losing everything kick in, and good money management offers the most protection.

On more ordinary trading days, be sure to supplement your position size and capital protection efforts with ordinary trading tools: trade planning and use of stop and limit orders. You can review these in Chapter 2.

Accounting for opportunity costs

Opportunity cost is the value you give up because you choose to do something else. In trading, each dollar you commit to one trade is a dollar that you cannot commit to another trade. Thus, each dollar you trade carries some opportunity cost, and good traders seek to minimize this cost. During the course of the trading day, you may see several great trades, and some opportunities will show up before you are ready to close out a different trade.

Because a money-management system holds back some of your capital, you are more likely to have funds to take advantage of these opportunities than if you allocate your cash willy-nilly. Your plan may cause you to miss some trades, and that's okay. If you believe that you are missing too many, though, you may want to experiment with another system to see whether it gives you better results. Whatever you do, don't ignore money management.

If you have committed all your capital to one trade, you miss out on the second. That alone is a good reason to keep some money on the table each time you trade.

Examining Styles of Money Management

Over the years, traders have developed many different ways to manage their money. Some money-management strategies are rooted in superstition, but most are based on different statistical probability theories. The underlying idea is that you should never place all of your money in a single trade. Instead, you should put in an amount appropriate given the level of volatility. Otherwise, you risk losing everything too soon.

Calculating position size under many of these formulas is tricky stuff. That's why brokerage firms and trading software packages often include money-management calculators. Check Chapter 11 for more information on the brokers and Chapter 12 for more on different software and research services.

In the following sections, I offer a sampling of the many different money-management methods available. Other methods are out there, and none is suitable to all markets all the time. If you trade both options and stocks, you may want to use one system for option trades and another for stock trades. And if that's your situation, you have one big money-management decision to make before you begin: how much money to allocate to each market!

Limiting portions: Fixed fractional

Fixed-fractional trading assumes that you want to limit each trade to a set portion of your total account, often between 2 and 10 percent. Within that range, you trade a larger percentage of money in less risky trades and a smaller amount of money for more risky trades. (In other words, this method isn't all that "fixed," but no one asked me to pick a name for the system!)

Here's the fixed fractional equation for calculating fixed-fractional trade proportions.

$$N = f\left(\frac{equity}{|trade\,risk|}\right)$$

N is the number of contracts or shares of stock you should trade, f is the fixed fraction of your account that you have decided to trade, *equity* is the value of your total account, and *trade risk* is the amount of money you could lose on the transaction. Because trade risk is a negative number, you need to convert it to a positive number to make the equation work. Those vertical bars in the equation ($|\;\;|$) are the sign for absolute value, and that means that you convert the number between them to a positive number.

Here's an example that uses the equation. Assume that you've decided to limit each trade to 10 percent of your account, you have a $20,000 account, and you are looking at contracts with a value of $3,500. You want to set your trade based on the assumption that the contracts go to zero, to look at the worst-case scenario. Plugging the numbers into the equation and doing the math gives you

$$0.57 = 0.10\left(\frac{20,000}{|-3,500|}\right)$$

Of course, you probably can't trade 0.57 of a contract, so in this case, you would have to round up to one.

Protecting profits: Fixed ratio

Developed by a trader named Ryan Jones, the *fixed-ratio* money-management system is used in trading options and futures. The idea behind fixed-ratio trading is to help you increase your exposure to the market while protecting your accumulated profits.

To find the optimal number of options or futures contracts to trade, you use this equation

$$N = 0.50 \left(\sqrt{1 + 8\,(P/\Delta)} + 1 \right)$$

_N_ is the number of contracts or shares of stock that you should trade, _P_ is your accumulated profit to date, and Δ (delta) is the dollar amount you would need before you could trade a second contract or another lot of stock. (Don't confuse this delta with the delta used to measure of volatility; see the sidebar "Measuring volatility" for more information.)

For example, the minimum margin for Chicago Mercantile Exchange E-mini S&P 500 futures contract, which gives you exposure to the Standard & Poor's 500 stock index, is $3,500. Until you have another $3,500 in your account, you can't trade a second contract. If you use fixed-ratio money management to trade this future, your delta is $3,500.

Here's an example that uses fixed-ration calculation. Assume your delta is $3,500 and that you have $10,000 in account profits. If you plug in the numbers and calculate, you see that you should trade 2.94 contracts:

$$2.94 = 0.50 \left(\sqrt{1 + 8\,(10{,}000/3{,}500)} + 1 \right)$$

What this means is that you can trade only one or two contracts, nothing in between. That's one of the imperfections of most money-management systems.

Sticking to 10 percent: Gann

William Gann developed a complicated system for identifying securities trades. Part of his system was a list of rules for managing money, and many traders follow that if nothing else.

The primary rule is this: Divide your money into ten equal parts and never place more than one 10 percent portion on a single trade. This strategy helps control your risk, whether or not you use Gann. (Gann is discussed in Chapter 7.)

Finding the ideal percentage: Kelly Criterion

The Kelly Criterion lets you determine the ideal percentage of your portfolio to put at risk. To calculate how much of your portfolio to put at risk, you need to know what percentage of your trades are expected to win, the return from a winning trade, and the ratio performance of winning trades to losing trades. The shorthand that many traders use for the Kelly Criterion is edge divided by odds, and in practice, the formula looks like this:

$$\text{Kelly}\% = W - \left(\frac{1 - W}{R} \right)$$

W is the percentage of winning trades, and R is the ratio of the average gain of the winning trades relative to the average loss of the losing trades.

To see this formula in action, consider a system that loses 40 percent of the time with a loss of 1 percent and that wins 60 percent of the time with a gain of 1.5 percent. (Look familiar? I used this same example at the beginning of the chapter.) Plugging that info into the Kelly formula, the right percentage to trade is 33.3 percent:

$$\text{Kelly}\% = W - \left(\frac{1 - W}{R} \right) = 0.60 - \left(\frac{1 - 0.60}{0.015/0.010} \right) = 3.33\%$$

In this situation, as long as you limit your trades to no more than 33 percent of your capital, you should never run out of money. The problem, of course, is that if you have a long string of losses, you can find yourself with too little money to execute a trade. Many traders use a "half-Kelly" strategy, limiting each trade to half the amount indicated by the Kelly Criterion, as a way to keep the trading account from shrinking too quickly. They are especially likely to do this if the Kelly Criterion generates a number greater than about 20 percent, as it does in this example.

This money-management method emerged from statistical work done at Bell Laboratories in the 1950s. The goal was to figure out the best ways to manage signal-noise issues in long-distance telephone communications. Very quickly, the mathematicians who worked on it saw that it could be applied to gambling, and in no time, the formula took off. In fact, a math professor, Edward O. Thorpe, used the Kelly Criterion with great success to win big at blackjack in Las Vegas in the early 1960s, which led to a change in casino rules.

In a casino, the rules are against you. If you find an edge, in no time, you'll be asked to leave, and the rules may be changed. In the financial markets, the odds are even or slightly in your favor, so you have a better opportunity to make money by practicing your strategies.

Doubling down: Martingale

The *martingale* style of money management is common with serious casino gamblers, and many traders apply it as well. It's designed to improve the amount of money you can earn in a game that has even odds. Most casino odds favor the house (roulette wheels used to be evenly black and red, but casinos found that they could make more money if they inserted a green slice for zero, thus throwing off the odds). Day trading, on the other hand, is a zero-sum game, especially in the options and futures markets. For every winner, there is a loser, so the odds of any one trade being successful are even. The martingale system is designed to work in any market where the odds are even or in your favor.

Under the martingale strategy, you start with a set amount per trade, say $2,000. If your trade succeeds, you trade another $2,000. If your trade loses, you double your next order (after you close or limit the first trade) so that you can win back your loss. (You may have heard gamblers talk about *doubling down?* Well, this is what they're doing.)

Under the martingale system, you always come out ahead *as long as you have an infinite amount of money to trade.* See the problem? You can run out of money before you have a trade that works. The market, on the other hand, has almost infinite resources because of the huge volume of participants coming and going all over the world. In short, you're at an enormous disadvantage. As long as you have a disadvantage, thoughtful money management is critical.

Letting a program guide you: Monte Carlo simulation

If you have the programming expertise or buy the right software, you can run what's called a *Monte Carlo simulation,* named for the famous casino town. In this calculation, you enter in your risk and return parameters and your account value and let the program run. It then returns the optimal trade size. The system is not perfect; it can't incorporate every market situation that you'll face, and it has the fractional trade problem that the other systems do. But it has one big advantage: It can incorporate random changes in the markets in ways that simpler money-management models cannot.

There are different schools of thought about the statistical theories that go into a Monte Carlo simulation. Fortunately, you don't have to know them to use the system's estimates of the return in the market to help you determine your position sizes as the market changes.

A Monte Carlo simulation is more dynamic than most of the other money-management systems, but it isn't as easy to use. For that reason, it isn't a do-it-yourself project unless you have extensive experience creating these programs. If you are interested, you need to find a suitable program. Many brokerage firms include Monte Carlo simulation packages in their day trading platforms. If you want to find stand-alone software, two options are offered by Probilitech, a low-end system available at `http://probilitech.com`, and Oracle Corporation's Crystal Ball, a high-end system discussed at `www.oracle.com/us/products/middleware/bus-int/crystalball/index.html`.

Considering past performance: Optimal F

The *Optimal F* system of money management was devised by Ralph Vince, and he's written several books about this and other money-management issues (see the appendix for more information). The idea is that you determine the ideal fraction of your money to allocate per trade based on past performance. If your Optimal F is 18 percent, then each trade should be 18 percent of your account — no more, no less. The system is similar to the fixed-fraction and fixed-ratio methods discussed earlier but with a few differences.

To find the number of shares of stock, N, to trade under Optimal F, you use this equation:

$$N = \frac{\left(F \times \frac{equity}{risk} \right)}{price}$$

F is a factor based on the basis of historical data, *risk* is the biggest percentage loss that you experienced in the past, *equity* is the amount of money in your account, and *price* is the current price. Using these numbers, you can find the contracts or shares you need to buy.

Here's an example: Assume your account has $25,000, your biggest loss (risk) was 40 percent, your F is 30 percent, and you're looking at a stock trading at $25 per share. Plug in the numbers and calculation to find that you should buy 750 shares:

$$750 = \frac{\left(0.30 \times \frac{25,000}{0.40} \right)}{25}$$

The Optimal F number itself is a mean based on historical trade results. The risk number is also based on past returns, and that's one problem with this method: It kicks in only after you have some trade data. A second problem is that you need to set up a spreadsheet to calculate it (so read Ralph Vince's book if you want to try it out). Some traders only use Optimal F in certain market conditions, in part because the history changes each time a trade is made, and that history doesn't always lead to usable numbers.

Seeing How Money Management Affects Your Return

Describing why you need money management is one thing, but showing you how it works is more fun. And because I love making spreadsheets (we all need a hobby, right?), I pulled one together to show you how different ways of managing your money may affect your return.

In Figure 6-2, I started with the expected return assumptions that I used in the earlier example: 40 percent of the time a trade loses, and it loses 1 percent. The trade wins 60 percent of the time, and winning trades are up 1.5 percent. I pick a hypothetical account of $20,000 and set up mock trades using these expected return numbers. Then I compared the performance of martingale and Kelly money management to betting the whole account each time.

As the calculations in Figure 6-2 show, you end up with the most money from trading the entire account. That doesn't mean you always get the most money this way, just that that's how the numbers worked out in this case, given the 60/40 win ratio and a 3/2 winning size/losing size ratio. (Keep in mind that if you were using a Kelly or martingale system, you'd probably be doing something with the rest of the account rather than just letting it sit there.)

This is just an example, applying some different strategies to different hypothetical returns. I'm not recommending any one system over another. The best system for you depends on what assets you're trading, your personal trading style, and how much money you have to trade.

Planning for Your Profits

In addition to determining how much to trade each time you place an order, you need a plan for what to do with the profits that accumulate in your account. That's as much a part of money management as calculating your probability of ruin and determining trade size.

Are you going to add the money to your account and trade it as before? Leverage your profits by trading them more aggressively than your core account? Pull money out and put it into long-term investments? Or a combination of the three? The following sections explore some of your options.

Martingale: Starting with 10% and Doubling Losses

	Performance	Intial Account Value	% Traded	Amount Traded	Ending Account Value	% Change
Trade 1	1.5%	$ 20,000	10%	$ 2,000	$ 20,030	
Trade 2	1.5%	$ 20,030		$ 2,000	$ 20,060	
Trade 3	-1.0%	$ 20,060		$ 2,000	$ 20,040	
Trade 4	-1.0%	$ 20,040		$ 4,000	$ 20,000	
Trade 5	1.5%	$ 20,000		$ 8,000	$ 20,120	
Trade 6	1.5%	$ 20,120		$ 2,000	$ 20,150	
Trade 7	-1.0%	$ 20,150		$ 2,000	$ 20,130	
Trade 8	-1.0%	$ 20,130		$ 4,000	$ 20,090	
Trade 9	1.5%	$ 20,090		$ 8,000	$ 20,210	
Trade 10	1.5%	$ 20,210		$ 2,000	$ 20,240	1.20%

Kelly: Trading 33%

	Performance	Intial Account Value	% Traded	Amount Traded	Ending Account Value
Trade 1	1.5%	$ 20,000	33%	$ 6,660	$ 20,100
Trade 2	1.5%	$ 20,100	33%	$ 6,693	$ 20,200
Trade 3	-1.0%	$ 20,200	33%	$ 6,727	$ 20,133
Trade 4	-1.0%	$ 20,133	33%	$ 6,704	$ 20,066
Trade 5	1.5%	$ 20,066	33%	$ 6,682	$ 20,166
Trade 6	1.5%	$ 20,166	33%	$ 6,715	$ 20,267
Trade 7	-1.0%	$ 20,267	33%	$ 6,749	$ 20,199
Trade 8	-1.0%	$ 20,199	33%	$ 6,726	$ 20,132
Trade 9	1.5%	$ 20,132	33%	$ 6,704	$ 20,233
Trade 10	1.5%	$ 20,233	33%	$ 6,738	$ 20,334

1.67%

Betting Everything

	Performance	Intial Account Value	% Traded	Amount Traded	Ending Account Value
Trade 1	1.5%	$ 20,000	100%	$ 20,000	$ 20,300
Trade 2	1.5%	$ 20,300	100%	$ 20,300	$ 20,605
Trade 3	-1.0%	$ 20,605	100%	$ 20,605	$ 20,398
Trade 4	-1.0%	$ 20,398	100%	$ 20,398	$ 20,194
Trade 5	1.5%	$ 20,194	100%	$ 20,194	$ 20,497
Trade 6	1.5%	$ 20,497	100%	$ 20,497	$ 20,805
Trade 7	-1.0%	$ 20,805	100%	$ 20,805	$ 20,597
Trade 8	-1.0%	$ 20,597	100%	$ 20,597	$ 20,391
Trade 9	1.5%	$ 20,391	100%	$ 20,391	$ 20,697
Trade 10	1.5%	$ 20,697	100%	$ 20,697	$ 21,007

5.04%

Figure 6-2: How money management affects your return.

Compounding interest

Compound interest is a simple concept: Every time you get a return, that return goes into your account. You keep earning a return on it, which increases your account size some more. You keep earning a return on your return, and pretty soon, the numbers get to be pretty big.

To benefit from that compounding, many traders add their profits back into their accounts and keep trading them as a way to build account size. Although day traders earn little to no interest (which is compensation for loaning out money — say, by buying bonds), the basic principle holds: By returning profits to the trading account to generate even more profits, the account should grow over time.

This practice of keeping profits in the account to trade makes a lot of sense for smaller traders who want to build their accounts and take more significant positions over time.

Pyramiding power

Pyramiding involves taking trading profits and borrowing heavily against them to generate even more profits. Traders usually do this during the day, using unrealized profits in trades that are not yet closed as collateral for loans used to establish new positions. If the new positions are profitable, the trader can keep borrowing until it's time to close everything at the end of the day.

Pyramiding works great as long as the markets are moving in the right direction. If all the positions in the pyramid remain profitable, you can make a lot of money during the course of the day. But if one of those positions turns against you, then the structure collapses and you end up with a call on your margin.

Figure 6-3 starts with an initial trade of $2,000 and assumes a return of 10 percent on each transaction — not realistic, necessarily, but it makes for a nice chart. If the profits from each trade are used as collateral for borrowing, and if that 10 percent return holds all day, then the trader can make 17 percent by pyramiding those gains. If a reversal hits before the end of the trading session and the positions lose 10 percent, then pyramiding magnifies the losses — assuming your broker would let you keep borrowing. After all, the borrowed money has to be repaid regardless of what happens in the market.

Pyramiding is not related to a pyramid scheme. In trading terms, *pyramiding* is a way to borrow against your profits to generate even bigger profits. A *pyramid scheme* is a fraud that requires participants to recruit new members, and fees paid by the new members go to the older ones. Eventually, the pyramid collapses because recruiting new members gets too difficult and those at the bottom get nothing. Be aware that some investment frauds have been structured as pyramid schemes. Steer clear of deals that sound fabulous and require you to recruit others.

Pyramiding increases your trading risk but also your expected return. It's a useful way to grow a portion of your trading account, especially when the market is favoring your trading system. This technique is good for medium-sized accounts, which have enough money that, if a pyramid were to collapse on you, you'd still have enough to stay in the market.

Making regular withdrawals

Because day trading can be so risky, many traders look to diversify their total financial risk. One way to do this is to pull money out of the trading account to put into a less volatile long-term investment. Many traders routinely pull out a percentage of their profits and put that money into government bonds, a low-risk mutual fund, or real estate. None of these investments is as glamorous or exciting as day trading, but that's the point: Trading is hard work, and anyone can lose money any day, no matter how big his account is or how much money he's made so far. By moving some money out, a trader can build a cushion for a bad trading stretch, prepare for retirement, and have some money to walk away for a short period or even forever. Having money in low-risk investments can greatly reduce the stress and the fear that go with trading.

The larger the account, the easier it is to pull money out, but even smaller traders should consider taking 5 or 10 percent of each quarter's profits and moving them into another type of investment. Many brokerage firms can set up automatic withdrawal plans that zap money from your trading account to a stock or bond mutual fund if you don't trust yourself to do it.

Pyramiding magnifies returns
Assume that you need to maintain 25% margin

	Initial Trade Equity	Amount Borrowed	Total Trade Size	Profit at Negative 10% Return
First trade	$ 2,000	$ -	$ 2,000	$ 200
Second trade	$ 200	$ 600	$ 800	$ 80
Third trade	$ 80	$ 240	$ 320	$ 32
Fourth trade	$ 32	$ 96	$ 128	$ 13
Fifth trade	$ 13	$ 38	$ 51	$ 5
Sixth trade	$ 5	$ 15	$ 20	$ 2
Return on initial $2,000 trade:	$ 332			
Percentage return:	17%			

... And pyramiding magnifies losses

	Initial Trade Equity	Amount Borrowed	Total Trade Size	Profit at Negative 10% Return
First trade	$ 2,000	$ -	$ 2,000	$ (200)
Second trade	$ 200	$ 600	$ 800	$ (80)
Third trade	$ 80	$ 240	$ 320	$ (32)
Fourth trade	$ 32	$ 96	$ 128	$ (13)
Fifth trade	$ 13	$ 38	$ 51	$ (5)
Sixth trade	$ 5	$ 15	$ 20	$ (2)
Return on initial $2,000 trade:	$ (332)			
Percentage return:	-17%			

Figure 6-3: Pyramiding magnifies returns and losses.

Chapter 7

Technical Analysis 101

● ●

In This Chapter

▶ Researching markets and trades

▶ Using technical analysis to forecast prices

▶ Gleaning information from the charts

▶ Reviewing schools of thought in technical analysis

▶ Avoiding the traps that technical analysts can fall into

● ●

*I*n some ways, day trading is easy. Open up an account with a brokerage firm and off you go, buying and selling securities! But how are you going to know when to buy and when to sell? That's not a simple matter. Most day traders fail because it's easy to place the order but hard to know whether the order is the right one.

Traders use different research systems to evaluate the market and have access to tools that can help them figure out when a security is likely to go up in price and when it is likely to go down. Two primary types of investment research systems exist: technical analysis and fundamental analysis. Technical analysis, which is widely used by day traders, looks at the supply and demand for a security and how it shows up in price data. Fundamental analysis, which is less commonly used by day traders, looks at the financial and operational factors that affect a security's value. This chapter tells you what you need to know about each.

Don't be fooled by anyone offering to sell you a guaranteed system for making money in day trading. Anyone with a surefire system has already made a fortune and retired to a private island in a tropical climate. He or she is too busy enjoying drinks with umbrellas in them to share that trading system with you.

Comparing Research Techniques Used in Day Trading

Day traders need to make decisions fast, and they need to have a framework for doing so. That's why they rely on research. But what kind? Most day traders rely heavily on *technical* research, which is an analysis of charts formed by price patterns to measure the relative supply and demand for the security. But some people use fundamental analysis to help inform their decisions, too.

Research systems fall into two categories: fundamental and technical:

- **Fundamental research looks at the specific factors that affect a security's value.** What's the relationship between the trade deficit and futures on two-year treasury notes? What's the prediction for summer rainfall in Iowa, and how will that affect December corn futures? How dependent is a company on new products to generate earnings growth?

- **Technical research looks at the supply and demand for the security itself.** Are people buying more and more shares? Is the price going up a lot as they buy more, or does the price go up just a little bit? Does it seem like everyone who is likely to buy has already bought, and what does that mean for the future price?

What direction is your research?

Securities are affected by matters specific to each type and by huge global macroeconomic factors that affect every security in different ways. Some traders prefer to think of the big picture first, whereas others start small. And some use a combination of the two approaches. Neither is better; each is simply a different perspective on what's happening in the markets.

Top-down research

With a *top-down* approach, the trader looks at the big economic factors: interest rates, exchange rates, government policies, and the like. How will these things affect a particular sector or security? Is this a good time to buy stocks or short interest-rate futures? The top-down approach can help evaluate the prices in big market sectors, and it can also help determine what factors are affecting trading in a subsector. You don't have to trade stock market index futures to know that the outlook for the overall stock market will have an effect on the trading of any specific company's stock.

Bottom-up research

Bottom-up analysis looks at the specific performance of the asset. It looks at the company's prospects and then works backward to figure out how it will get there. What has to happen for a company's stock price to go up 20 percent? What earnings does it have to report, what types of buyers have to materialize, and what else has to happen in the economy?

Fundamental research

Day traders do very little fundamental research. Sure, they know that demand for ethanol affects corn prices, but they really want to know what the price will do right now relative to where the price was a few minutes ago. How a proposed farm bill might affect ethanol prices in six years doesn't figure into day trading.

Knowing a little bit about the fundamentals — those basic facts that affect the supply and demand for a security in all markets — can help the day trader respond better to news events. It can also give you a better feel for when *swing trading* (holding a position for several days) will generate a better profit than closing out every night. But knowing a lot can drag a day trader down.

Fundamental analysis can actually *hurt* you in day trading, because you may start making decisions for the wrong reasons. If you know too much about the fundamentals, you may start considering long-term outlooks instead of short-term activity. For example, many people buy Standard & Poor's (S&P) 500 Index mutual funds for their retirement accounts because they believe that in the long run, the market will go up. That does not mean that people should trade E-mini S&P futures or an S&P exchange-traded fund today, because a lot of zigzagging can happen between now and the arrival of the long-run price appreciation.

Fundamental research falls into two main categories: top-down and bottom-up. As I mention earlier, top-down starts with broad economic considerations and then looks at how those will affect a specific security. Bottom-up looks at specific securities and then determines whether those are good buys or sells right now.

If you love the very idea of fundamental research, then day trading is probably not for you. Day trading requires quick responses to price changes, not a careful understanding of accounting methods and business trends. A little fundamental analysis can be helpful in day trading, but a lot can slow you down.

Technical analysis

Information about the price, time, and volume of a security's trading can be plotted on a chart. The plots form patterns that can be analyzed to show what happened. How did the supply and demand for a security change, and why? And what does that mean for future supply and demand? Technical analysis is based on the premise that securities prices move in trends and that those trends repeat themselves over time. Therefore, a trader who can recognize a trend on the charts can determine where prices are most likely to go until some unforeseen event comes along that creates a new trend.

Most traders rely on software to spot patterns because it makes them easier to find and to act upon. Remember that the vast volume of short-term trading takes place by computer algorithm. You can't beat them, so join them.

The basic element of technical analysis is a *bar,* which shows you the high, low, open, and closing price of a security for a given day. It looks like the one shown in Figure 7-1.

Figure 7-1:
A bar
displays
high, low,
open, and
closing.

Bulls and bears and pork bellies

Traders work cattle and hogs at the Chicago Mercantile Exchange, but bulls and bears are in every market. What do those animals symbolize?

✔ *Bulls* believe that the market is going up, and bullish news and bullish patterns are good for them.

✔ *Bears* believe that the market is going down, so bearish news and bearish patterns are good for them.

No one is exactly sure why the words came to symbolize market behavior, but the best guess for the symbolism is that, when attacked, bulls charge and bears retreat.

In most markets, every day generates a new *bar* (many traders talk about bars instead of days, and they aren't talking about where they go after work). A collection of bars, with all their different high, low, open, and close points, is put together into a larger *chart*. Often, a plot of the volume for each bar runs underneath, with the result looking like Figure 7-2.

Figure 7-2:
A plot of volume underneath a year's worth of bars.

Many patterns formed in the charts are associated with future price moves. Technical analysts thus spend a lot of time looking at the charts to see whether they can predict what's going to happen. Many software packages (some of which are discussed in Chapter 12) send traders signals when certain technical patterns occur so that the traders can place orders accordingly.

Technical analysis is a way to measure the supply and demand in the market. It's a tool for analyzing the markets, not predicting them. If deciphering the meaning of the data were that easy, everyone would be able to make money in the markets.

Price changes

Market observers debate *market efficiency* all the time. In an efficient market, all information about a security is already included in the security's price, so there's no point to doing any research at all. Few market participants are willing to go that far, but they concede the point that the price is the single most important summary of information about a company. That means that technical analysis, looking at how the price changes over time, is a way of learning about whether a security's prospects are improving or getting worse.

Volume changes

The basic bar shows how price changed during the day, but adding *volume* information tells the other part of the story: how much of a security was demanded at that price. If demand is going up, then more people want the security, so they are willing to pay more for it. The price tells traders what the market knows; the volume tells them how many people in the market know it.

Using Technical Analysis

Technical analysis helps day traders identify changes in the supply and demand for a security that may lead to profitable price changes ahead. It gives traders a way to talk about and think about the market so that they can be more effective.

Most brokerage firm quote systems generate charts, sometimes with the help of additional software that automatically marks the chart with trendlines. Technical traders look for those trendlines. Before placing an order to buy or sell, a trader needs to know whether the security's price is going up and whether that trend is going to continue.

One interesting aspect of technical analysis is that the basics hold no matter what market you're looking at. Technical analysis can help you monitor trends in the stock market, the bond market, the commodity market, and the currency market. Anywhere people try to match their supply and their demand to make a market, technical analysis can be used to show how well they're doing it.

First things first: Should you follow a trend or deviate from it?

The next sections go into all sorts of detail about how to spot a trend, but the key thing to understand as a day trader is whether you should follow a trend or not. Sometimes a trend is good to follow, but sometimes deviating from it is better.

Remember when you were a kid wanting to do something that all your friends were doing and your mother would invariably say, "If all your friends jumped off of a bridge, would you have to jump off, too?"

Well, Mom, guess what? If the bridge were on fire, the escape routes blocked by angry mobs, and the water just a few feet down, then yes, I just might jump off the bridge like everyone else. Likewise, if someone were paying us good money to jump and I knew I wasn't likely to get hurt on the way down,

I'd be over the railing in a flash. Sometimes being a follower is good. But if my friends were idiots, there were no fire and no angry mob, and I couldn't swim, I might not be so hasty to leap.

Trend following is like those mythical childhood friends on that mythical hometown bridge. Sometimes, you should join the crowd. Other times, deviating is best. When should you follow and when should you deviate? Well, that depends. You need to know what you're trading and what the other people trading that asset are considering when they place their orders. That's why a good understanding of what trends are and how they work can help you.

Finding trends

A technical analyst usually starts off by looking at a chart and drawing lines that show the overall direction of the price bars for the period in question. Rather than plot the graph on paper or print out the screen, she probably uses software to draw the lines. Figure 7-3 shows what this basic analysis looks like.

With the basic trendlines in place, the trader can start thinking about how the trends have played out so far and what may happen next.

Figure 7-3:
Basic analysis of trends in price bar changes draws lines showing the general movement.

Drawing trendlines

As shown in the preceding section, the most basic trendline is a line that shows the general direction of the trend. And that's a good start, but it doesn't tell you all you need to know. The next step is to take out your ruler, or set your software, to find the trendlines that connect the highs and the lows. Doing so creates a channel that tells you the *support level* (the trendline for the lows) and the *resistance level* (the trendline for the highs), as Figure 7-4 shows. Unless something happens to change the trend, securities tend to move within the channel, so extending the line into the future can give you a sense of where the security is likely to trade.

Figure 7-4:
Drawing
trendlines
to identify
channels.

When a security hits its support level, it is usually seen as relatively cheap, so that's a good time to buy. When a security hits its resistance level, it is usually seen as relatively expensive, so that's a good time to sell. Some day traders find that simply moving between buying at the support and selling at the resistance can be a profitable strategy, at least until something happens that changes those two levels.

Calculating indicators

In addition to drawing lines, technical analysts use their calculators — or have their software make calculations — to come up with different *indicators,* numbers used to gauge performance. The following sections cover some common indicators, with definitions.

Pivot points

A *pivot point* is the average of the high, low, and close price for the day. If the next day's price closes above the pivot point, that sets a new support level, and if the next day's price is below the pivot point, that sets a new resistance level. Hence, calculating pivot points and how they change may indicate new upper and lower stops for your trading. (Refer to Chapter 2 for more about using stops.)

For markets that are open more or less continuously, such as foreign exchange, the close price is set arbitrarily. The usual custom in the United States is to use the price at 4 p.m. Eastern time, which is the closing time for the New York Stock Exchange.

Moving averages

Looking at all those little high-low-open-close lines on a chart will give your bifocals a workout. To make the trend easier to spot, traders calculate a *moving average* by averaging the closing prices for a given time period. Some traders prefer to look at the last 5 days; some at the last 60 days. Every day, the latest price is added, and the oldest price is dropped to make that day's calculation. Given the wonders of modern computing technology, pulling up moving averages for almost any time period you want is easy. The average for each day is then plotted against the price chart to show how the trend is changing over time. Figure 7-5 shows an example of a 10-day moving average chart.

Figure 7-5: A price chart showing a 10-day moving average.

Traders use the moving average line to look for crossovers, convergences, and divergences. A *crossover* occurs whenever the price crosses the moving average line. Usually, buying is a good idea when the price crosses above the moving average line, and selling is a good idea when the price crosses below it.

To use *convergence* and *divergence* in analysis, the trader looks at moving averages from different time periods, such as 5 days, 10 days, and 20 days. Figure 7-6 shows what convergence and divergence look like.

Figure 7-6:
Moving
average
conver-
gence and
divergence.

Three Moving Averages
5-day _____
10-day _____
20-day _____

When two or three of the moving average lines converge (come together), that means that the trend may be ending. That often makes it a good time to buy if the trend has been down and a good time to sell if the trend has been up. If two or three of the moving average lines split up and diverge, the trend is likely to continue. That means it's probably a good time to buy if the trend is up and sell if the trend is down.

A moving average is a lagging indicator. It sums up trading activity in the last 5, 10, 30, or 60 days, which means that the line smooths out changes in the trend that may affect future prices, giving you a more accurate picture of the overall trend over the time period.

Observing trend phases

Price trends tend to move in cycles that can be seen on the charts or observed in market behavior. Knowing the phases of a trend can help you better evaluate what's happening. Here is a summary of some phases of a trend:

- **Accumulation:** This is the first part of the trend, where traders get excited about a security and its prospects. They start new positions or add to existing ones.

- **Main phase (also called *continuation*):** Here, the trend moves along nicely, with no unusual price action. The highs get higher on an uptrend, and the lows get lower on a downtrend. A trader may make money — but not big money — following the trend here.

✔ **Consolidation (also called *congestion*):** This phase indicates a sideways market. The security stays within the trend but without hitting higher highs or lower lows. It just stays within the trading range. A consolidation phase is good for scalpers, who make a large volume of trades in search of very small profits. It can be boring for everyone else.

✔ **Retracement (also called *correction* or *pullback*):** Retracement is a secondary trend, a short-term pullback away from the main trend to the support level. Retracements create buying opportunities, but they can also kill day traders who are following the trend.

✔ **Distribution:** In the distribution phase, traders don't think that the security can go up in price any more. Hence, they tend to sell in large volume.

✔ **Reversal:** At this point, the trend changes. It's time to sell if you've been following an uptrend and buy if you've been following a downtrend. Many reversals follow classic patterns, which are discussed later in this chapter.

Those ever-changing trends

Although technical traders look to follow trends, they also look for situations where the trend changes so that they can find new profit opportunities. In general, day traders are going to follow trends, and swing traders — those who hold securities for a few days or even weeks — are going to be more interested in identifying changes that may play out over time.

Monitoring momentum

Following the trend is great, but if the trend is moving quickly, you want to know so that you can get ahead of it. If the rate of change on the trend is going up, then rising prices are likely to occur.

To calculate momentum, take today's closing price for a security, divide that by the closing price ten days ago, and then multiply the result by 100. This gives you a *momentum indicator*. If the price didn't go anywhere, the momentum indicator is 100. If the price went up, the indicator is greater than 100. And if the price went down, the indicator is less than 100.

In technical analysis, trends are usually expected to continue, so a security with a momentum indicator above 100 is expected to keep going up, all else being equal. But that "all else being equal" is the sticky part. Technical analysts usually track momentum indicators over time to see whether the positive momentum is, itself, a trend. In fact, momentum indicators are a good confirmation of the underlying trend.

Momentum is a leading technical indicator. It tells you what is likely to happen in the future, not what has happened in the past.

Momentum trading is usually done with some attention to the fundamentals. When key business fundamentals, such as sales or profits, are accelerating at the same time that the security is going up in price, the momentum is likely to continue for some time. You can learn more about momentum trading and investing in Chapter 17.

Finding breakouts

A *breakout* occurs when a security price passes through and stays above — or below — the resistance or support line, which creates a new trend with new support and resistance levels. A one-time breakout may just be an anomaly (what technicians sometimes call a *false breakout*), but pay attention to two or more breakouts. Figure 7-7 shows what breakouts look like.

Figure 7-7:
A breakout
indicates a
new trend.

When a true breakout occurs, a new trend starts. That means an upward breakout is accompanied by rising prices, and a downward breakout is accompanied by falling prices.

False breakouts can wreak havoc for a day to two of trading. With a false breakout, some traders buy or sell, thinking that the trend will continue. When they see that it doesn't, they then turn around and reverse their positions at a loss. During these times, the ability to size up the intelligence of the other traders in the market can come in handy.

Good technical analysts look at several different indicators to determine whether a change in trend is real or just one of those things that goes away quickly as the old trend resumes. For example, they may look at short interest or overall market volatility. You can learn more about these indicators in Chapter 8.

Reading the Charts

How long does it take to find the trend? How long does it take for the trend to play out? When do you act on it? Do you have minutes, hours, or days to act?

Because markets tend to move in cycles, technical analysts look for patterns in the price charts that give them an indication of how long any particular trend may last. In this section, I show you some of the common patterns that day traders look for when they do technical analysis. Alas, some patterns are obvious only in hindsight, but knowing what the patterns mean can help you make better forecasts of where a security price should go.

This section provides just an introduction to some of the better-known (and cleverly named) patterns. Technical analysts look for many others, and you really need a book on the subject to understand them all. Check out the appendix for books that provide more information on technical analysis so that you can get a feel for how you can apply it to your trading style.

Wave your pennants and flags

Pennants and *flags* are chart patterns that show *retracements,* short-term deviations from the main trend. With a retracement, no breakout occurs from the support or resistance level, but the security isn't following the trend, either. Because there is no breakout, the trend is more short-term.

Figure 7-8 shows a pennant. Notice how the support and resistance lines of the pennant (which occur within the support and resistance lines of a much larger trend) converge almost to a point.

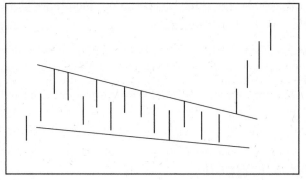

Figure 7-8: In a pennant, support and resistance begin to converge.

Figure 7-9, by contrast, is a flag. The main difference between a flag and a pennant is that the flag's support and resistance lines are parallel.

Figure 7-9: A flag, like a pennant, usually indicates falling volume.

Pennants and flags are usually found in the middle of the main phase of a trend, and they seem to last for two weeks before going back to the trendline. They are almost always accompanied by falling volume. In fact, if the trading volume isn't falling, you are probably looking at a *reversal* — a change in trend — rather than a retracement.

Not just for the shower: Head and shoulders

The *head and shoulders* formation is a series of three peaks within a price chart. The peaks on the left and right (the shoulders) should be relatively smaller than the peak in the center (the head). The shoulders connect at a price known as the *neckline,* and when the right shoulder formation is reached, the price plunges down.

The head and shoulders is one of the most bearish technical patterns, and Figure 7-10 shows an example.

Figure 7-10: In a head and shoulders formation, the price goes down after the right shoulder formation.

The head and shoulders formation seems to result from traders holding out for a last high after a security has had a long price run. At some point, though, the trend changes, because nothing grows forever. And when the trend changes, the prices fall.

An upside-down head and shoulders sometimes appears at the end of a downtrend, and it signals that the security is about to increase in price.

Drink from a cup and handle

When a security hits a peak in price and falls, sometimes because of bad news, it can stay low for a while. But eventually, the bad news works itself out, the underlying fundamentals improve, and the time comes to buy again. The technical analyst sees this scenario play out in a *cup and handle* formation, and Figure 7-11 shows you what one looks like.

The handle forms as those who bought at the old high and who felt burned by the decline take their money and get out. But other traders, those who haven't the same history with the security, recognize that the price will probably resume going up now that those old sellers are out of the market.

Figure 7-11:
A cup and
handle for-
mation is a
long-term
trend.

A cup and handle formation generally shows up over a long period of trading — sometimes as long as a year — and many subtrends occur during that time. As a day trader, you'll probably care more about those day-to-day changes than the underlying trend taking place. Still, if you see that cup formation and the hint of a handle, you can interpret that as a sign that the security will probably start to rise in price.

Mind the gap

Gaps are breaks in prices that show up all the time, usually when some news event takes place between trading sessions that causes an adjustment in prices and volume. Whether the news is about an acquisition, a product line disappointment, or a war that broke out overnight, it's significant enough to change the trend, and that's why traders pay attention when they see gaps.

A gap is a break between two bars, as shown in Figure 7-12.

Gaps are usually great signals. A security that gaps up at the open usually means a strong uptrend is beginning, so it's time to buy. Likewise, if the security gaps down, that's often the start of a downtrend, so it's better to sell.

Day traders can get sucked into a gap, a situation known as a *gap and crap* (or *gap and trap,* if you prefer more genteel language). Many traders view the security going up in price as a great time to sell, so the day trader who buys on the gap up immediately gets slammed by all the selling pressure. For that reason, some day traders prefer to wait at least 30 minutes before trading on an opening gap, while others rely on their knowledge of the buyers and sellers in a given market to decide what to do.

Figure 7-12:
A gap
down often
means it's
time to sell.

Grab your pitchforks!

A *pitchfork* is sometimes called an *Andrews pitchfork* after Alan Andrews, the technical analyst who popularized it. This pattern identifies long-run support and resistance levels for subtrends by creating a channel around the main trendline. Figure 7-13 shows what a pitchfork looks like.

Figure 7-13:
A pitchfork
makes a
channel
around the
main
trendline.

The upper line shows the resistance level for upward subtrends, and the lower line shows the support level for lower subtrends. The middle line forms a support and a resistance line, depending on which side of it trading takes place. If the price crosses above the midline, it can be expected to go no higher than the highest line. Likewise, if the price crosses below the midline, it can be expected to go no lower than the lowest line.

Considering Different Approaches to Technical Analysis

Technical analysts tend to group themselves under different schools of thought. Each approaches the charts differently and uses them to glean different information about how securities prices are likely to perform. In this section, I offer an introduction to a few of these approaches. If one strikes your fancy, you can look in the appendix for resources to help you learn more.

Dow Theory

The *Dow Theory* was developed by Charles Dow, the founder of *The Wall Street Journal.* The theory and the market indexes that are part of it helped sell newspapers; they also helped people make money in the markets. The Dow Theory is the basis for the traditional technical analysis described in this chapter.

Dow believed that securities move in trends, that the trends form patterns that traders can identify, and that those trends remain in place until some major event takes place that changes them. Further, trends in the Dow Jones Industrial Average and the Dow Jones Transportation Average can predict overall market performance.

Not all technicians believe that the Dow Jones Industrial Average and Dow Jones Transportation Average are primary indicators in the modern economy, but they rely on the Dow Theory for their analysis, and they still read the *Journal.*

Fibonacci numbers and the Elliott Wave

Remember back when you had to take standardized tests, you'd often have to figure the next number in a series? Well, here's such a test. What's the next number in this series? (Hint: This is not a phone number in Chad.)

0, 1, 1, 2, 3, 5, 8, 13, 21

If you answered 34, you're right! The series is known as the *Fibonacci numbers,* sometimes called the *Fibonacci series* or just the *Fibs*. You find this number by adding together the preceding two numbers in the series, starting with the first two digits on the number line. $0 + 1 = 1$; $1 + 1 = 2$; $1 + 2 = 3$; and so on into infinity. Furthermore, when the series gets well into the double digits, the ratio of one number to the one next to it settles at 0.618, a number known as the *golden ratio,* which means that the ratio of the smaller and the larger of two numbers is the same as the ratio of the larger number to the sum of the two numbers. In nature, this is the proportion of a perfect spiral, like that found on a pinecone and a pineapple.

Ralph Elliott was a trader who believed that over the long run the market moved in waves described by the Fibonacci series. For example, Elliott believed that a bull market would be characterized by three down waves and five up waves. He also believed that support and resistance levels would be found 61.8 percent above lows and below highs. Under the Elliott Wave system, if a security falls 61.8 percent from a high, it's a good time to buy.

Elliott believed that these waves ranged from centuries to minutes, so both traders and investors use the system to identify the market trends that suit their timeframes. Others — including me — think it's highly unlikely that the human activity in the stock market would follow the same natural order as the ratio of the spiral on a mollusk shell.

Japanese candlestick charting

Candlestick charts were developed by traders in the Japanese rice futures markets in the 18th century, and they've carried through into the present. The basic charts are similar to the high-low-close-open bars that I talk about earlier in this chapter, but they are shaped a little differently to carry more information. Figure 7-14 shows an example of a candlestick.

Figure 7-14: Candle- sticks are like slightly more sophisti- cated bars.

High

Open or close

Open or close

Low

The length of the rectangle (the so-called *candle,* also known as the *body*) between the open and the close prices gives a sense of how much volatility the security has, especially relative to the high and low prices above and below the rectangle (the so-called *wick,* also known as the *shadow*). The shapes and colors create different patterns that traders can use to discern the direction of future prices. (Most technical-analysis packages color the candlesticks green on up days and red on down days, to make finding trends even easier.)

The Gann system

William Gann supposedly made $50 million in the stock and commodities markets in the first half of the 20th century by using a system that he may or may not have taught to others before his death. A lot of mystery and mythology surrounds the Gann system; some traders rely on what they perceive to be his method, whereas others dismiss it, in part because Gann relied on astrology to build his forecasts.

The *Gann system,* as it is defined nowadays, looks at the relationship between price and time. If a security moves one point in one day, that's a 1 × 1 Gann angle, and that's normal trading. If a security moves two points in one day, it is said to create a 2 × 1 Gann angle, which is bullish. An angle of less than 1 × 1 is bearish.

Furthermore, Gann recognized that the market moves back and forth while in a general upward or downward cycle, but some of those fluctuations are more positive than others. Just as the system looks for price movements over time with even proportions (1 × 1, 2 × 1, and so on), it also looks for orderly retracements. When a security moves back 50 percent, say from a low of $20 to a high of $40 and then back to $30, it would be a good time to buy under the Gann system.

Many traders swear by the 50 percent retracement guide — even those who think that Gann is an otherwise crazy system. This may be the origin of one hoary trading chestnut: Buy whenever a price dips, because it's likely to be heading on its way back up.

Avoiding Technical-Analysis Pitfalls

A lot of people make a lot of money selling services to day traders. They produce videos, organize seminars, and (ahem) write books to tell you how to be a success. But in the financial world, success is a combination of luck, skill, and smarts.

Before you commit wholeheartedly to any particular school of research and before you plunk down a lot of money for some "proven" system demonstrated on an infomercial, think about who are you are and what you are trying to do. Despite all the books and all the seminars and all the business-school debates, every form of research has its drawbacks. Keep them in mind as you develop your day-trading business plan.

If it's obvious, there's no opportunity

Many day trading systems work much of the time. For example, a security gaps up, meaning that, due to positive news or high demand, the price jumps from one trade to the next (refer to Figure 7-12 for a gap formation). This is good, and the security is likely to keep going up. So you buy the security, you make money. Bingo! But here's the thing: Everyone is looking at that gap, everyone is assuming that the stock will go up, so everyone buys, and that bids up the security. The profit opportunity is gone. So maybe you're better off going short? Or avoiding the situation entirely? Who knows? And that's the problem. Looking for obvious patterns like gaps tells you a lot about what is happening in the market, but only your own judgment and experience can tell you what the next move should be.

Overanalyzing the data

Technical analysis is a useful way to gauge market psychology. That's what it was designed to do. However, when it was developed, most traders were human beings, with all their crazy human emotions. Nowadays, you aren't trading against a person. In almost all cases, you will be trading against machines that do what they are programmed to do. They don't suffer from doubt, fear, or greed — but you do. The market is an aggregation of everyone in it, but you don't want to assign human emotions to nonhumans.

When trying to determine the mood of the market, you can easily start overanalyzing and working yourself into a knot. Should you follow the trend or trade against it? But if everyone trades against it, would you be better off following it?

Instead of puzzling over what's really going on, develop a system that you trust. Do that through backtesting, simulation, and performance analysis. Chapter 16 has plenty of advice on how to use these techniques. The more confident you feel in how you should react given a market situation, the better your trading will be.

Success may be the result of an upward bias

Under the efficient markets theory, all information is already included in a security's price. Until new information comes into the market, the prices move in a random pattern, so any security is as likely to do as well as any other. In some markets, like the stock market, this random path has an *upward bias,* meaning that as long as the economy is growing, companies should perform well, too; therefore, the movement is more likely to be upward than downward, but the magnitude of the movement is random.

If price movements are random, some people are going to win and some are going to lose, no matter what systems they use to pick securities. If price movements are random with an upward bias, then more people are going to win than lose, no matter what systems they use to pick securities. Some of those who win are going to tout their systems, even though random chance was really what led to their success.

Technical analysis is a useful way to measure the relative supply and demand in the market, and that in turn is a way to gauge the psychology of those who are trading. But it's not perfect. Before you plunk down a lot of money to learn a complex trading system or to subscribe to a newsletter offering a can't-miss method of trading, ask yourself if the person selling it is smart or just lucky. A good system gives you discipline and a way to think about the market relative to your trading style. A bad system costs a lot of money and may have worked for a brief moment in the past, with no relevance to current conditions.

Chapter 8

Following Market Indicators and Tried-and-True Day-Trading Strategies

In This Chapter

▶ Studying the psychology and moods of the market

▶ Following the flow of funds

▶ Knowing what to look for during the trading day

▶ Avoiding dangerous situations

▶ Looking at strategies that many day traders use

▶ Learning how to program your trades

Day traders put their research to work through a range of different strategies. All strategies have two things in common: They're designed to make money, and they're designed to work in a single day. And the best ones help traders cut through the psychology of the market.

In this day and age, most trading takes place via computers. The trading is often directed by human beings, of course, but the machines are doing the work. Short-term profit potentials can be very small. As much as they want to be dispassionate, human traders get sucked into hope, fear, and greed — the three emotions that ruin people every day. To complicate matters, many markets, such as options and futures, are zero-sum markets, meaning that for every win, someone has to lose. Some markets, such as the stock market, have a positive bias, meaning that winners outnumber losers in the long run, but that doesn't mean that'll be the case today.

With thin profit potential and so much emotional upheaval, making money in the long run as a day trader can be tough. This chapter may help. In it, I cover some common day-trading strategies, and I discuss some of the cold analysis that goes into figuring out the psychology of the markets.

Psyching Out the Markets

For every buyer, there's a seller. (There has to be, or no transaction will take place.) The price changes to reach the point where the buyer is willing to buy the security and the seller is willing to part with it. This interaction is basic supply and demand. The financial markets are more efficient at matching supply and demand than almost any other market in existence. There are no racks of unsold sweaters at the end of the season, no hot new cars that can't be purchased at any price, no long lines to get a table. The prices change to match the demand, and those who want to pay the price or receive the price are going to make a trade.

Despite the ruthless capitalistic efficiency underlying trading, the markets are also dominated by human emotion and psychology. All the buyers and all the sellers look at the same information, but they reach different conclusions. There's a seller out there for every buyer, so the trader looking to buy needs to know why the seller is willing to make a deal.

Why would someone be on the other side of your trade?

- ✔ **The other trader may have a different time horizon.** For example, long-term investors may sell on bad news that changes a security's outlook. A short-term trader may not care about the long-term outlook if the selling in the morning is overdone, creating an opportunity to buy now and sell at a higher price in the afternoon.

- ✔ **The other trader may have a different risk profile.** A conservative investor may not want to own shares in a company that's being acquired by a high-flying technology company. That investor will sell, and some-one with more interest in growth will buy. A trading algorithm may place a trade to manage the risk on another trade.

- ✔ **The other trader may be engaging in wishful thinking, acting out of fear, or trading from sheer greed.** He or she may not be thinking rationally about what is happening, creating an opportunity for you.

- ✔ *You* **may be engaging in wishful thinking, acting out of fear, or trading from sheer greed.** You may be the irrational trader, making mistakes that cost you. Hey, it happens to the best of us sometimes, but the more aware you are of your emotional tendencies, the better you can trade past them.

Don't try to psych out the trader on the other side. You won't face the same traders each time you trade, and more likely than not, the trader you're facing is a machine. Worry about yourself instead.

Betting on the buy side

Every market participant has his or her own set of reasons and rationales for placing an order today. In general, though, although many reasons to sell exist — to pay taxes, generate cash for college tuition, or meet a pension obligation, among many others — there's only one reason to buy: You think the security is going up in price.

For that reason alone, traders often pay more attention to what is happening to buy orders than to sell orders. To get a sense of who is projecting a profit, traders look at the number of buy orders coming in, how large they are, and at what price. I cover volume and price indicators in more detail later in the chapter.

Because there are so many good reasons to sell but only one good reason to buy, the market can take a long time to recognize bearish (pessimistic) sentiment indicators. Even if you see that prices should start to go down in the near future, you have to consider that the market today can be very different from what you see coming up. And as a day trader, you only have today.

Avoiding the projection trap

If you took a peek at some of the technical analysis charts in Chapter 7, you may have noticed that you can see what you want to see in some price charts. And if you thought a little about fundamental analysis, you may have seen that interpreting information the way you want to is just as easy. Instead of looking objectively at what the market is telling them, some traders see what they want to see. That's one reason why knowing your system and using your limits are so important. Information in Chapters 2 and 16 can help you with both.

The best traders are able to figure out the psychology of the market almost by instinct. They can't necessarily explain what they do — which makes it hard for those trying to learn from them. But they can tell you this much: If you can rationally determine why the person on the other side of the trade is trading, you can be in a better position to make money and avoid the big mistakes brought on by hope, fear, and greed.

Taking the Temperature of the Market

For decades, most traders were rooted on the floors of the exchanges. They had a good sense of the mood of the market because they could pick up the mood of the people in the pits with them. They often knew their fellow traders well enough to know how good they were or the needs of the people they were working for. It made for a clubby atmosphere, despite all the shouting and arm waving. It wasn't the most efficient way to trade big volume, but it allowed traders to read the minds of those around them.

Now, almost all trading is electronic, without the paper and the jackets and the excitement. Professional traders, who work for brokerage firms or fund companies, trade electronically, but along long tables (known as trading desks) where they sit next to colleagues trading similar securities. Even though everyone is trading off a screen, they share a mood and thus a sense of what's happening out there. Some day traders can replicate this camaraderie by working for a proprietary trading firm, but most traders work alone at home, with nothing but the information on their screens to tell them what's happening in the market.

Fortunately, ways do exist to figure out what's happening, even when you're just looking at the screen. They include paying attention to price, volume, and volatility indicators, and you're in the right place to find out more about them.

Some traders rely on Internet chat rooms to help them measure market sentiment. Doing so can be risky. Some chat rooms have smart people who are willing to share their perspectives on the market, but many are dominated by novice traders who have no good information to share or by people who are trying to manipulate the market in their favor. Check out a chat room carefully before participating.

Pinpointing with price indicators

In an efficient market, all information about a security is included in its price. If the price is high and going up, then the fundamentals are doing well. If the price is low and going lower, then something's not good. And everything in between means something else.

The change in a security's price gives you a first cut of information. Price changes can be analyzed in other ways to help you know when to buy or when to sell.

Momentum

Momentum, which is also discussed in Chapter 7, is the rate at which a security's price is increasing (or decreasing). If momentum is strong and positive, then the security shows both higher highs and higher lows. People want to buy the security for whatever reason, and the price reflects that. Likewise, momentum can be strong and negative. Negative momentum is marked with lower highs and lower lows. No one seems interested in buying, and that keeps dragging the price down.

The exact amount of momentum that a security has can be measured with indicators known as *momentum oscillators.* A classic momentum oscillator starts with the moving average, which is the average of the closing prices for a past time period, say the last ten trading days. Then the change in each day's moving average is plotted below the price line. When the oscillator is positive, traders say that the security is *overbought;* when it's negative, they say that the security is *oversold.* Figure 8-1 shows a momentum oscillator plotted below a price line.

Figure 8-1:
A momentum oscillator indicates (no surprise here) momentum.

If a momentum oscillator shows that a security is overbought (the line is above the center line), too many people own it relative to the remaining demand in the market, and some of them will start selling. Remember, some of these people have perfectly good reasons for selling that may have nothing to do with the underlying fundamentals of the security, but they are going to sell anyway, and that brings the price down. Traders who see that a security is overbought want to sell in advance of those people.

If a momentum oscillator shows that a security is *oversold* (the line is below the center line), the security is probably too cheap. Everyone who wanted to get out has gotten out, and now it may be a bargain. When the buyers who see the profit opportunity jump in, the price goes up.

The trend is your friend . . . until the end. Although great reasons exist to follow price trends, remember that they all end, so you still need to pay attention to your money management and your stops, no matter how strong a trend seems to be.

Given that most trends end — or at least zig and zag along the way — some traders look for securities that fit what they call the *1-2-3-4 criterion*. If a security goes up in price for three consecutive days, then it's likely to go down on the fourth day. Likewise, if a security has fallen in price for three days in a row, it's likely to be up on day four. Be sure to run some simulations (see Chapter 16) to see whether this strategy works for a market that interests you.

Trading on the tick

A *tick* is an upward or downward price change. For some securities, such as futures contracts, the tick size is defined as part of the contract. For others, such as stocks, a tick can be anywhere from a penny to infinity (at least in theory).

You can also calculate the tick indicator for the market as a whole. (In fact, most quotation systems calculate the market tick for you.) The tick for the market is the total number of securities in that market that traded up on the last trade minus the number that traded down on the last trade. If the tick is a positive number, that's good: The market as a whole has a lot of buying interest. Although any given security may not do as well, a positive tick shows that most people in the market have a positive perspective right now.

By contrast, a negative tick shows that most people in the market are watching prices fall. Sure, some prices are going up, but unhappy people outnumber happy ones (assuming that most people are trading on the long side, meaning that they make money when prices go up, not down). This shows that the sentiment is negative in the market right now.

Tracking the trin

Trin is short for *trading indicator,* and it's another measure of market sentiment based on how many prices have gone up relative to how many have gone down. Most quotation systems pull up the trin for a given market, but you can also calculate it on your own. The math looks like this:

$$\frac{\dfrac{advances}{declaines}}{\dfrac{advance\ volume}{declaine\ volume}}$$

The numerator is based on the tick: the number of securities that went up divided by (not less) the number that went down. The denominator includes the volume: the number of shares or contracts that traded for those securities that went up divided by the number of securities traded for those that went down in price. This solution tells you just how strongly buyers supported the securities that were going up and just how much selling pressure faced those securities that went down.

A trin of less than 1.00 usually means that a lot of buyers are taking securities up in price, and that's positive. A trin above 1.00 indicates that the sellers are acting more strongly, which means a lot of negative sentiment is in the market.

Volume

The trin indicator looks at price in conjunction with volume. *Volume* tells you how much trading is taking place in the market. How excited are people about the current price? Do they see this as a great opportunity to buy or to sell? Are they selling fast, to get out now, or are they taking a more leisurely approach to the market these days? This information is carried in the volume of the trading, and it's an important adjunct to the information you see in the prices. Volume tells you whether enough support exists to maintain price trends or whether price trends are likely to change soon.

Force index

The *force index* gives you a sense of the strength of a trend. It starts with information from prices, namely that if the closing price today is higher than the closing price yesterday, that's positive for the security. Conversely, if today's closing price is lower than yesterday's, then the force is generally negative. Then that price information is combined with volume information. The more volume that goes with that price change, the stronger that positive or negative force.

Although many quotation systems calculate force for you, you can do it yourself, too. For each trading day, run this calculation:

Force index = volume × (today's moving average – yesterday's moving average)

In other words, the force index simply scales the moving average momentum oscillator (discussed in the earlier section "Pinpointing with price indicators") for the amount of volume that accompanies that price change. That way, the trader has a sense of just how overbought or oversold the security is on any particular day.

On-balance volume

The *on-balance volume* is a running total of the amount of trading in a security. To calculate the on-balance volume, first look at today's closing price relative to yesterday's and then do one of the following:

- ✔ **If today's close is higher than yesterday's:** Add today's volume to yesterday's on-balance volume.

- ✔ **If today's closing price is less than yesterday's:** Subtract today's volume from yesterday's total.

- ✔ **If today's close is the same as yesterday's:** Don't do anything! Today's balance is the same as yesterday's.

Many traders track on-balance volume over time, and here's why: A change in volume signals a change in demand. The change in demand may not show up in price right away if enough buyers exist to absorb volume from sellers. But if still more buyers are out there, then the price is going to go up. Hence, the volume from even small day-to-day increases in price need to be added up over time. If the volume keeps going up, then at some point, prices are going to have to go up to meet the demand.

On the downside, the volume from small price declines add up over time, too. Over time, this volume may show that very little pent-up interest exists, indicating that prices could languish for some time.

Many traders look to on-balance volume to gauge the behavior of so-called *smart money,* such as pension funds, hedge funds, and mutual fund companies. Unlike individual investors, these big institutional accounts tend to trade on fundamentals rather than emotion. They generally start buying a security at the point where the dumb money is tired of owning it, so their early buying may show big volume with little price change. But as the institutions keep buying, the price has to go up to get the smarter individuals and the early institutions to part with their shares.

Open interest

Open interest has a different meaning in the stock market than in the options and futures markets, but in both cases, it gives traders useful information about demand:

- ✔ In the stock market, open interest is the number of buy orders submitted before the market opens. When the open interest is high, people are ready to add shares to their positions or initiate new positions, which means that the stock is likely to go up in price on the demand.

✔ In the options and futures markets, open interest is the number of contracts at the end of every day that have not been exercised, closed out, or allowed to expire.

Day traders don't have open interest, because by definition, day traders close out at the end of every day. But some traders keep open interest, either because they think that their position has the ability to increase in profitability or because they're hedging another transaction and need to keep that options or futures position in place. If open interest in a contract is increasing, new money is coming into the market, and prices are likely to continue to go up. This is especially true if volume is increasing at about the same rate as open interest. On the other hand, if open interest is falling, people are closing out their positions because they no longer see a profit potential, and prices are likely to fall.

Volatility, crisis, and opportunity

The *volatility* of a security is a measure of how much that security tends to go up or down in a given time period. The more volatile the security, the more the price fluctuates. Most day traders prefer volatile securities, because they create more opportunities to make a profit in a short amount of time. But volatility can make gauging market sentiment tougher. If a security is volatile, the mood can change quickly. What looked like a profit opportunity at the market open may be gone by lunchtime — and back again before the close.

Average true range

The *average true range* is a measure of volatility that's commonly used in commodity markets, but some stock traders use it, too. It's a measure of how much volatility occurred each day. When averaged over time, this measure shows how much volatility takes place during the period in question. The higher the average true range is, the more volatile a security is.

Many quotation systems calculate the average true range automatically, but if you want to do it yourself, start with finding each day's *true range,* which is the greatest of

✔ The current high less the current low

✔ The absolute value of the current high less the previous close

✔ The absolute value of the current low less the previous close

Calculate those three numbers and then average the highest of them with the true range for the past 14 days.

Each day's true range number shows you just how much the security swung between the high and the low or how much the high or the low that day varied from the previous day's close.

Beta

Beta is the *covariance* (that is, the statistical measure of how much two variables move together) of a stock relative to the rest of the market. The number comes from the *capital assets pricing model,* which is an equation used in academic circles to model the performance of securities. Traders don't use the capital assets pricing model, but they often talk about beta to evaluate the volatility of stocks and options.

What does beta mean?

- A beta of 1.00 means that the security is moving at a faster rate than the market. You would buy high betas if you think the market is going up but not if the market is going down.

- A beta of less than 1.00 means that the security is moving more slowly than the market — a good thing if you want less risk than the market.

- A beta of exactly 1.00 means that the security is moving at the same rate as the market.

- A negative beta means that the security is moving in the opposite direction of the market. The easiest way to get a negative beta security is to *short* (borrow and then sell) a positive beta security.

The VIX

VIX is short for the Chicago Board Options Exchange Volatility Index. Calculating VIX is complex enough to border on being proprietary, but it's available on many quotation systems and on the exchange's website, www.cboe.com/micro/vix/introduction.aspx.

The VIX is based on the implied volatility of options on stocks included in the S&P 500 Index. The greater the volatility, the more uncertainty investors have; the more options that show great volatility, the more widespread is the concern about prospects for the financial markets. In fact, the VIX is often called *the fear index* and is used to gauge the amount of negative sentiment investors have. The greater the VIX, the more bearish the outlook for the market in general. The more bearish the outlook, the more likely the market is to be volatile. And volatility is the day trader's best friend.

Traders can use the VIX to help them value options on the market indexes. (For that matter, traders who want to take a position on market volatility can use options and futures contracts on the VIX, including a mini-sized future, offered by the Chicago Board Options Exchange.) The VIX can also be used to help confirm bullish or bearish sentiment that shows up in other market signals, such as the tick or the on-balance volume measures described earlier. The CBOE also calculates a VIX number on a handful of common stocks, if you are trading those issues or the options on them.

In addition to the VIX, the exchange also tracks the *VXN* (volatility on the NASDAQ 100 Index) and the *VXD* (volatility on the Dow Jones Industrial Average).

Volatility ratio

The *volatility ratio* tells traders what the implied volatility of a security is relative to the recent historical volatility. This ratio shows whether the security is expected to be more or less volatile right now than it has been in the past, and it's widely used in option markets. The first calculation required is the *implied volatility,* which is backed out using the Black-Scholes model, an academic model for valuing options. When you plug in to the model certain variables — time until expiration, interest rates, dividends, stock price, and strike price — the implied volatility is the volatility number that then generates the current option price. (You don't have to perform these calculations yourself because most quotation systems generate implied volatility for you.)

After you have the implied volatility, you can compare it to the historical volatility of the option, which tells you just how much the price changed over the last 20 or 90 days. If the implied volatility is greater than the statistical volatility, the market may be overestimating the uncertainty in the prices, and the options may be overvalued. If the implied volatility is much less than the statistical volatility, the market may be underestimating uncertainty, so the options may be undervalued.

Measuring Money Flows

Money flows tell you how much money is going into or out of a market. They are another set of indicators telling you where the market sentiment is right now and where it may be going soon. Money-flow indicators combine features of price and volume indicators to help traders gauge the market. Although amounts spent to buy and sell have to match — otherwise, the market wouldn't exist — the enthusiasm of the buyers and the anxiousness of the sellers show up in the volume traded and the direction of the price change. Just how hard was it for the buyers to get the sellers to part with their positions? And how hard will it be to get them to part with their positions tomorrow? That's the information contained in money-flow indicators.

The most basic money-flow indicator is the change in closing price multiplied by the number of shares traded. If the closing price was higher than the closing price yesterday, then the number is positive; if the closing price today was lower than the price yesterday, then the number is negative. Other indicators out there use midpoint values and don't go negative; instead, the numbers range from higher to lower. Whether positive or negative, a high money flow indicates strong buying activity, and that indicates that a positive price trend is likely to continue.

Accumulation/distribution index

In trading terms, *accumulation* is controlled buying, and *distribution* is controlled selling. This kind of buying and selling doesn't lead to big changes in securities prices, usually because the action was planned. No one accumulates or distributes a security in a state of panic.

But even if the buying and selling activity isn't driven by madcap rushes in and out of positions, it's still important to know whether, on balance, the buyers or the sellers have the slight predominance in the market, because that may affect the direction of prices in the near future. For example, if a security has been in an upward trend but more and more down days occur with increasing volume, the sellers are starting to dominate the trading, and the price trend is likely to go down.

To determine the accumulation/distribution index, you use this equation:

$$\frac{accumulation}{distribution} = \frac{(close - low) - (high - close)}{(high - low) \times period's\ volume}$$

Some traders look at accumulation/distribution from day to day, whereas others prefer to look at it for a week or even a month's worth of trading. One way isn't inherently better than the other; it depends on what you trade and how you trade it.

Money-flow ratio and money-flow index

Money flow is closing price multiplied by the number of shares traded. That basic statistic can be manipulated in strange and wonderful ways to generate new statistics carrying even more information about whether the markets are likely to have more buying pressure or more selling pressure in the future.

The first is the *money-flow ratio,* which is simply the total money flow for those days where prices were up from the prior day (days with positive money flow) divided by the total money flow for those days where prices were down from the prior day (which are the days with negative money flow). Day traders tend to calculate money-flow ratios for short time periods, such as a week or ten days, whereas swing traders and investors tend to care about longer time periods, like a month or even four months of trading.

The money-flow ratio is sometimes converted into the *money-flow index,* which can be used as a single indicator or tracked relative to prices for a given period of time. The equation used to figure out the money-flow index looks like this:

$$MFI = 100 - \frac{100}{1 + money\ ratio}$$

If the money-flow index is more than 80, the security is usually considered to be overbought — meaning that the buyers are done buying, and the sellers will put downward pressure on prices. If the money-flow index is less than 20, the security is usually considered to be oversold, and the buyers will soon take over and drive prices up. In between, the money-flow index can help clarify information from other market indicators.

Short interest ratios

Short selling is a way to make money if a security falls in price. In the options and futures markets, one simply agrees to sell a contract to someone else. In the stock and bond markets, short selling is a little more complicated. The short seller borrows stock or bonds through the brokerage firm and then sells them. Ideally, the price falls, and then the trader can buy back the stock or bonds at the lower price to repay the loan. The trader keeps the difference between the security's selling price and its repurchasing price. (The process is described in more detail in Chapter 9.)

People take the short side of a position for only one reason: They think that prices are going to go down. They may want to hedge against this, or they may want to make a big profit if it happens. In the stock market in particular, monitoring the rate of short selling can give clues to investor expectations and future market direction.

The New York Stock Exchange and NASDAQ report the short interest in stocks listed with them. The data are updated monthly, as it can take a while for brokerage firms to sort out exactly how many shares have been shorted and then report that data to the exchanges. The resulting number, the *short interest ratio,* tells the number of shares that have been shorted, the percentage change from the month before, the average daily trading volume in the same month, and the number of days of trading at the average volume that covering the short positions would take.

The loans that enable short selling have to be repaid. If the lender asks for the securities back or if prices go up so that the position starts to lose money, the trader is going to have to buy shares to make repayment. The harder it is to get the right number of shares in the market, the more desperate the trader will become, and the higher prices will go.

An increase in short interest shows that investors are becoming nervous about a stock. However, given that short interest is not calculated frequently, the number would probably not give a trader a lot of information about the prospects for the company itself. This doesn't mean short interest doesn't carry a lot of useful information for traders. It does. If the short interest is high, then the security price is likely to go up when all the people who are short need to buy back stock. Likewise, if short interest is low, there will be little buying pressure in the near future.

High short interest, along with other bullish indicators, is a sign that prices are more likely to go up than down in the near future.

Considering Information That Crops Up during the Trading Day

Technical analysis (described in Chapter 7) and all the indicators discussed in this chapter offer useful information about what's happening in the markets, but there's one problem: Because so many of those indicators are based on closing prices and closing volume, they aren't much use during the trading day. In fact, many traders read through the information in the morning before the open to sort out what is likely to happen and what the mood of the market is likely to be, but then they have to recalibrate their gauge of the market as information comes to them during the trading day. That information doesn't show up on charts or in neat numerical indicators until the day ends. Fortunately, several sources of information that are updated while the market is open can give a trader a sense of what's happening at any given time.

Price, time, and sales

The most important information for a trader is the current price of the security, how often and in what volume it has been trading, and how much the price has moved from the last trade. This information is the most basic real-time info out there, and it's readily available through a brokerage firm's quotation screens.

Chapter 11 discusses the different quotation services that traders can obtain from their brokerage firms. Although your broker may charge you more to get more detailed quotes, doing so is worth it for most trading strategies. Knowing how the price is moving can give you a sense of whether the general mood of the market is being confirmed or contradicted — information that can help you place more profitable trades.

Order book

High-level price-quote data, such as that available through NASDAQ Level 2 or NASDAQ TotalView-ITCH, include information on who is placing orders and just how large those orders are. (Flip to Chapter 13 to see what such high-level price-quote data looks like.) The order book gives you key data because it gives you a sense of how smart the other buyers and sellers are. Are they day traders just trying not to be killed? Or are they institutions that have done a lot of research and are under a lot of performance pressure? Sure, day traders are often very right and institutions are often very wrong, but the information you see in the order book can help you sense whether people are trading on information or on emotion.

An additional piece of information from the order book can help you figure out what's happening in the market now — namely, the presence of an *order imbalance.* An order imbalance means that the number of buyers and sellers doesn't match. This situation often occurs during the open because some traders prefer to place orders before the market opens, whereas others prefer to wait until after the open. These imbalances tend to be small and clear up quickly. However, if a major news event takes place or a great deal of fear exists in the market, large imbalances can occur during the trading day. These imbalances can be disruptive, and in some cases, the exchange stops trading until news is disseminated and enough new orders are placed to balance out the orders.

The order book doesn't show all the orders. Most brokerage firms maintain *dark pools* (also known as *dark books* or *dark liquidity*) for large clients or for their trading desks. Dark pools are collections of orders above or below market prices that aren't advertised except in the pool or on electronic communication networks (also known as ECNs, covered in Chapter 3). Traders use this technique to help buy or sell securities without affecting the price and to reduce trading costs. The order is executed only if someone matches it inadvertently rather than the market price changing to meet the changing supply and demand. The bad news for a day trader is that these trades can contribute to market volatility without giving any advance warning.

Quote stuffing

Quote stuffing is the practice of placing a really large number of orders for a security, often at a price significantly above or below the current market price. Almost as soon as the orders are placed, they're cancelled. The transaction is completely handled by computerized trading systems, not people. The people behind the placement of these orders are sometimes referred to as *quote-rate pirates.*

The official idea seems to be to hide customer orders in order to reduce their effect on the market, especially to keep them hidden from other computer trading systems, but in practice, these quotes seem to be a way to lead the market up or down by placing an unusually high or low order out there. Hence, quote stuffing may be outright market manipulation. In some cases, it may simply be that the algorithms in the computer programs place wacky orders for reasons that make sense only to other computer programs. Either way, these orders contribute to market volatility. That may be just the way it goes, unless the orders are placed for nefarious purposes.

Regulators aren't happy with quote stuffing, and it is prohibited — if it's caught.

News flows

Although much of the discussion in this chapter is about the information contained in price, volume, and other trade data, the actual information that comes from news releases is at least as important.

Much of the news is regularly scheduled and much predicted: corporate earnings, Federal Reserve discount rates, unemployment rates, housing starts, and the like. When this information comes in, traders want to know how the actual results compare with what was expected and how this info fits with the overall bullish or bearish sentiment of the market.

The second type of news is the unscheduled breaking event, such as corporate takeovers, horrible storms, political assassinations, or other happenings that were not expected and that take more time for the market to digest. That's in part because these events have the ability to change trends rather than play out against them. In some cases, the markets will halt trading to allow this information to disseminate; in others, traders have to react quickly based on what they know now and what they suspect will happen in the near future.

Many day traders track Twitter and other social-media feeds for information during the trading day, and some brokers include these feeds as part of the services that they offer to their customers. Social media is a permitted way for companies to disseminate information to the market, but it can also be spoofed in such a way as to cause headaches. In April of 2013, someone hacked the Associated Press's Twitter feed to announce that there were two explosions in the White House and that President Barack Obama had been injured. The story was false, but it created a lot of havoc in the markets and elsewhere before it was retracted.

What's the difference between risk and uncertainty? *Risk* is something that happens often enough that people can quantify the damage. *Uncertainty* is something that may happen, but no one can figure out the likelihood. A fire that knocks out power to Midtown Manhattan sometime in the next ten years is a risk; the invasion of the planet by aliens from outer space is uncertainty.

News can happen at any time. It can change a trend and throw all your careful analysis into disarray. For this reason, careful analysis is no substitute for risk management. Watch your position sizes and have stops in place so that you exit when you need to. Chapter 2 has a lot of information on these topics.

Identifying Anomalies and Traps

Traders can be superstitious, and that superstition shows up in different anomalies and traps that affect the mood of the market even when there is no logical reason for their existence. You want to be aware of them, because they can affect trading.

An *anomaly* is a market condition that occurs regularly but for no good reason. It can be related to the month of the year, the day of the week, or the size of the company involved. A *trap* is a situation where the market doesn't perform the way you expect it to given the indicators that you are looking at. You have a choice: Go with what the market is telling you or go with what your indicators are telling you.

To a long-term investor, perception is perception. When perception is different from reality, an opportunity exists to make money. To a short-term trader, perception is reality because it affects what happens before everyone figures out what's real.

Bear traps and bull traps

Traders talk about getting caught in traps, which neatly fits the language of bulls and bears. When they stumble into a trap, they're stuck moving against the market, which causes them big trouble. After all, day trading is about identifying trends and moving with them. You only have a few hours to work before the time comes to close out. In this section, I list a few common traps to help you identify and, I hope, avoid them.

The best antidote for a trap is to take your loss and move on to the next trade.

Chart traps

If you flip back to Chapter 7 and look at some of the sample charts and if you look at actual price charts created in the market every day, you may notice that sometimes it's really hard to tell whether a breakout is false or real and whether a trend is changing or just playing out with a smaller subtrend. A ton of subjectivity goes into reading charts, and some days you read them wrong. You think you're ahead of the market when you're actually just trading against it. Ouch!

Some traders try to work around these types of chart traps by automating their trading. Several different software packages are available that can scan the market and identify potential trading opportunities (see Chapter 13 for more information). But even the best software misreads the market on some occasions, which is why you need to monitor your positions and make sure you stick to your loss limits.

Contrarian traps

Way back in Chapter 1, I note that about 80 percent of day traders lose money. So maybe you're thinking that the way to make money is to just do the opposite of what everyone else is doing. But the reason that day traders lose money isn't so much that they're wrong about the trend; it's because they're sloppy in their trading and don't limit their losses. (That's why so much of this book is about the business of trading rather than the actual mechanics of placing buy and sell orders.)

In a *contrarian trap,* the trader has made the decision to trade against the market, and that's exactly what happens: He or she loses money because the market is moving in the opposite direction. Taking a contrary position doesn't work too well in day trading. In most cases, you have to go with the flow, not against it, to make money in a single day's session. The market is always right in the short term.

A lot of people make money with a contrarian strategy, but they need to pay attention to avoid the traps.

Calendar effects

Many trading anomalies follow time periods — which is not completely unexpected — because many economic and business trends follow the calendar. Companies report their results quarterly. Most close their books for tax purposes at the end of the year. Investors are also evaluated quarterly. Retail sales follow holiday seasons, demand for commodities follows the growing season, and fuel demand varies with the weather. Whatever you decide to trade, you need to do enough fundamental research (the study of the business and economic factors that affect the security, described in Chapter 7) so that you know how your chosen securities move over time.

But some of the calendar effects — the January effect, the Monday effect, and the October effect — make little logical sense, yet they still influence trading.

The January effect

Many years, the stock market goes up in the early part of January. Why? No one is entirely sure, but the guess is that people tend to sell at the end of December for tax reasons and then buy back those securities in January. It may also be that in the new year everyone is flush with excitement and ready to see the market go up, so they put money to work and start buying.

If stocks go up in January, then you can get a jump on the market by buying in December, right? And that would make prices go up in December. To get a jump on the December rally, you could buy in November. And that's exactly what people started to do, and the once-pronounced January effect is now weak to nonexistent. (People still talk about it, though.) In an efficient market, people eventually figure out these unexplained phenomena and then trade on them until they disappear. Use these anomalies as a way to gauge psychology, not as hard and fast trading rules.

The Monday effect

The market seems to do more poorly on Monday than on the other days of the week. And no matter what the evidence shows (the research is ambiguous, and the findings vary greatly based on the time period and the markets examined), many traders believe this to be true, so it has an effect. Why? There are two thoughts. The first is that people are in a bad mood on Monday because they have to go back to work after the weekend. The second is that people spend all weekend analyzing any bad news from the end of the prior week and then sell as soon as they get back to the office.

The 2008 stock market crash happened on a Monday. Over the previous weekend, the different regulatory agencies decided to allow the old-line brokerage firm of Lehman Brothers to fail. The firm failed to open on Monday, September 15, and the rest of the market went into a tailspin.

The October effect

The stock market has had two grand crashes and one smaller but profound one in October:

- **October 29, 1929:** On this day, known as Black Tuesday, the Dow Jones Industrial Average declined 12 percent in one day as market speculators caught up with the less rosy reality of the economy. This crash kicked off a general decline that contributed to the Great Depression of the 1930s.

- ✓ **October 19, 1987:** This day, known as Black Monday, saw the Dow Jones Industrial Average decline 23 percent. No one is really sure why this crash happened, but it did.

- ✓ **October 13, 1989:** On this day, the Dow Jones declined 7 percent in the last hour of trading when a leveraged buyout for United Airlines fell through.

Because of these crashes, many traders believe that bad things happen in October, and they act accordingly. Of course, bad things happen in other months. The crash in the NASDAQ market that marked the end of the 1990s tech bubble took place in March 2000, but no one talks about a March effect. The 2008 crash took place in September; maybe, like the January effect, the October effect is starting to roll earlier into the year.

Building on Some Standard Strategies

This chapter has a lot of information about different indicators that you can look at, and this information can be used to form all types of trading strategies. Many traders work out their own systems after they've been trading for a while, but they often start with something standardized.

You can start trading in a lot of ways (many of which you can read about in this book; Chapter 13 in particular has advice on how to evaluate different trading systems that you can subscribe to, if you are looking for a system). In this section, I cover a few basic styles that you can use to launch your trading business. All the strategies outlined in the following sections are based on the indicators discussed in this chapter. They include *range trading,* or working within normal high and low movements; *contrarian trading,* or going against the momentum; *news trading,* or looking to buy and sell as soon as a juicy tidbit comes across the newswire; and *pairs trading,* in which a trader goes long a strong stock and short a weaker one in the same category. The idea is that in an up market, gains on the long will outpace losses on the short, and in a down market, gains on the short will outpace losses on the long.

No one of these strategies is better than another. Each has advantages in different market conditions. The key is finding a strategy that fits your temperament and style so that you can act on it. A strategy is only as good as the trader who executes it.

Many brokerage firms offer practice accounts and backtesting services that you can use to play around and see what fits. And then you can start working with real money.

Range trading

Range trading, sometimes called *channel trading,* starts with an understanding of the recent trading history of a given security. Getting this history involves looking at the charts (see Chapter 7) to identify typical highs and lows during the day as well as the typical difference between these two prices. With this information, the trader simply buys low and sells high. When the security dips in price, the order to buy is placed; when it rises, the order to sell goes in.

Most range traders use stops and limits to keep their trading in line with what they see. Covered in more detail in Chapter 2, a *stop* limits the loss if the security keeps dropping below your entry point, and the *limit order* gets you out at a profit if the security moves to the top of the range.

Range trading works in a normal market with just enough volatility to keep the price wiggling around during the day but not so much that it breaks out of the range and starts a new trend.

Contrarian trading

Momentum traders buy securities when prices are rising and sell when prices are falling. These traders figure that something that goes up in price will continue to go up and something going down will continue to go down. Momentum trading is one strategy, and it works well for many traders, especially in a strong bull market.

Contrarian trading, on the other hand, is just the opposite of momentum trading, and it can work well, too. The logic behind a contrarian strategy is that nothing goes up forever; for that matter, nothing falls forever, either. The contrarian trader looks for assets than have been rising in price and sells them; she prefers to buy things that have been falling. The point is not to buy cheap or sell dear, but rather to sell what seems to be overpriced and buy what seems to be a bargain. Contrarian traders may just be quick to spot when a trend ends. For example, they may buy on a rumor and sell on the news, jumping out right when everyone else is ready to jump in.

The people I've known who use this strategy well tend to be bargain hunters in every aspect of their lives. They stock up on frozen vegetables when the grocery store has a once-a-year loss leader, and they sell their apartment if their neighborhood's real estate gets too hot. They have a nose for value and put that to work during the trading day.

Contrarian traders are fighting the trend, and that can work against them sometimes. This style favors people who know a market inside and out so that they know when to move against it.

News trading

News trading is possibly the most traditional form of day trading. This type of trader doesn't pay much attention to charts. Instead, he waits for information that will drive prices. This information may come in the form of a company announcement about earnings or new products; a general economic announcement about interest rates or unemployment; or just a lot of rumors about what may or may not be happening in a given industry.

Traders who do well with news trading usually have some understanding of the markets they're working in. They're not hard-core fundamental researchers, but they know enough to know what kind of news would be taken well by the markets and what would be taken poorly. They also have the attention span needed to pay attention to a few different news sources simultaneously, as well as the ability to place the order when the time comes.

The downside of news trading is that really good events may be few and far between; more often, the hype is already built into the price by the time you see it. Also, news trading is difficult to automate, although more and more computer programs draw signals from news and social-media feeds. You can't place a limit order to buy when a price level is hit; you have to wait until you see the news and then place the order yourself. Thus, news trading works well only for traders who can commit to placing the order.

Pairs trading

A pairs trader looks for two related assets and goes long on the stronger one and short on the weaker. Many pairs traders work with stocks and look for two companies in the same industry, but a pairs strategy can be worked in futures and currency markets, too — going long on metals and short on interest-rate futures, for example, or long on the dollar and short on the euro. The idea is to get the maximum return possible from a trend that affects both assets. For example, if one retail stock does really well, it may be because the company is taking market share from a weaker one. These trades are a little more complex because you have to plan both sides.

Developing a Program

Most modern day traders find that they need to program their trades. By this, I mean that they need to determine what they are trading, identify the signals they use to buy and sell securities, and set their trading platform to execute the orders automatically. Instead of working on your reflexes, you do the work of planning and testing.

Of course, a program is only as good as its inputs, and even the biggest of the big trading firms have had huge losses because of trading glitches.

You don't need to be a software engineer to develop trading programs. Many of the charting services offer program templates that you can follow or adapt; the brokerage firms that work with day traders offer trading platforms that can be programmed without too much effort, usually by clicking on icons or inserting widgets of prewritten code.

How do you get started?

- ✔ If you already know a programming language, look for a broker or trading platform that uses it.

- ✔ If you don't know a programming language, expect to spend a lot of time and trial and error learning it. The broker probably has online tutorials; spend time with them. If you're stuck on something, ask the broker's customer service rep for help and look for additional tutorials on YouTube.

- ✔ Write out your process step by step with a pen on paper before you attempt to convert it to code.

- ✔ Buy a book or take a class if you need more help.

And if the very idea of programming gives you the heebie-jeebies, consider another way to make money!

Chapter 9

Increasing Risk and Potential Return with Short Selling and Leverage

*I*n a certain sense, day trading isn't risky at all. Day traders close out their positions overnight to minimize the possibility of something going wrong while the trader isn't paying attention. Each trade is based on finding a small price change in the market over a short period of time, so nothing is likely to change dramatically. But here's the thing: Trading this way leads to small returns. Trading full time is hard to justify if you aren't making a lot of money when you do it, no matter how low your risk is.

And some days, there aren't many good trades to make. You may be looking for securities to go up, but they don't. Zero trades lead to zero risk — and zero return. For this reason, savvy traders think about other ways to make money on their trades, even when doing so involves taking on more risk. That risk is what generates the return that many traders crave.

In this chapter, I cover two techniques for finding trades and increasing returns: *short selling* and *leverage*. Both involve borrowing, and both increase risk.

The Magic of Margin

The dollars you make from trading depend on two things: your percentage return on your trades and the dollars you have to start out with. If you double your money but have only a $1,000 account, you're left with $2,000. If you get a 10 percent return but have a $1,000,000 account, you make $100,000. Which would you rather have? (Yes, I know, you'd rather double your money with the $1,000,000 account. But I didn't give you that choice, alas.)

The point is that the more money you have to trade, the more dollars you can generate, even if the return on the trade itself is small. If you have $500,000 and borrow $500,000 more, then your 10 percent return gives you $100,000 to take home, not $50,000. You've doubled the dollars returned to you by doubling the money you used to place the trades, *not* by doubling the performance of the trade itself. Clever, huh?

Here are two important things to remember about borrowing, which is known in trading as *leverage:*

- ✔ Leverage gives you more money to trade, which helps you generate more dollars for your account — or lose more dollars, if you aren't careful or have a string of reversals.

- ✔ When you borrow money or shares of stock, you have to pay it back, no matter what happens. That's why borrowing can be risky.

Day traders and other short-term traders aren't looking to make big money on any single trade. Instead, the goal is to make small money on a whole bunch of trades. Unfortunately, all those little trades don't easily add up to something big. That's why many day traders turn to leverage. They either borrow money or stock from their brokerage firm or they trade securities that have built-in leverage, such as futures and foreign exchange.

Making margin agreements

Leverage not only adds risk to your own account but also adds risk to the entire financial system. If everyone borrowed money and then some big market catastrophe happened, no one would be able to repay their loans, and the people who lent the money would go bust, too.

As a result, an incredible amount of oversight goes with leverage strategies. The Securities and Exchange Commission, the Commodity Futures Trading Commission, the different exchanges, and even the U.S. Treasury Department regulate how much money a trader can borrow. Many brokerage firms have even stricter rules in place as part of their risk management, and they're expected to demonstrate to FINRA and the National Futures Association that they follow their practices.

This extensive oversight means that you have about as much flexibility when you borrow from your broker to buy and sell securities as you would have if you borrowed from your friendly neighborhood loan shark to play a high-stakes poker game. In other words, not much. Margin loans, which are loans from your broker that increase your buying power, are highly regulated, and you must meet the broker's terms. If you fail to repay the loan, your positions will be sold from underneath you. If you try to borrow too much, you will be cut off. No amount of begging and pleading will help you.

Your brokerage firm makes you sign a margin agreement, which says that you understand the risks and limits of your activities. You probably can't have a margin account unless you meet a minimum account size, maybe $10,000 or more, and the amount you can borrow depends on the size of your account. Generally, a stock or bond account must hold 50 percent of the purchase price of securities when you borrow the money. The price of those securities can go down, but if they go down so much that the account ends up holding only 25 percent of the value of the loan, you get a margin call. (Some brokers call in loans faster than others; their policies are disclosed in their margin agreements.)

Brokerage firms handle margin trades all the time. You do the paperwork once, when you sign a margin agreement. Then each time you place an order, you're asked whether you're making the trade with cash or on margin. Click the box marked "Margin," and you've just borrowed money. It's that easy.

Understanding the costs and fees of margin

Every brokerage firm charges interest on margin. The stated number is usually an annualized rate; if the rate given is 8 percent, for example, then you'd owe that much if your loan was outstanding for the entire year. (Some investors have margin loans in place that long.) A day trader, whose loan may only be outstanding for a few hours, probably has to pay interest, too. Some brokerage firms charge by the day; others may charge interest over three days because it takes three days for a trade to settle.

On top of margin interest, some firms charge a higher commission on margin trades than for cash trades. They justify this policy with the higher levels of paperwork and risk management required on margin accounts. Some firms go with the higher commission rather than charge interest on intraday loans. Your trading life will be easier if you find out your firm's policies and fees before you open a margin account.

If you trade derivatives, margin works differently. The contract itself is leveraged, so you aren't charged interest. You have to settle your profits and losses at the end of the day, however (don't worry; the exchange's clearinghouse does it for you). You can't use the money held as margin for other trades.

Managing margin calls

If the value of your account starts falling and it looks like it's falling below the 25 percent maintenance margin limit, you get a *margin call,* in which your broker calls you and asks you to deposit more money in your account. If you can't make the necessary deposit, the broker starts selling your securities to close out the loan. And if you don't have enough to pay off the loan, the broker closes your account and puts a *lien,* which is a claim on your assets, against you.

Most brokerage firms have risk-management limits in place, so you'll probably get plenty of warning before you get a margin call or see your account closed out. After all, neither you nor your brokerage firm wants to lose money. Just keep in mind that a margin call is a possibility. If your account falls to the maintenance level, ask yourself, as objectively as you can, whether your idea is still good or whether you're just wishing and hoping that it is.

At least one brokerage firm advertises that, as a service to you, it will close out your account as soon as you lose the amount in it in order to keep you from losing more money. This service helps the brokerage firm as much as it helps you, because it keeps the firm from dealing with the hassles of chasing down additional margin. This is one example of the built-in risk management policies that firms use to limit risks to everyone.

Enjoying margin bargains for day traders

Day traders are often able to avoid margin calls because they borrow money for such short periods of time. Good day traders look for small market moves and cut their losses early, which minimizes the risk of using other people's money. And by definition, day traders close out their positions every night.

If you qualify as a pattern day trader, you get two benefits. First, your brokerage firm probably won't charge you any interest as long as you don't hold a margin loan balance overnight. Second, you may be allowed to borrow more than 50 percent of the purchase price of securities. Some firms allow pattern day traders to borrow 75 percent or more of their trade value.

The Financial Industries Regulatory Association defines a *pattern day trader* as one with a margin account holding at least $25,000. This trader must also buy then sell, or sell short then buy, the same security on the same day four or more times in five business days. The number of day trades should be more than 6 percent of the customer's total trading activity for that same five-day period.

The Switch-Up of Short Selling

Traditionally, investors and traders want to buy low and sell high. They buy a position in a security and then wait for the price to go up. This strategy isn't a bad way to make money, especially because, if the country's economy continues to grow even a little bit, businesses are going to grow and so are their stocks.

But even in a good economy, some securities go down. The company may be mismanaged, it may sell a product that's out of favor, or maybe it's just having a string of bad days. For that matter, maybe it went up a little too much in price, and investors are now coming to their senses. In these situations, you can't make money buying low and selling high. Instead, you need a way to reverse the situation.

The solution? Selling short. In short — hah! — *selling short* means that you borrow a security and sell it in hopes of repaying the loan of the shares by buying back cheaper shares later on.

In trading lingo, when you own something, you are considered to be *long*. When you sell it, especially if you do not already own it, you are considered to be *short*. You don't have to be long before you go short.

Selling short

Most brokerage firms make selling short easy. You simply place an order to sell the stock, and the broker asks whether you're selling shares that you own or selling short. After you place the order, the brokerage firm goes about borrowing shares for you to sell. It loans the shares to your account and executes the sell order.

You can't sell short unless the brokerage firm is able to borrow the shares. Sometimes so many people have sold a stock short that no shares are left to borrow. In that case, you have to find another stock or another strategy.

When the shares are sold, you wait until the security goes down in price, and then you buy the shares in the market at a bargain. You then return these purchased shares to the broker to pay the loan, and you keep the difference between where you sold and where you bought — less interest, of course.

The stock exchanges are in the business of helping companies raise money, so they have rules in place to help maintain an upward bias in the stock market. These rules can work against the short seller. The key regulation is what's called the *uptick rule,* which means you can only sell a stock short when the last trade was a move up. You can't short a stock that's moving down.

Figure 9-1 shows how short selling works. The trader borrows 400 shares selling at $25 each and then sells them. If the stock goes down, she can buy back the shares at the lower price, making a tidy profit. If the stock stays flat, she loses money because the broker will charge her interest based on the value of the shares she borrowed. And if the stock price goes up, she not only loses money on the interest expense but also is out on her investment.

Figure 9-1:
Looking at short selling in the equities market.

The trader borrows 400 shares of SuperCorp shares to sell. The shares are trading at $25 each. She sells them for $10,000. The brokerage firm charges 10% interest.

Beginning Price	Shares Borrowed	Proceeds from Sale	Repurchase Price	Repurchase Cost	Loan Value	Net Profit	Interest Expense	Rate of Return	% Change in Stock Price
$ 25	400	$ 10,000	$ 40	$ (16,000)	$ 10,000	$ (6,000)	$ 1,000	-70%	60%
$ 25	400	$ 10,000	$ 25	$ (10,000)	$ 10,000	$ -	$ 1,000	-10%	0%
$ 25	400	$ 10,000	$ 15	$ (6,000)	$ 10,000	$ 4,000	$ 1,000	30%	-40%

The interest and fees that the broker charges traders who borrow stock accrue to the broker, not to the person who actually owns the stock. In fact, the stock's owner will probably never know that his shares were loaned out.

Choosing shorts

Investors — those people who do careful research and expect to be in their positions for months or even years — look for companies that have inflated expectations and are possibly fraudulent. Investors who work the short side of the market spend hours doing careful accounting research, looking for companies that are likely to go down in price some day.

Day traders don't care about accounting. They don't have the time to wait for a short to work out. Instead, they look for stocks that go down in price for more mundane reasons, like more sellers than buyers in the next ten minutes. Most day traders who sell short simply reverse their long strategy. For example, some day traders like to buy stocks that have gone down for three days in a row, figuring that they'll go up on the fourth day. They'll also short stocks that have gone up three days in a row, figuring that they'll go down on the fourth day. You don't need a CPA to do that!

Trading strategies are covered in more detail in Chapters 7 and 8, if you are looking for some ideas.

Losing your shorts?

Shorting stocks carries certain risks because a short sale is a bet on things going wrong. Because, in theory, there's no limit on how much a stock can go up, there's no limit on how much money a short seller can lose. Two traps in particular can get a short seller. The first is a short squeeze due to good news; the second is a concerted effort to hurt traders who are short.

Squeeze my shorts

With a *short squeeze,* a company that has been popular with a lot of short sellers has some good news that drives the stock price up. Or, maybe some other buyers simply drive up the price in order to force the shorts to sell, which is a common form of market manipulation. When the price goes up, short sellers lose money, and some may even have margin problems. And the original reason for going short may be proven to be wrong. Those who are short start buying the stock back to reduce their losses, but their increased demand drives the stock price even higher, causing even bigger losses for people who are still short. Ouch!

Calling back the stock

All is not sweetness and light in the world of short selling. Many market participants distrust those folks who are doing all the careful research, in part because they are often right. Company executives are often optimists who don't like to hear bad news, and they blame short sellers for all that is wrong with their stock price. Meanwhile, some short sellers have been known to get impatient and start spreading ugly rumors if their sale isn't making money.

Many companies, brokers, and investors hate short sellers and try tactics to bust them. Sometimes they issue good news or spread rumors of good news to create a squeeze. Other times, they collectively ask holders of the stock to request that their brokerage firm not loan out their shares, which means that those who shorted the stock have to buy back and return the shares even if doing so makes no sense.

Leveraging All Kinds of Accounts

Leverage is the use of borrowed money to increase returns. Day traders use leverage a lot to get bigger returns from relatively small price changes in the underlying securities. And as long as they consistently close their positions out at the end of the day, day traders can borrow more money and pay less interest than people who hold securities for a longer term.

The process of borrowing works differently in different markets. In the stock and bond markets, it's straightforward: When you place the order, you just tell your broker you're borrowing. In the options and futures markets, the contracts you buy and sell have leverage built in to them. Although you don't borrow money outright, you can control a lot of value in your account for relatively little money down. The following sections go into more detail on these points.

In stock and bond markets

Leverage is straightforward for buyers of stocks and bonds: You simply click the box marked "Margin" when you place your order, and the brokerage firm loans you money. Then when the security goes up in price, you get a greater percentage return because you've been able to buy more for your money. Of course, that also increases your potential losses. (For more detail on the margin process, head to the earlier section "The Magic of Margin.")

Figure 9-2 shows how leverage works. The trader borrows money to buy 400 shares of SuperCorp. If the stock goes up 4 percent, she makes 8 percent. Whoo-hooo! But if the stock goes down 4 percent, she still has to repay the loan at full dollar value, so she ends up losing 8 percent. That's not so good.

A trader buys $10,000 of SuperCorp with $5,000 of her own cash and a $5,000 loan. SuperCorp trades at $25/share, so the trader purchases a total of 400 shares. The trader closes out at the end of the day, so no interest is charged. What happens as the stock price changes?

	Ending Price	Ending Value	Loan Value	Net Equity	Trader's Rate of Return	% Change in Stock Price
Figure 9-2: An example of trading stocks on margin.	$ 26.00	$ 10,400	$ 5,000	$ 5,400	8%	4%
	$ 25.50	$ 10,200	$ 5,000	$ 5,200	4%	2%
	$ 25.00	$ 10,000	$ 5,000	$ 5,000	0%	0%
	$ 24.50	$ 9,800	$ 5,000	$ 4,800	-4%	-2%
	$ 24.00	$ 9,600	$ 5,000	$ 4,600	-8%	-4%

REMEMBER

If you hold your margin position overnight or longer, you have to start paying interest, which cuts into your returns or increases your losses.

In options markets

An *option* gives you the right, but not the obligation, to buy or sell a stock or other item at a set price when the contract expires. A *call option* gives you the right to buy, so you would buy a call if you think the underlying asset is going up. A *put option* gives you the right to sell, so you would buy a put if you think the underlying asset is going down. (You can read more about options in Chapter 3.) By trading an option, you get exposure to changes in the price of the underlying security without actually buying the security itself. That's the source of the leverage in the market.

A day trader can use options to get an exposure to price changes in a stock for a lot less money than buying the stock itself would cost. Suppose a call option is *deeply in the money,* meaning that its *strike price* (the price at which you would buy the stock if you exercised the option) is far below the current stock price. In this event, the obvious thing to do is to set option price at the difference between the current stock price and the strike price, which is more or less what happens — more in theory, less in practice. When the stock price changes, the option price changes by almost exactly the same amount, enabling you to buy the price performance of the stock at a discount, with the discount being the strike price of the option.

Figure 9-3 shows the performance-boosting leverage from this strategy. The trader buys call options with an exercise price of $10 on a stock trading at $25. The option price changes the same amount that the stock price does, but the call holder gets a greater percentage return than the stockholder.

Figure 9-3:
What happens to the option value when the stock price changes?

A trader buys deep in-the-money call options on SuperCorp. The exercise price is $10, and the stock is trading at $25.

Stock Price	Initial Option Price	Exercise (Strike) Price	New Option Price	Stock Price Change	Option Price Change
$ 26.00	$ 15.00	$ 10.00	$ 16.00	4%	7%
$ 25.50	$ 15.00	$ 10.00	$ 15.50	2%	3%
$ 25.00	$ 15.00	$ 10.00	$ 15.00	0%	0%
$ 24.50	$ 15.00	$ 10.00	$ 14.50	-2%	-3%
$ 24.00	$ 15.00	$ 10.00	$ 14.00	-4%	-7%

Day traders can use many other options strategies, but a discussion of them goes beyond the scope of this book. The appendix has some resources to help you in your research.

In futures trading

A *futures* contract gives you the obligation to buy or sell an underlying financial or agricultural commodity, assuming you still hold the contract at the expiration date. That underlying product ranges from the value of treasury bonds to barrels of oil and heads of cattle, and you're only putting money down now when you purchase the contract. You don't have to come up with the full amount until the contract comes due — and almost all options and futures traders close out their trades long before the contract expiration date. Futures are discussed in Chapter 3, but here I talk about how leverage works in the futures market.

Although most options and futures contracts settle with cash long before the due date, contract holders have the right to hold them until the due date and, in the case of options on common stock and agricultural derivatives, demand physical delivery. It's rare, but the commodity exchanges have systems in place for determining the transport, specifications, and delivery of grain, cattle, or ethanol. One advantage of day trading is that you close out the same day, without ever even thinking about the fine print of physical delivery.

Because *derivatives* have built-in leverage that allows a trader to have big market exposure for relatively few dollars up front, they've become popular with day traders. Figure 9-4 shows how derivative leverage works. Here, a trader is buying the Chicago Mercantile Exchange's E-mini S&P 500 futures contract, which gives her exposure to the performance of the Standard and Poor's 500 Index, a standard measure of the stock performance of a diversified list of 500 large American companies. The futures contract trades at 50 times the value of the index, rounded to the nearest $0.25. The minimum margin that this trader must put down on the contract is $3,500. Each $0.25 change in the index leads to a $12.50 ($0.25 × 50) change in the value of the contract, and that $12.50 is added to or subtracted from the $3,500 margin.

Figure 9-4: Margin and the derivatives trade with built-in leverage.

A day trader buys a Chicago Mercantile Exchange E-Mini S&P 500 futures contract. The contract price is $50 x the index level. To buy it, the trader must post margin of $3,500.

Initial Index Value	Ending Index Value	Multiplier	Initial Contract Value	Contract Value	Value Change in Dollars	Value Change in Percent	Initial Margin	Ending Margin	Percent Change in Margin
1,457.50	1,458.50	$ 50.00	$ 72,875.00	$ 72,925.00	$ 50.00	0.07%	$ 3,500.00	$ 3,550.00	1.43%
1,457.50	1,458.00	$ 50.00	$ 72,875.00	$ 72,900.00	$ 25.00	0.03%	$ 3,500.00	$ 3,525.00	0.71%
1,457.50	1,457.50	$ 50.00	$ 72,875.00	$ 72,875.00	$ -	0.00%	$ 3,500.00	$ 3,500.00	0.00%
1,457.50	1,457.00	$ 50.00	$ 72,875.00	$ 72,850.00	$ (25.00)	-0.03%	$ 3,500.00	$ 3,475.00	-0.71%
1,457.50	1,456.50	$ 50.00	$ 72,875.00	$ 72,825.00	$ (50.00)	-0.07%	$ 3,500.00	$ 3,450.00	-1.43%

Some exchanges use the term *margin,* and others prefer to use *performance bond.* Either term refers to the same thing: money you put in up front to ensure that you can meet the contract terms when it comes due. If you hold the contract overnight, your account is adjusted up or down to reflect the day's profits. If it gets too low, you're asked to add more money.

In foreign exchange

The *foreign exchange,* or *forex,* market is driven by leverage. Despite the nervous reports you may hear in the financial news, exchange rates tend to move slowly, by as little as a tenth or even a hundredth of a penny a day. And the markets are so huge that hedging risk is easier in the currency markets than in other financial markets. You may have trouble borrowing shares of stock that you want to short, but you should have no trouble ever borrowing yen. To get a big return, forex traders almost always borrow huge amounts of money.

In the stock market, day traders can borrow up to three times the amount of cash and securities held in their accounts (although not all firms let you borrow the statutory maximum), and that amount is set by outside regulatory organizations. In the forex market, there is no regulation on lending, and some forex firms allow traders to borrow as much as 400 times the amount in their accounts.

Forex firms allow such huge borrowing because they can hedge their risks so that if you lose money, they make money. If you sell dollars to buy euros, for example, the firm can easily go in and sell euros to buy dollars. This capability makes its position net neutral. If the euro goes down relative to the dollar, you lose money, but the firm can offset its risk because its counter-trade went up.

The reason that a forex firm hedges its risks against its day-trading customers is that most day traders lose money. The firm knows that if it bets against the aggregate trades held by its customers, it'll probably come out ahead. Don't trade in forex or any other market until you've worked out a strategy and practiced it so that you can avoid becoming a statistic. Chapter 16 has information on testing and evaluating trading strategies.

Figure 9-5 shows how leverage in foreign exchange makes good returns possible. Here, the trader starts with a $1,000 account and borrows the maximum amount the forex firms allow, $400 for each dollar in the account. All $401,000 are put to work buying euros. Note that the euro value stays constant, but the dollar value of those euros changes by hundredths of a penny. Thanks to leverage, the return is 11 percent — not bad for a day's trading! Of course, you could lose 11 percent, which wouldn't be so good.

A trader has a $1,000 forex account. He borrows 400 times that amount — $400,000 — to buy euros.

Figure 9-5:
Trading foreign exchange on margin.

Initial Dollar/Euro Rate	Ending Dollar/Euro Rate	Initial Account Value	Amount Purchased ($)	Amount Purchased (€)	Ending Value (€)	Ending Value ($)	Loan Value	Ending Account Value	Trader's Rate of Return	% Change in Exchange Rate
0.7477	0.7475	$ 1,000	$ 401,000	€ 299,828	€ 299,828	$ 401,107	$ 400,000	$ 1,107	11%	-0.03%
0.7477	0.7476	$ 1,000	$ 401,000	€ 299,828	€ 299,828	$ 401,054	$ 400,000	$ 1,054	5%	-0.01%
0.7477	0.7477	$ 1,000	$ 401,000	€ 299,828	€ 299,828	$ 401,000	$ 400,000	$ 1,000	0%	0.00%
0.7477	0.7478	$ 1,000	$ 401,000	€ 299,828	€ 299,828	$ 400,946	$ 400,000	$ 946	-5%	0.01%
0.7477	0.7479	$ 1,000	$ 401,000	€ 299,828	€ 299,828	$ 400,893	$ 400,000	$ 893	-11%	0.03%

An exchange rate is just the price of money. If the dollar/euro rate is 0.7477, $1.00 will buy €0.7477.

Borrowing in Your Trading Business

Leverage is only part of the borrowing involved in your day-trading business. Like any business owner, sometimes you need more cash than your business generates. Other times, you see expansion opportunities that require more money than you have on hand. In this section, I discuss why and how day traders can borrow money over and above leveraged trading.

Taking margin loans for cash flow

If day trading is your job, then you face a constant pressure: How do you cover the costs of living while keeping enough money in the market to trade? One way to do so is to have another source of income — from savings, a spouse, or a job that doesn't overlap with market hours. Other day traders take money out of their trading account.

If the market hasn't been cooperative, your account may not have enough in it to allow you to withdraw funds while still maintaining enough capital to trade. One option is to arrange a margin loan through a brokerage firm. With a margin loan, the firm lets you take out a loan against the cash in your account (or securities that you are holding, not trading). You can spend the money any way you like, but you're charged interest and you have to repay it. Still, a margin loan is a good option to know about because day-trade earnings tend to be erratic.

Borrowing for trading capital

Some day traders use a double layer of leverage: They borrow the money to set up their trading accounts and then they borrow money for their trading strategies. If the market cooperates, this type of borrowing can be a great way to make money, but if the market doesn't cooperate, you could end up owing a lot of people money that you don't have.

If you want to take the risk, though, you have a few resources to turn to other than your relatives: You can borrow against your house, use your credit cards, or find a trading firm that will give you some money to work with.

Borrowing against your house

Yes, you can use a mortgage or a home equity line of credit to get the money for your day-trading activities. In general, this option carries low interest rates because your house is your collateral. In most cases, however, the interest isn't tax deductible (ask your accountant, but generally, you can only deduct interest used to purchase or improve your house). Still, borrowing against your house can be a relatively low-cost way to pull value stored in your house for use in trading.

The risk? If you can't pay back the loan, you can lose your residence. If you decide to pursue this strategy, just don't borrow against your car, too, because you'll need a place to live when the bank forecloses.

Putting it on the card

The business world is filled with people who started businesses using credit cards. And you can do that. If you have good credit, credit card companies are happy to lend to you.

Naturally, credit card companies charge you a mighty high rate of interest, one that even the sharpest traders will have trouble covering from their returns. If the only way you can raise the capital for day trading is through your credit card, consider waiting a few years and saving your money before taking the plunge. Because day trading income can be erratic, you may end up using your credit cards to cover your living expenses some months. You may want to save your credit for that rather than dedicate it directly for your day trading.

Accepting risk capital from a prop trading firm

Some firms that are in the business of trading are willing to stake new traders. You may have to go through a training period or pay a fee to rent a desk at their office or to use their software remotely. The firm watches your trading patterns, including both your profits and your risk management. If the principals like what they see, they may offer you money to manage along with your own capital. You will receive a cut of the profits on the funds you trade for them.

The costs of free riding

Some traders figure that they don't need margin accounts if they buy a security in a cash account and then sell it before they have to pay for it. This is known as *free riding,* and the SEC doesn't look kindly upon it. In fact, brokerage firms are required to freeze a customer's account for 90 days when they identify free riding. The customer can then trade only if he or she pays for each trade as it is made rather than receiving the three days normally allowed.

If you're trading in a cash account, you can avoid a free-riding freezeout by paying for any securities that you buy within three days, without relying on money from the sale of those securities to cover the payment. The alternative is to trade in a margin account.

Assessing Risks and Returns from Short Selling and Leverage

Leverage introduces risk to your day trading, and that can give you greatly increased returns. Most day traders use leverage, at least part of the time, to make their trading activities pay off in cold, hard cash. The challenge is to use leverage responsibly. Chapter 6 goes into money management in great detail, but here I cover the two issues most related to leverage: losing your money and losing your nerve. Understanding those risks can help you determine how much leverage you should take and how often you can take it.

Losing your money

Losing money is an obvious hazard. Leverage magnifies your returns, but it also magnifies your risks. Any borrowings have to be repaid regardless. If you buy or sell a futures or options contract, you are legally obligated to perform, even if you have lost money. That can be really hard.

Day trading is risky in large part because of the amount of leverage used. If you don't feel comfortable with that, you may want to use little or no leverage, especially when you are new to day trading or when you are starting to work a new trading strategy.

Losing your nerve

The basic risk and return of your underlying strategy isn't affected by leverage. If you expect that your system will work about 60 percent of the time, that should hold no matter how much money is at stake or where that money came from. However, trading with borrowed money likely *does* make a difference to you on some subconscious level.

Trading is very much a game of nerves. If you hesitate to make a trade, cut a loss, or otherwise follow your strategy, you're going to run into trouble. Say you're trading futures and decide that you'll accept three downticks before selling and that you'll look for five upticks before selling. This strategy means you're willing to accept some loss, cut it if it gets out of hand, and then be disci-plined about taking gains when you get them. It keeps a lid on your losses while forcing some discipline on your gains. Now, suppose you're dealing with lots and lots of leverage. Suddenly, those downticks become too real to you — it's money you don't have. Next thing you know, you only accept two downticks before closing out. But doing so keeps you from getting winners. Then you decide to ride with your winners, and suddenly you aren't taking profits fast enough, and your positions move against you. Your fear of loss is making you sloppy. That's why many traders find it better to borrow less money and stick to their system rather than borrow the maximum allowed and let that knowl-edge cloud their judgment. Head to Chapter 14 for more on the mental aspects of day trading.

Lenders can lose their nerve, too. Your brokerage firm may close your account because of losses, even though waiting just a little longer may turn a losing position into a profit. Remember Bear Stearns, the big fancy broker-age firm that was shut down in March 2008? Or Lehman Brothers, the big fancy brokerage firm that was shut down in September 2008? Both were shut down because they had big losses and their lenders would no longer give them cash.

Chapter 10

Looking for Easy Profits: Navigating the Tricky World of Arbitrage and High-Frequency Trading

....

In This Chapter

▶ Finding out about the law of one price

▶ Making quick profits through scalping

▶ Considering the costs of your transactions

▶ Checking out tools used to conduct arbitrage

▶ Looking at the various types of arbitrage

....

*D*ay traders work fast, looking to make lots of little profits during a single day. *Arbitrage* is a trading strategy that looks to make profits from small discrepancies in securities prices. The idea is that the *arbitrageur,* or *arb* (the person who does arbitrage), works back and forth among the prices in the market to reach one final level. In theory, arbitrage is riskless. It's illogical for the same asset to trade at different prices, so eventually the two prices must converge. The person who buys at the lower price and sells at the higher one makes money with no risk.

Good arbitrageurs have a paradoxical mix of patience (to wait for the right opportunity) and impatience (to place the trade the instant the opportunity appears). If you have the fortitude to watch the market or are willing to have software do it for you (see information on research services in Chapter 13), you'll probably find enough good arbitrage opportunities to keep you busy.

True arbitrage involves buying and selling the same security, often with high levels of *leverage* (borrowing — see Chapter 9) to boost returns. Other traders follow trading strategies involving similar, but not identical, securities. These fall under the category of *risk arbitrage.* Because brokerage firms, hedge funds, and other institutions have a huge advantage over day traders, day traders are more likely to rely on risk arbitrage than on other forms.

In this chapter, I cover the terms and strategies that day traders who engage in arbitrage use, discuss the basics of arbitrage and how a patient trader can put those to good use, outline the tools you can use to profit from price differences among similar securities, and list the many types of arbitrage you may want to include in your arsenal of trading strategies.

The challenge is that everyone is looking for these easy profits, so there may not be many of them out there.

Arbitrage and the Law of One Price

The key to success in any investment is buying low and selling high. But what's low? And what's high? Who knows?

In the financial markets, the general assumption is that, at least in the short run, the market price is the right price. Only investors, those patient, long-suffering accounting nerds willing to hold investments for years, see deviations between the market price and the true worth of an investment. For everyone else, especially day traders, what you see is what you get.

Under *the law of one price,* the same asset has the same value everywhere. If markets allow for easy trading — and the financial markets certainly do — then any price discrepancies are short-lived because traders immediately step in to buy at the low price and sell at the high price. In the following sections I explore how market efficiency limits arbitrage opportunities and how you can step in when the moment is right.

Understanding how arbitrage and market efficiency interact

The law of one price holds as long as markets are efficient. Market efficiency is a controversial topic in finance. In academic theory, markets are perfectly efficient, and arbitrage simply isn't possible. That makes a lot of sense if you are testing different assumptions about how the markets would work in a perfect world. A long-term investor would say that markets are inefficient in the short run but perfectly efficient in the long run, so they believe that if they do their research now, the rest of the world will eventually come around, allowing them to make good money.

Traders are in between. The market price and volume are pretty much all the information they have to go on. The price may be irrational, but that doesn't matter today. The only thing a trader wants to know is whether an opportunity exists to make money given what's going on right now.

In the academic world, market efficiency comes in three flavors, with no form allowing for arbitrage:

- ✔ **Strong form:** Everything, even inside information known only to company executives, is reflected in the security's price.

- ✔ **Semi-strong form:** Prices include all public information, so profiting from insider trading may be possible.

- ✔ **Weak-form:** Prices reflect all historical information, so research that uncovers new trends may be beneficial.

Those efficient-market true believers are convinced that arbitrage is imaginary because someone would've noticed a price difference between markets already and immediately acted to close it off. But who are those mysterious someones? They are day traders! Even the most devout efficient markets adherent would, if pressed, admit that day traders perform a valuable service in the name of market efficiency. The 2008 financial crisis and the 2010 flash crash thinned the ranks of the efficient-market true believers.

Those with a less-rigid view of market activity admit that arbitrage opportunities exist but that they are few and far between. A trader who expects to make money from arbitrage had better pay close attention to the markets to act quickly when a moment happens.

Finally, people who don't believe in market efficiency believe that market prices are usually out of sync with asset values. They do research in hopes of learning things that other people don't know. This mindset favors investors more than traders because it can take time for these price discrepancies to work themselves out.

Because arbitrage requires traders to work fast, it tends to work best for traders who are willing and able to automate their trading. If you are comfortable with programming and relying on software to do your work, arbitrage may be a great strategy for you. Remember that the big players have an advantage.

Taking advantage of price discrepancies

So how can you as a day trader take advantage of what you know about the one-price rule? Suppose that what you see in New York is not what you see in

London, or that you notice that futures prices are not tracking movements in the underlying asset. How about if you see that the stock of every company except one in an industry has reacted to a news event?

Well, then, you have an opportunity to make money, but you'd better act fast because other people will probably see the discrepancy, too. What you do is simple: You sell as much of the high-priced asset in the high-priced market as you can, borrowing shares if you need to, and then you immediately turn around and buy the low-priced asset in the low-priced market.

Think of the markets as a scale, and you, the arbitrageur, must bring fairness to them. When the markets are out of balance, you take from the high-priced market (the heavier side of the scale) and return it to the low-priced market (the lighter side) until both even out at a price in between.

If you start with a high price of $8 and a low price of $6 and then buy at $6 and sell at $8, your maximum profit is $2 — with no risk. Until the point where the two assets balance at $7, you can make a profit on the difference between them.

Of course, most price differences are on the order of pennies, not dollars, but if you can find enough of these little pricing errors and trade them in size, you can make good money.

Sometimes, the price differences are less than a penny, a situation the traders call *subpennying*. A day trader really can't work with that. To see if subpennying is going on with an asset that you trade, set your price screens to display four decimal places rather than only two.

Reducing arbitrage opportunities: High-frequency trading

Most of the large brokerage firms and many large hedge funds have invested crazy amounts of time and money to develop *high-frequency* and *algorithmic* trading strategies. These strategies use computer programs that control billions of dollars and make extremely short-term trades — sometimes holding only for seconds — whenever the programs spot short-term discrepancies in the market. In some ways, this practice has made the market more efficient, because these program traders fix prices that are out of whack in no time. But they have also added to volatility, sometimes due to program glitches and sometimes because the trades go on even when they shouldn't, because no human is there to stop them. In fact, many observers of the *market microstructure,* which is the underlying trading environment, think that the amount of high-frequency and algorithmic trading has reduced efficiency. They see evidence that the larger number of market participants have led to knee-jerk reactions when different programs malfunction or entire systems fail. The downside for the day trader is that these programs have eliminated many arbitrage opportunities that once made up the bread and butter of many a trader's earnings.

Scalping, the Dangerous Game

The law of one price is all well and good, but prices change constantly during the day. They go up a little bit, they go down a little bit, and they move every time an order is placed.

Once upon a time, day traders could profit from these movements. The process, known as *scalping,* is not exactly arbitrage. Especially active in commodities markets, scalpers look to take advantage of changes in a security's *bid-ask spread.* This spread is the difference between the price that a broker will buy a security for from those who want to sell it (the *bid*) and the price that the broker will charge those who want to buy it (the *ask* — also called the *offer* in some markets).

In normal trading, the bid-ask spread tends to be more or less steady over time because the usual flow of supply and demand stays in balance. After all, under market efficiency, everyone has the same information, so their trading is consistent and allows the broker-dealers to generate a steady profit. Sometimes, however, the spread is a little wider or narrower than normal, not because of a change in the information in the market but because of short-term imbalances in supply and demand.

A basic scalping strategy looks like this:

- ✔ **If the spread between the bid and the ask is wider than usual,** the ask is higher and the bid is lower than it should be. That's because slightly more people want to buy than to sell, so the brokers charge the buyers higher prices. The scalper uses this as a sign to sell.

- ✔ **If the spread between the bid and the ask is narrower than usual,** the ask is lower and the bid is higher than it would normally be. This situation occurs when sellers slightly outnumber buyers and the broker wants to find buyers to pick up the slack. The scalper would be in there buying — and hoping that the selling pressure is short lived.

The scalper has to work quickly to make many small trades. He may buy at $20.25, sell at $20.50, and buy again at $20.30. He has to have a low *trade cost structure* in place (discussed later in this chapter) or else he'll pay out all his profits and more to the broker. He also has to be sure that the price changes aren't driven by real information, because that makes market prices too volatile to make scalping profitable. Scalping is akin to "picking up nickels in front of a steamroller," some traders say, because of the risk of focusing on small price changes when bigger changes are underway.

For years, scalping was a common day-trading strategy. It was always tricky business, given how quickly prices could move within a trend. With the presence of so many high-frequency traders, scalping has become downright dangerous, if not impossible. High-frequency traders can and will move before you can. Nowadays, scalping is like picking up pennies as steamrollers come at you from all sides.

Scalping, as defined here, is perfectly legal. However, the word is also used to describe some illegal activities, such as promoting a security in public and then selling it in private. (Another term for this is *pump and dump*.) If a celebrity goes on his Twitter feed and talks about how great a stock is so that the price goes up and then he sells the stock the next day when everyone else is buying, he has committed the crime of scalping.

Those Pesky Transaction Costs

Pure arbitrage works best in a world where trading is free. In reality, trading costs good money. Sometimes you may notice a price discrepancy that seems to last forever, but you can't work it because the profit wouldn't cover your costs. And that actually may be true for everyone else out there.

In the real world, trading costs money. Consider all the costs of getting started: buying equipment, paying for Internet access, learning how to trade. Add to those costs the costs of doing business that vary with each transaction: commissions, fees, interest, the bid-ask spread, and taxes. You don't make a profit on a trade unless it covers those costs.

Even if you work with a broker who charges little or no commission and even if your broker charges no interest on day trading margin (loans against your securities account), you can bet that your broker is making money off you. That broker's profit is showing up in the spread and the speed of execution, so arbitrage still has a cost that must be covered, even on a seemingly free account. Trust me, brokerage firms are in business to make money, whether or not their customers do.

Add up those trading costs, and you can find yourself in a frustrating situation: You can see the opportunity staring you in the face, but you can't take it. So the opportunity either sits there, taunting you, or it gets picked off by a trader who has lower costs than you do.

Does that mean you're out of luck? Not at all. If you know what your costs are, you can avoid unprofitable opportunities and take advantage of profitable ones. When determining how much you have to clear, don't consider your fixed costs, like your office and your equipment. Those expenses don't change with any given trade. (Yes, you have to cover them in the long run to stay in business, but you can ignore them in the short run.) Instead, figure out how much money you give to your broker on any given trade, on an order, per share, or per contract basis. Write that number down on a sticky note and put it on your monitor so that you remember what you have to clear before you risk a trade. Then don't get so fixated on covering your costs that you avoid exiting trades at the right time.

Risk Arbitrage and Its Tools

In its purest form, arbitrage is riskless because the purchase of an asset in one market and the sale of the asset in another happen simultaneously — you just let those profits flow right into your account. This situation does occur, but not often, and not in a way that lets most day traders compete with algorithmic traders.

Because so few opportunities for true arbitrage exist, most day traders looking at arbitrage strategies actually practice *risk arbitrage*. Like true arbitrage, risk arbitrage attempts to generate profits from price discrepancies, but like the name implies, risk arbitrage involves taking some risk. Yes, you buy one security and sell another in risk arbitrage, but it's not always the same security and not always at the same time. For example, a day trader may buy the stock of an acquisition target and sell the stock of an acquirer in the hopes of making a profit as the deal nears the closing date.

Risk arbitrage usually involves strategies that unfold over time — possibly hours, but usually days or weeks. Pursuing these strategies puts you into the world of swing trading (described in Chapter 2), which carries a different set of risks than day trading.

In risk arbitrage, a trader is buying and selling similar securities. Much of the risk draws from the fact that the securities are not identical, so the law of one price isn't absolute. Nevertheless, it forms the guiding principle, which is this: If you have two different ways to buy the same thing, then the prices of each purchase should be proportional. If the prices aren't proportional, there's an opportunity to make money. And what day trader doesn't want to make money?

Return is a function of risk. The more risk you take, the greater the return you expect to make.

Arbitrageurs use a mix of different assets and techniques to create these different ways of buying the same thing. The following sections describe some of their favorites.

Arbitrating derivatives

Derivatives are options, futures, and related financial contracts that draw or derive their value from the value of something else, such as the price of a stock index or the current cost of corn. Derivatives offer a lower-cost, lower-obligation method of getting exposure to certain price changes. In the case of agricultural and energy commodities, derivatives are the only practical way for a day trader to own them. Because they are so closely tied to the value of the underlying security, derivatives form a useful, almost-but-not-quite asset for traders looking for arbitrage situations. A trader may see a price discrepancy between the derivative and the underlying asset, thus noticing a profitable trading opportunity.

Using a derivative in tandem with its underlying security, traders can construct a range of risk arbitrage trades (and you can read more about them later in this section). For example, a trader looking to set up arbitrage on a merger could trade options on the stocks of the buying and selling companies rather than trading the stocks themselves. The more arbitrage opportunities there are, the greater the likelihood of making a low-risk profit.

Levering with leverage

Leverage is the process of borrowing money to trade in order to increase potential returns. The more money the trader borrows, the greater the return on capital that she can earn. Leverage is commonly used by day traders, because most trades with a one-day time horizon carry low returns unless they are magnified through borrowing. (Go to Chapter 9 for detailed coverage of leverage.)

That magic of magnification becomes especially important in arbitrage, because the price discrepancies between securities tend to be really small. The primary way to get a bigger return is to borrow money to do it.

 Leverage has a downside: Along with improving returns, it increases risk. Because even risk arbitrage strategies tend to have low risk, the risk associated with leverage may be acceptable. Just remember that you have to repay all borrowed money, no matter what happens to prices. Chapter 9 has more information on that.

Short selling

Short selling (another topic from Chapter 9) creates another set of alternatives for setting up an arbitrage trade — one that's almost necessary to the process. Short selling allows a day trader to profit when a security's price goes down. The short seller goes to her broker, borrows the security that she thinks will decline in price, sells it, and then buys it back in the market later so that she has the shares to repay the loan. In essence, the trader is selling high (with borrowed money) and buying back low. Assuming she's right and the price does indeed fall, she pockets the difference between the price where she sold the security and the price where she bought it back. Of course, that difference is her loss if the price goes up instead of down. The arbitrageur can use this to bet on assets that are likely to go down in price when another asset goes up.

By adding short selling to the bag of tricks, an arbitrageur can find a lot more ways to profit from a price discrepancy in the market. New combinations of cheap and expensive assets — and more ways to trade them — give a day trader more opportunities to make trades during the day.

Creating synthetic securities

Feeling creative? Well, then, consider creating synthetic securities when looking for arbitrage opportunities. A *synthetic security* is a combination of assets that have the same profit-and-loss profile as another asset or group of assets. For example, a stock is a combination of a short *put option,* which has value if the stock goes down in price, and a long *call option,* which has value if the stock goes up in price. By thinking up ways to mimic the behavior of an asset through a synthetic security, a day trader can find more ways for an asset to be cheaper in one market than in another, leading to more potential arbitrage opportunities.

A typical arbitrage transaction involving a synthetic security, for example, involves shorting the real security and then buying a package of derivatives that match its risk and return. Many of the risk-arbitrage techniques covered later in this chapter involve the creation of synthetic securities.

Complex arbitrage trading strategies require more testing and simulation trading (covered in Chapter 16) and may possibly involve losses while you fine-tune your methods. Be sure you feel comfortable with your trading method before you commit big time and big dollars to it.

Arbitrage Strategies for Day Traders

You can use the tools of arbitrage — derivatives, leverage, short selling, synthetic securities — in all sorts of ways to generate potentially profitable trades, and that's what this section of the chapter covers. If you decide to do arbitrage, you may discover a few useful strategies to follow. Beware of picking too many: The trader who tries to do too much is the trader who will soon be looking for a new job! Instead, look for an arbitrage strategy that matches your approach to the market and make it your own.

The varieties of arbitrage transactions are listed here in alphabetical order. Some are more complex than others, some generate more opportunities than others, and some work best if you are willing to swing trade (hold for a few days) rather than day trade (close out all positions at the end of the day). Keep in mind that this list is not exhaustive; you can find plenty of other ways to exploit price differences in the market, but some involve more time than a day trader is willing to commit.

Many arbitrage strategies work best in combination with other strategies, such as news-driven trading (discussed in Chapter 8). For example, a news announcement may cause people to pay attention to a company's stock, resulting in enough trading activity that day to close a price gap. If you know about the pricing problem ahead of time, you can swoop in and make the arbitrage that day.

Other types of arbitrage are certainly out there. Wherever people pay close attention to the markets and price changes, they find small price differences to turn into large, low-risk profits. If you think you've found an arbitrage strategy not listed here, by all means, go and test it to see whether it will work for you.

Convertible arbitrage

As part of designing their capital structure, some companies issue *convertible bonds* (sometimes called a *convertible debenture*) or *convertible preferred stock*. These securities are a cross between stocks and bonds. Like an ordinary bond, convertibles pay regular income to those who hold them (interest for convertible bonds and dividends for convertible preferred stock), but they also act a little like stock because the holders have the right to exchange the convertible security for ordinary common stock.

Here's an example: A $1,000 convertible bond pays 7.5 percent interest and is convertible into 25 shares of stock. If the stock is less than $40 per share, the convertible holder will prefer to cash the interest or dividend checks. If the company's stock trades above $40, the convertible holder would make more money giving up the income in order to get the stock cheap. Because of the benefit of conversion, the interest rate on a convertible security is usually below that on a regular corporate bond.

Because a convertible security carries a built-in option to buy the underlying stock, it generally trades in line with the stock. If the convertible's price gets too high or too low, then an arbitrage opportunity presents itself.

Consider this case: A day trader notices that a convertible bond is selling at a lower price than it should be, given the current level of interest rates and the price of the company's common stock. So he buys the convertibles and sells the common stock short (see Chapter 9 for more on short selling). When the stock's price moves back into line, he collects a profit from both sides of the trade.

ETF arbitrage

An exchange-traded fund, or ETF, is a security based on a stock market index. It may be a recognized index or one that has been invented by the company that created the ETF to track a particular investment strategy.

ETFs have been designed with a built-in mechanism to keep the price of the funds in line with the underlying securities. A typical ETF has two classes of shareholders. The first are *authorized participants,* which are large trading firms that agree to buy the securities in the ETF. The authorized participants then give the securities to the ETF company in exchange for *creation units,* which are shares of the fund that the authorized participant can hold, sell on the open market, or trade back to the ETF company for the shares. The authorized participant will do whatever had the greatest profit potential, some built-in arbitrage designed to keep the ETF's value in line for the second class of shareholders, the regular ETF traders.

Despite this mechanism, an ETF's value may swing out of line with the underlying index or the underlying fundamentals of the sector that it represents. When this happens, a trader can look for an arbitrage opportunity between the ETF and an index future, between two different ETFs, or between an ETF and a representative stock.

Fixed income and interest-rate arbitrage

Fixed-income securities are bonds, notes, and related securities that give their owners a regular interest payment. They are popular with conservative investors, especially retirees, who want to generate a regular income from the quarterly interest payments. They are considered to be safe, predictable, long-run investments, but they can fluctuate wildly in the short term, which makes them attractive to arbitrageurs.

Interest rates are the price of money, and so they affect the value of many kinds of securities. Fixed-income securities have a great deal of interest-rate exposure because they pay out interest. Some stocks have interest-rate exposure, too. Trading in foreign exchange is an attempt to profit from the changing price of one currency relative to another, and that's usually a function of the difference in interest rates between the two countries. Derivatives have a regular expiration schedule, so they have some time value, and that's measured through interest rates.

With so many different assets affected by changes in interest rates, arbitrageurs pay attention. With *fixed-income arbitrage,* the trader breaks out the following:

- The time value of money
- The level of risk in the economy
- The likelihood of repayment
- The inflation-rate effects on different securities

If one of the numbers is out of whack, the trader constructs and executes an arbitrage trade to profit from it.

Buying bonds outright is rarely practical for a day trader. Instead, day traders looking at fixed-income arbitrage and other interest-rate sensitive strategies usually rely on interest-rate futures, offered by the CME Group. You can read more about interest-rate futures in Chapter 3.

How would such a trade work? Think of a day trader monitoring interest rates on U.S. government securities. He notices that two-year treasury notes are trading at a lower yield than expected — especially relative to five-year treasury notes. He sells futures on the two-year treasury notes and then buys futures on the five-year treasury notes. When the difference between the two rates falls back where it should be, the futures trade will turn a profit.

Index arbitrage

Market observers talk a lot about the performance of the S&P 500 Index and the Dow Jones Industrial Average. These *market indexes* represent the activity of the market and are widely published for market observers to follow. The performance of the index is based on the performance of a group of securities, ranging from the 3,000 largest companies in the market (the Russell 3,000) to a mere 30 large companies (the Dow Jones Industrial Average).

Sure, an arbitrageur could buy all the stocks, and some hedge funds do just that. But very few people can afford to pursue that strategy. Instead, they get exposure to index performance through the many different securities based on the indexes. Buy-and-hold mutual fund investors can buy funds that hold all the same stocks in the same proportion as the index. Those with shorter-term profits in mind can buy exchange-traded funds, which are baskets of stocks listed on organized exchanges, or they can trade futures and options on the indexes.

Arbitrageurs love the idea of an asset — like an index — that has lots of different securities based on its value because it creates lots of opportunities for mispricing. Unless the index, the futures, the options, and the exchange-traded funds are all in line, some canny day trader can step in and make some money.

Suppose, for example, that the S&P 500 futures contract is looking mighty cheap relative to the price of the S&P 500 Index. A trader can short an exchange-traded fund on the index and then buy futures contracts to profit from the difference.

Merger arbitrage

Every day, companies get bought and sold, and that creates arbitrage opportunities. In fact, one of the better-known arbitrage strategies out there is *merger arbitrage*, in which traders try to profit from the change in stock prices after a merger has been announced. This kind of trade starts with the trader looking at the following details in the merger announcement:

- ✔ The name of the acquiring company
- ✔ The name of the company being taken over (and no matter what PR people say, there are no mergers of equals)
- ✔ The price of the transaction
- ✔ The currency (cash, stock, debt)
- ✔ The date the merger is expected to close

Until the date that the merger actually closes, which may be different from the date in the merger announcement, any and every one of the announced details can change. The acquiring company may learn new information about the target company and change its mind. A third company may jump in and make an offer for more money. The shareholders may agree to support the deal only if they get cash instead of stock. All that drama creates opportunity, both for traders looking for one-day opportunities and for those willing to hold a position until the merger closing date.

Here's an example. Say that Major Bancorp offers to buy Downtown Bank for $50 per share in cash. Major Bancorp's shares will probably fall in price because its shareholders will be concerned that the merger will be a lot of trouble. Downtown Bank's shares will go up in price, but not all the way to $50, because its shareholders understand the risk that the deal won't go through. An arbitrageur would short Major Bancorp and buy Downtown Bank to profit from the concerns. If Overseas Banque decides to step in, the trader may think it a profitable idea to buy Major Bancorp and short Overseas Banque. (If another bidder steps in and places a higher offer for Downtown Bank, then the whole arbitrage unravels — hence, the risk.)

Option arbitrage

Options, discussed in detail in Chapter 3, form the basis of many arbitrage strategies, especially for those day traders who work the stock market. First, many different types of options are available, even on the same security. The two main categories are *puts,* which bet on the underlying security price falling, and *calls,* which bet on the underlying security price rising. Puts and calls on the same security come in many different strike prices, depending on where you want to bet the price goes. Some options, known as *American options,* can be cashed in at any time between the date of issue and the expiration date, and you can exercise others, known as *European options,* only at the expiration date. (To complicate matters, American and European options can be issued anywhere.) With all those choices, the alert arbitrageur is bound to notice a few price discrepancies.

Maybe a day trader notices that on a day when a company has a big announcement, the options exchanges seem to be assuming a slightly higher price for the stock than where the stock is actually trading. He decides to buy the underlying stock as well as a put; he also sells a call with the same strike price and expiration date as the put. This strategy creates a synthetic security (refer to the earlier section "Creating synthetic securities") that has the same payoff as shorting the security, meaning that the trader has pulled off a riskless arbitrage transaction. He effectively bought the security cheap in the stock market and sold it at a higher price in the options market.

Garbitrage

Traders get sloppy when an exciting merger is announced. If one company in an industry gets taken over, the stock in all the companies in the industry will go up, often for no good reason. Some traders get so carried away that they buy the wrong stock entirely, usually because of confusion over ticker symbols. If Lowe's Companies, a hardware chain with the ticker symbol LOW, were to be taken over, chances are good that the stock in Loews Corporation — an insurance company with the ticker symbol L — would also go up. Such bad trading is known as *garbitrage.*

Chapter 11

All About Accounts

. . . .

In This Chapter

▶ Knowing what to look for in a brokerage firm

▶ Choosing from the many brokers available

. . . .

*Y*ou can't day trade without a trading account at a brokerage firm. It's that simple. Although every trader needs one, and although the rates charged are similar, brokerage accounts are not commodities. Not only do different brokers offer different services, but most brokers also have tiers of services available for different types of investors and traders. You aren't just buying a way to execute a trade but rather a set of services.

Some brokerage services will be worth the money and then some to you. Others will be inappropriate for your style. To help you get started on your research, this chapter covers the different types of accounts, with information on their features and benefits. After all, you want to make a good trade from the start!

Choosing a Brokerage

If you are going to trade, you need a brokerage account. What kind of broker you need depends on what you plan to trade (head to Chapter 3 for some of the basics of different types of securities and where they trade):

- ✔ If you plan to trade stocks, you need a full-service broker that belongs to NASDAQ, the New York Stock Exchange, and other major exchanges.

- ✔ If you'd rather trade the stock market through the CME Group's E-Mini index futures, or if you're interested in other types of derivatives, then you need a futures trading account with a broker holding a seat on the Chicago Mercantile Exchange or other derivatives exchange.

Many day traders pursue two or three strategies, which may require holding different brokerage accounts. Having multiple brokerage accounts isn't unusual. If you are going to trade both grain futures and tech stocks, for example, you may want one account with a futures brokerage that belongs to the Chicago Mercantile Exchange and another account with a stock brokerage that offers fast execution.

The following sections tell you what to look for when choosing a brokerage firm.

Getting proper pricing

All brokerage firms offer *price quotes:* a summary of the current bid and offer prices for selling or buying the security in question. But not all these price quotes are the same. Some are offered in *real time,* meaning that you see the prices as soon as your modem can transmit the change to you. Others are delayed, sometimes by seconds, sometimes by minutes. If you're buying a bond with plans to hold it for ten years, the difference in price between now and 15 minutes ago probably isn't material. But if you're looking to day trade in the bond market, using short-term changes in treasury futures, a delay of even 30 seconds may be the difference between your strategy succeeding or failing.

Almost all day-trading strategies need direct access in order to maximize profitability. Direct-access brokers allow you to see the price quotes in real time so that you can act on them immediately, and they allow you to work through different electronic communications networks rather than going through the firm's own traders.

To help you with the pricing, some brokers offer access to *liquidity pools,* also known as *dark pools, dark liquidity,* or *dark books.* These pools are private execution networks that can sometimes wreak havoc with the market, but when used properly, they can improve the pricing on a stock trade. Brokers that participate in these pools may place your order in the liquidity pool, and then your order will be executed only if a matching trade exists. In this situation, the trade happens faster and often with better pricing than it would if it had been executed in the open market.

Unlike those brokerage services aimed at day traders, a traditional retail brokerage offers customers more research and advice and may even offer to improve order execution by waiting until market conditions are more favorable. That's fine for investors but not so good for day traders.

In addition to different levels of market access, brokerage firms offer different types of price quotes with different amounts of detail. Read on for descriptions and pictures to see what you need for your strategy.

Faster, detailed price quotes are valuable to traders, so brokerage firms usually charge more for them. Don't skimp on price services at the expense of your trading profitability.

Level I quotes

Level I quotes give you the current bid and ask, or bid and offer, prices for a given security. The *bid,* of course, is the price at which the broker buys the security from you, and the *ask* (also called *offer* in some markets) is the price at which the broker offers to sell the security to you. A Level I quote also shows the size of the most recent buy and sell orders.

Most brokerage firms offer real-time Level I quotes for free, but these numbers do not have enough detail for day trading.

Level II quotes

Level II quotes not only tell you what the current bid and offer prices are but also who the market makers are — the brokerage firm traders who are buying and selling the security — and what size orders they have at different prices (see Figure 11-1). This information can help you gauge the volatility and direction of trading in the market, which can help you make more profitable trades. Most brokerage firms that specialize in day trading offer Level II quotes in most markets.

SYMBOL	**AMAT**	Applied Materials (NGS)		
LAST SALE	20.15 q	NASDAQ Bid Tick (+)		
NATIONAL BBO	20.15 q	20.16 q	6900 × 3000	

MPID	Bid	Size	MPID	Ask	Size
NSDQ	20.15	3000	NSDQ	20.16	2000
ARCX	20.15	2600	ARCX	20.16	1900
BEST	20.15	1500	TDCM	20.16	1000
NITE	20.15	1400	OPCO	20.17	2100
CINN	20.15	1200	BARD	20.17	1000
BOFA	20.15	1000	CLYP	20.18	2000
AUTO	20.14	5000	SCHB	20.18	1500
LEHM	20.14	1000	NITE	20.18	1100
ABLE	20.14	1000	DAIN	20.18	100
SCHB	20.14	500	TEJS	20.18	100
GSCO	20.14	100	GSCO	20.18	100
RAJA	20.12	1200	MSCO	20.19	1500
TDCM	20.12	1000	JPMS	20.19	100
MONR	20.12	1000	BEST	20.20	1200
SWST	20.12	1000	NFSC	20.20	1000
NORT	20.12	400	FBRC	20.20	800
JPMS	20.12	100	FACT	20.20	100
PERT	20.11	800	UBSW	20.21	1100
PIPR	20.11	100	GSCO	20.21	1000
PRUS	20.10	500	FBCO	20.21	100
FBCO	20.09	1400	LEHM	20.21	100
COWN	20.09	800	RHCO	20.21	100
HDSN	20.09	400	WCHV	20.22	1200
UBSW	20.09	400	GLBT	20.22	1000

Figure 11-1: A NASDAQ Level II quote.

TotalView quotes

TotalView quotes show all orders in the market for a given security, both attributed to market makers and anonymous (see Figure 11-2). This information gives traders the most detailed information about what's happening in the market. Although all this detail may be overkill for some trading strategies, it's vital to the success of most. You'll have a better idea of how much information your trading strategies need after you test them, using the advice in Chapter 16.

SYMBOL	**AMAT**	Applied Materials (NGS)
LAST SALE	20.15 q	NASDAQ Bid Tick (+)
NATIONAL BBO	20.15 q	20.16 q 6900 × 3000

Bid Price	Total Depth	Ask Price	Total Depth
20.15	10700	20.16	4900
20.14	56100	20.17	9100
20.13	26300	20.18	13400
20.12	9900	20.19	11200
20.11	1700	20.20	8700

MPID	Bid	Size	MPID	Ask	Size
NSDQ	20.15	3000	NSDQ	20.16	2000
ARCX	20.15	2600	ARCX	20.16	1900
BEST	20.15	1500	TDCM	20.16	1000
NITE	20.15	1400	NSDQ	20.17	6000
CINN	20.15	1200	OPCO	20.17	2100
BOFA	20.15	1000	BARD	20.17	1000
NSDQ	20.14	28500	NSDQ	20.18	5000
BEST	20.14	12500	OPCO	20.18	2500
NITE	20.14	7500	CLYP	20.18	2000
AUTO	20.14	5000	SCHB	20.18	1500
LEHM	20.14	1000	NITE	20.18	1100
ABLE	20.14	1000	TDCM	20.18	1000
SCHB	20.14	500	DAIN	20.18	100
GSCO	20.14	100	TEJS	20.18	100
NSDQ	20.13	10000	GSCO	20.18	100
GSCO	20.13	8800	NSDQ	20.19	5500
SCHB	20.13	7500	NITE	20.19	3000
NSDQ	20.12	2200	MSCO	20.19	1500
BEST	20.12	2000	OPCO	20.19	1000
RAJA	20.12	1200	JPMS	20.19	100
LEHM	20.12	1000	SCHB	20.19	100
TDCM	20.12	1000	BAR	20.19	4000
MONR	20.12	1000	BEST	20.20	1200
SWST	20.12	1000	NFSC	20.20	1000
NORT	20.12	400	NSDQ	20.20	1000
JPMS	20.12	100	FBRC	20.20	800
PERT	20.11	800	SCHB	20.20	500
GSCO	20.11	500	NITE	20.20	100
LEHM	20.11	100	FACT	20.20	100
NSDQ	20.11	100	UBSW	20.21	1100
NORT	20.11	100	GSCO	20.21	1000
PIPR	20.11	100	NITE	20.21	1000
NSDQ	20.10	13500	NSDQ	20.21	500
SCHB	20.10	3500	TDCM	20.21	100
TDCM	20.10	2000	FBCO	20.21	100
PRUS	20.10	500	LEHM	20.21	100
GSCO	20.09	100	RHCO	20.21	100
NSDQ	20.09	2500	LEHM	20.22	5000
RAJA	20.09	2200	WCHV	20.22	1200
FBCO	20.09	1400	GLBT	20.22	1000
MONR	20.09	1000	NSDQ	20.22	500
NITE	20.09	1000	FBRC	20.22	500
COWN	20.09	800	DAIN	20.22	100
HDSN	20.09	400	NITE	20.22	100
UBSW	20.09	400	BEST	20.22	100

Figure 11-2:
A NASDAQ
TotalView
quote is
the most
detailed
available.

Evaluating types of platform

When you have an account with a brokerage firm, you have a way to get information about the markets and place your orders. The conduit is the Internet, but you need a way to get your orders to it. Some brokerage firms have their own software that you can use; others allow you to log in through a website. The following sections detail your options.

Software-based platforms

With a software-based platform, you must download and install the brokerage firm's proprietary system onto your computer. When you're ready to start your trading day, you connect to the Internet first, launch the software to see what's happening, and place your trades. Software systems generally offer more features and analytical tools than web-based platforms, but you can only trade on a machine that has the software loaded on it.

Web-based platforms

With a web-based trading platform, you go to the broker's website and log in to trade. With these types of platforms, you can trade from any computer that has Internet access, which is a boon if you travel or work from several different locations. In exchange, you may give up some of the analytic and backtesting tools offered through software-based platforms.

Note that web-based platforms may be designed to work on specific web browsers. Given the importance of having a stable connection and full functionality in a fast-moving market, if the firm recommends using Internet Explorer, accept that. Don't cling to a preferred alternative.

What about mobile platforms? Some brokerage firms allow you to get price quotes and place trades through a mobile phone. This capability may be useful to some people, especially as a backup system, but relying on it solely is a bad idea for most day traders. Day trading is a business, and that means you need some discipline about setting regular hours and working from a regular workspace. You'll probably need more information to work a trade than will fit on your phone's screen (most day traders work off more than one full-sized screen, in fact). Finally, you need to take a break from the market to maintain balance in your life. If you're making trades at your cousin's wedding, you have a problem.

Opening an account

When you open a brokerage account, you must fill out a lot of paperwork to comply with government and exchange regulations. Basically, these forms help the firm ensure that you're suitable for day trading; that you understand the risks of options, futures, and margin strategies; and that your trading money did not come from ill-gotten gains. (I explain all the laws behind these in Chapter 5.)

After you complete and sign the paperwork, you need to transfer funds. Most brokers require a minimum investment of $25,000 to open a day-trading account (to meet the FINRA pattern day-trading rules, although some brokers set lower or higher minimums). Write a check or set up a wire or Internet transfer from an existing bank, brokerage, or mutual fund account.

Brokers for Day Traders

Following is a list of brokerage firms with services for day traders. It's arranged by specialty (stocks and general trading, options and futures, foreign exchange) and then alphabetically within each category. This list is not exhaustive. Also keep in mind that every year new firms are formed and existing firms are acquired or merged away, so be sure to do your own research. Also, this list does not imply an endorsement of anyone's services.

Barron's (www.barrons.com), the weekly financial newspaper, has a regular column discussing electronic trading firm issues and concerns, many of which are of interest to day traders. Each winter *Barron's* conducts a survey of online brokerage firms with updates on the latest features and rankings based on such criteria as technology, usability, additional features, customer service, and trading costs. Check it out when you're ready to research.

Brokers for stocks and a bit of the rest

Day traders almost always work through online brokerage accounts. Many firms offering these accounts handle trading in almost all securities. The firms usually belong to all the exchanges, so you can trade almost anything anywhere in the world through them. These brokerage accounts often offer a range of news and charting services to help you plan your trading. In some cases, their offerings may be overkill; you may find them distracting and their services unnecessary. Some may not handle your security of choice well.

Brokerage firms don't make money just on the commission charged per trade. Other sources of revenue include monthly service charges, fees for real-time quotes, interest on margin loans to customers, and the *spread,* which is the difference between what you pay for a security and what the firm paid to get it. So don't let the commission be the critical factor in deciding among brokerage firms. Think about the services you need and the relative cost to you of different account offerings.

By the way, the brokerage industry has been consolidating — and not because of the financial crisis. (Most of these brokers had no involvement with the mortgage market.) There are huge advantages to being big, including both the payoff from technology investments and the ability to get good execution on trades.

Charles Schwab Active Trading

Charles Schwab was one of the first discount retail brokerage firms, and it now offers just about every financial service one could want: financial planning, banking, and mutual funds. The Schwab Active Trading account includes trading demonstrations and education services that are particularly useful for active stock traders, although the firm has trading and support capabilities for options and ETFs, too. The platform works directly through an Internet browser. Schwab participates in different electronic communications networks and liquidity pools, which may improve execution.

For more information, go to www.schwab.com/public/schwab/active_trader.

ChoiceTrade

ChoiceTrade offers software-based equity stock and option trading services to individuals and small trading firms. Customers can opt for a basic platform or pay a monthly fee for additional charting, analytic, and money-management services. Traders can opt for direct access trading, which may offer faster execution for some strategies. Some of ChoiceTrade's platforms include mobile trading capabilities, which may be useful as a backup system.

For more information, go to www.choicetrade.com.

Cobra Trading

Started as a stock brokerage firm, Cobra now offers trading in futures, options, and foreign exchange. It has a lot of features for short sellers, such as an "easy to borrow" list that helps identify stocks that can be shorted with little market disruption. The firm offers different software platforms to suit different trading styles, as well as a web-based platform.

For more information, go to www.cobratrading.com.

E*TRADE

E*TRADE offers trading in stocks, options, and futures as well as services for active traders through its web-based trading platform. It also offers a software-based platform, Power E*TRADE Pro, with direct-access trading and customization abilities. The company also has market scanners, to help you spot when a target pattern shows up, and efficient backtesting systems. If you really want to trade from your phone, E*TRADE has platforms for that. (I still think it's a bad idea.)

For more information, go to www.etrade.com.

Fidelity Active Trader Pro

Fidelity started life as a mutual fund company and continues to dominate that business. It now also offers a wide range of financial services, including online trading. Fidelity Active Trader Pro is a software-based system with lots of bells and whistles, including systems for analyzing and testing options strategies. (A web-based version is available but has less functionality.) To use Active Trader Pro, you need to place 36 trades over a rolling 12-month period; placing 120 trades over a year gets you free Level II quote access. Both levels should be a slice of cake for most day traders.

For more information, go to http://personal.fidelity.com/accounts/activetrader.

Firstrade

Designed for stock traders, Firstrade offers screeners, alerts, and commentary through its web-based trading platform. The education features include some good advice about taxes, and community features help traders with ideas. In addition, Firstrade offers its platforms in both traditional and simplified Chinese, if you'd rather not work in English. (No surprise, Firstrade has a lot of Chinese-speaking customers.)

For more information, go to www.firstrade.com.

Interactive Brokers

Interactive Brokers offers software-based direct-access trading, with special expertise in international markets. It has options, futures, and foreign-exchange trading services, as well as trading in stocks. Traders can use a range of order types and order-management features to work complicated strategies. Interactive Brokers has a small stake in TradeStation, mentioned later in this list, and some observers think it's just a matter of time before the firms merge.

For more information, go to www.interactivebrokers.com.

Just2Trade

Just2Trade targets equity day traders with low commissions. The company's goal is to provide fast execution through its web-based platform, which is useful to day traders who are looking to move quickly. Its services include real-time Level I and Level II quotes at no extra fee. It doesn't offer the analysis tools that some of the other brokerage firms do, but its system is nice and simple.

For more information, go to www.just2trade.com.

Lightspeed Trading

In 2010, Lightspeed Trading acquired Terra Nova, another brokerage firm that worked with active traders. The combined firm specializes in low commission trades and has robust information services for day traders. Lightspeed also offers programming and testing services for traders who want to develop their own automated trading systems that include high-frequency trading capabilities. In addition, Lightspeed promotes its community services to help people just learning trading or looking for order ideas.

For more information, go to www.lightspeed.com.

ScottradeELITE

Scottrade is an online stock broker that offers additional services for customers with more than $25,000 in their accounts. Under the name ScottradeELITE, it gives these customers web-based access to NASDAQ Level II and detailed NASDAQ TotalView quotes as long as they do 15 trades a month; otherwise, this access costs $15. The firm can handle stock, bond, option, ETF, and international trading.

For more information, go to www.scottradeelite.com.

SogoTrade

SogoTrade started life as a stock brokerage firm, but the company has added a lot of features for options traders. Its commissions are low: $3 for stock trades, $5 for options. The website has basic educational services, screeners, and other tools to help people get started.

For more information, go to www.sogotrade.com.

thinkorswim

Although thinkorswim began as a trading platform for options strategies, it has since been acquired by TD Ameritrade, a more-traditional discount brokerage firm, and is now TD Ameritrade's service for active traders. thinkorswim offers a full range of products, including mutual funds, on web, software, and mobile platforms. In addition to an auto-execute feature for subscribers of different trading newsletters, it has a paper-trading feature that lets you practice your trades before you commit real dollars. It also offers what it calls *swimming lessons,* which are seminars on trading techniques and tools offered each day that the market is open. And it has services to help traders keep track of their gains and losses, the better to simplify tax time.

For more information, go to www.thinkorswim.com.

TradeKing

TradeKing offers a range of basic trading services in stocks, bonds, and options, both online and through mobile applications. The company's most unique feature is the community offerings on its site, where customers can create blogs, track each other's trades, share commentary, and send messages in hopes that they all make better, smarter trades. A lot of traders appreciate the support and the ability to share ideas through the community features.

For more information, go to www.tradeking.com.

TradeStation

TradeStation offers a huge range of services for people who day trade stocks, options, futures, and foreign exchange. A software-based system, TradeStation includes a rich set of features, especially for developing and testing trading strategies. Traders who have strong systems will like the automatic trading features that signal — and can even act — when appropriate trading opportunities occur. TradeStation's services are especially popular with traders who like to develop their own systems and work on their own programs.

For more information, go to www.tradestation.com.

Brokers for options and futures

To effectively day trade options and futures, you need an account with a broker that has direct access to the exchanges' electronic communications networks. Several of the full-service firms listed in the preceding section offer that service, as do the brokers listed here, which specialize in these particular markets.

Infinity Futures

Infinity Futures offers software-based trading in the options, futures, and foreign exchange markets; it also has trading education services and access to live brokers who can answer questions. Customers can choose from several platforms, depending on trading needs. The firm particularly supports traders working in the stock index futures offered by the CME Group.

For more information, go to www.infinityfutures.com.

MB Trading

MB Trading handles stocks and foreign exchange as well as derivatives, but the company is best known for its services for forex traders. The company seems to add features constantly. The firm has both software and web platforms, training programs, community features, and customer alert settings to help you find trades that suit your system. In addition, MB Trading offers a lot of support for developers who want to build software around its platform.

For more information, go to www.mbtrading.com.

OptionsHouse

OptionsHouse was founded by a major options-trading firm and has its offices on the original Chicago Board of Trade trading floor. Between that pedigree and the company's name, it's no surprise that it offers direct access web-based trading in options and their underlying stocks. Its software tools are designed to help you identify and analyze profitable opportunities in the options market. The firm also has online training programs, blogs, and other information to help you learn more about options and different strategies for trading them.

For more information, go to www.optionshouse.com.

optionsXpress

The company optionsXpress is designed for people trading options and the stocks underlying them. It offers a lot of educational services and live customer support as well as phone apps, if you're so inclined. The optionsXpress platform has changed over the years as the company adds more services to meet customer demand. One of its nifty features is an automatic execution service for subscribers of participating research services (you can find out more about research services in Chapter 13). The company is owned by Charles Schwab, but its platform is independent — at least as I write this.

For more information, go to www.optionsxpress.com.

TradeMONSTER

TradeMONSTER is designed for options and futures traders, although this broker handles stock and mutual fund trades as well. The company offers a suite of tools to help traders do research, develop and test strategies, and refine them over time. Some of its features are wonderfully practical, like the ability to rearrange the data windows across multiple screens to suit your preferences.

For more information, go to www.trademonster.com.

Brokers for foreign exchange

The foreign exchange, or forex, market is the largest trading market in the world and offers lots of opportunities for day traders to make (or lose) money. Most forex trades take place between banks, corporations, and hedge funds directly, without the use of a broker. If you want to trade foreign currency directly, you need to use a trading firm that is tied in to these networks. Many of the brokers listed in the preceding sections offer forex. The following sections list those that do little else.

Gain Capital Group's FOREX.com

Gain Capital Group deals mostly with institutional investors and money managers, but it makes its platform available to individual day traders through its FOREX.com site. There, you can download software that lets you analyze markets and place trades. The company offers a lot of educational programs and practice accounts for traders interested in foreign exchange; it also has a mobile application for those who want to trade by phone.

For more information, go to www.forex.com.

InterbankFX

Want to try your hand at trading forex? In addition to demo accounts, InterbankFX lets customers start trading with as little as $250, making it an option for day traders who want to trade currency along with other types of securities. It also offers charting and automatic trading services to help customers design and adhere to their strategies.

For more information, go to `www.ibfx.com`.

Part III

Necessities and Niceties for Successful Day Trading

A Sample Profit-and-Loss Spreadsheet

Profit and Loss					
	Initial Capital	Net Profit (Loss)	Ending Capital	Percentage Change	Hourly Wage
1/3/07	$ 161,298	$ 134	$ 161,432	0.08%	$ 16.75
1/4/07	$ 161,432	$ (268)	$ 161,164	-0.17%	$ (33.50)
1/5/07	$ 161,164	$ 450	$ 161,614	0.28%	$ 56.25
1/8/07	$ 161,614	$ (183)	$ 161,431	-0.1 1%	$ (22.88)
1/9/07	$ 161,431	$ 192	$ 161,623	0.12%	$ 24.00
1/10/07	$ 161,623	$ 598	$ 162,221	0.37%	$ 74.75
1/11/07	$ 162,221	$ (168)	$ 162,053	-0.10%	$ (21.00)
1/12/07	$ 162,053	$ 987	$ 163,040	0.61%	$ 123.38
1/16/07	$ 163,040	$ (196)	$ 162,844	-0.12%	$ (24.50)
1/17/07	$ 162,844	$ 59	$ 162,903	0.04%	$ 7.38
1/18/07	$ 162,903	$ (273)	$ 162,630	-0.17%	$ (34.13)
1/19/07	$ 162,630	$ (124)	$ 162,506	-0.08%	$ (15.50)
1/22/07	$ 162,506	$ 689	$ 163,195	0.42%	$ 86.13
1/23/07	$ 163,195	$ (397)	$ 162,798	-0.24%	$ (49.63)
1/24/07	$ 162,798	$ 967	$ 163,765	0.59%	$ 120.88
1/25/07	$ 163,765	$ (387)	$ 163,378	-0.24%	$ (48.38)
1/26/07	$ 163,378	$ 469	$ 163,847	0.29%	$ 58.63
1/29/07	$ 163,847	$ 798	$ 164,645	0.49%	$ 99.75
1/30/07	$ 164,645	$ (129)	$ 164,516	-0.08%	$ (16.13)
1/31/07	$ 164,516	$ 723	$ 165,239	0.44%	$ 90.38
January:	$ 161,298	$ 3,941	$ 165,239	2.44%	$ 24.63
2/1/07	$ 165,239	$ 743	$ 165,982	0.45%	$ 92.88

Ever wondered if you could get great tips from chat rooms? Get the lowdown on online forums at www.dummies.com/extras/daytrading.

In this part...

- ✓ Approach day trading as a business. Develop a plan, set a budget, and treat it like a job.

- ✓ Find the support services you need to research trades and to get through the treacherous days with your sanity intact and your positions under control.

- ✓ Discover how to pay taxes on your gains and figure out how well your time, energy, and trading paid off. (Yes, day trading is a taxable activity.)

- ✓ Develop the discipline that can set you apart from traders who don't take the markets or their time seriously.

Chapter 12

Equipping to Day Trade

. . . .

. . . .

To perform the job of day trader well, you need to commit to the necessary space and the equipment at home. If you skimp on your Internet connection, for example, it may be unable to handle the data on a big market day. If you skimp on your PC, it may go down, leaving you scrambling to get it back up — a rotten position to be in if you have open positions.

In this chapter, I go over the basics of your office setup, discuss the pros and cons of mobile trading, and give you some advice on finding trading apps — even if you trade on a big old computer.

Setting Up Your Trading Laboratory

Twenty years ago, you would have had to pay millions of dollars for the equipment and telecommunications networks that you can now have in your own home for just a few thousand bucks or so.

You may be thinking, I can do it for free! I have an iPhone, so what else do I need? Ah, but you need plenty. Remember, successful day traders approach trading as a professional activity. That means starting with an adequate work space and dedicated equipment, as the following sections explain.

Where to sit, where to work

First, you need to find an area to work. If you can't give up an entire room in your house, find a corner or hallway where you can put a desk and a computer just for day trading. Going to an area dedicated to day trading will clear your mind so that you can focus on the work at hand.

You also need a table and a chair. Instead of borrowing a chair from the dining room, get a good desk chair that swivels and that you can adjust as necessary while you work. You also need a shelf and a cabinet of some sort to hold your files and documents.

Want to get more comfort for the dollar in a desk chair? Consider shopping for used chairs at office-equipment dealers. They may come with a few scuffs but will probably have more ergonomic settings than chairs at office-supply superstores.

Although no rule stipulates the proper layout of your equipment, the more you can see and do without getting up from your chair, the better off you'll be. If you find yourself getting sore at the end of the day, investigate ergonomic products such as special keyboards, contoured mice, wrist pads, and foot rests, all of which are readily available at office-supply stores.

Counting on your computer

You can't day trade without at least one computer, and you may want two or three: one to trade from and one for everything else (such as spreadsheets, e-mail, and instant messaging). Some traders keep a spare computer on hand in case the trading computer goes down, but many smartphones can be set up to work as a backup instead. (See the section "The department of redundancy department: Backing up your systems" later in this chapter.)

Almost every personal computer on the market today has the power to handle day-trading activities, so you don't need to sweat over the details. In general, faster processing speeds are better than slower ones, and more memory and storage are preferable to less.

What about the manufacturer? Well, you may not want an Apple computer for day trading, because you may discover that not all the software packages you need will be Mac-compatible. If you are one of those die-hard Mac heads, though, be sure to ask brokers and software vendors about compatibility. Other than that, the manufacturer doesn't matter much.

Seeing it on the big screen

Do yourself a favor and spend money on a big flat-screen monitor. Prices have been falling and sizes have been increasing, so you should have no trouble finding one. Or two! Or three! If you need to look at more than one window at a time — to see charts and Level II quotes at the same time, for example — consider using two or more monitors hooked to the same PC. This arrangement gives you a clear view of necessary data. Most traders work with at least two monitors, often extra-large ones, because the information they need is too valuable to be hidden by overlapping windows during a work session.

Connecting to the Internet

If you're day trading, hook up to the Internet with as much bandwidth as possible. Ask around to find out the fastest time in your area. Your Internet service provider may charge more for faster performance, but most day traders find the extra cost worth it. If prices are changing quickly, a delay of half a second can be costly.

You need fast service, but don't base your strategy on speed. Even if you pay up for the fastest service in your area, the brokers and hedge funds of the world will probably have faster service. NYSE Technologies, the data-services business of exchange-operator NYSE Euronext, allows brokerage and trading firms to put their servers on the floor of the exchange. This colocation can reduce trade execution times to fractions of a second, allowing more trades to be executed in less time than if the server were in, say, midtown Manhattan. NYSE Euronext colocation isn't cheap, but if you make thousands of trades a day, it may be worth it.

As a day trader, you're playing in a market with traders who pay good money for the edge they can get from moving their servers closer to the exchange's servers. Hence, when choosing your Internet provider, you don't want to go with the low bidder.

Also make sure your trading computer is hooked up to the Internet provider's wire. Wireless routers are less reliable and can slow you down. If other people in your household want Internet access, consider getting two Internet lines so that your son downloading videos in the family room doesn't slow you down.

A great source of information about the performance of different broadband Internet providers is Broadband Reports, www.broadbandreports.com.

Staying virus- and hacker-free

Most operating systems have built-in firewall and virus protection that can handle most likely threats with aplomb. You can also subscribe to different virus protection services. No matter which way you go, be careful how you set these up. Some pointers:

- ✔ **Check compatibility.** Check with your brokerage firm to make sure that its system is compatible with the virus protection package you choose; some are not. (That potential problem increasingly makes the built-in options more practical.)

- ✔ **Determine whether there's a trade-off in access speed.** Some types of antivirus software protect your system at the expense of data speed, which will hurt your trading execution.

If you decide to *go naked* — operate without a firewall or virus scanner in order to maintain optimal speed — be sure to have a backup computer at the ready.

Whether you go with the built-in software or buy an outside package or are a Mac or a PC, be sure to set automatic downloads, software upgrades, and background scans to take place after market hours. You don't want to be slowed down because of an operating system update.

The department of redundancy department: Backing up your systems

When you day trade, you are intentionally looking at volatile markets and fast-moving securities because that's where you have the most opportunity to make money in a short time. You may very well be leveraged, either through the use of borrowed money or by trading securities with built-in leverage, such as futures. (I have a lot more to say about leverage in Chapter 9.) If you're in a position that moves against you and you can't get out, you're sunk.

Not being able to get out because the markets are melting down due to some kind of global catastrophe is bad enough. But suppose you can't get out because the batteries in your wireless mouse have died and you can't find new ones? What if you spill your drink and short out your keyboard — or your PC? What if the developer building a McMansion next door accidentally knocks out your phone line and your DSL service? All these little workaday calamities have happened to me — and trust me, they're downright annoying even if you aren't trading. If you *are* trading, they can be ruinous. If you're serious about making money as a day trader, build in redundant systems as much as possible:

- ✔ Have high-speed data service on your smartphone or tablet computer in case your primary Internet access goes out.

- ✔ Load your broker's mobile app on your phone so that you can switch to it should something odd happen to crash your computer.

✔ Keep extra supplies on hand: extra batteries, extra keyboard, and extra mouse. You want to be able to react quickly when things go wrong. (These items are all cheap to keep in inventory, too, because the computer makers give keyboards and mice away with every new PC.)

✔ Invest in an uninterruptible power supply (UPS) backup for your PC so that if the power goes down, your computer stays up. The backup doesn't have to last for hours, just long enough that you can close out your positions. You don't need a backup generator, though — unless you think that you'd still want to trade after your town was devastated by an earthquake or a hurricane. (Hey, crisis creates opportunities!)

✔ Finally, back up your computer regularly. You don't want to lose your tax records! You can back up online through Mozy (`www.mozy.com`) or Carbonite (`www.carbonite.com`), or you can use an external hard drive connected to your PC. Most backup systems can be set up to work automatically — but don't back up during trading hours! It'll slow you down.

Getting Mobile with the Markets

A growing number of brokerage firms and software developers are coming up with applications that let you trade from a smartphone or a tablet computer. At the time I'm writing this, I think these options are a bad idea for most day traders. Even with 4G service, mobile networks can be slow and drop out, and you can't get enough information on a little screen to trade well.

However, technology changes fast, so maybe by the time you're reading this, mobile speeds have become as fast as wired ones. This may be especially true if you live in a rural area without reliable high-speed Internet service. The different brokerage firms (including those listed in Chapter 11 and others) are adding new and better mobile capabilities. Some of the things to look for are signaling and charting capabilities, ease of order entry, and synching to your desktop information. Also, make sure that the mobile service handles whatever asset you usually trade. Mobile apps are still relatively new as far as the trading world goes, and some can handle your strategy better than others. Still, I remain skeptical that mobile trading is a good idea for an active day trader. I live in Chicago near Wrigley Field, and cellphone service slows to a crawl on game days. Some 40,000 fans all e-mailing pictures of themselves at the Friendly Confines to their friends takes a toll on cell towers. Sometimes, my provider slows so much that only emergency service is available on game days. It's not a typical problem, to be sure, but it's also not something you want to deal with as a trader. Keep that in mind when you see brokerage-firm commercials that talk about trading at the game.

If you're a business traveler who gets a great idea on the road and who wants to place one order to buy and hold, then great! Use your phone. If you are a swing trader or an investor who trades more than average, using a mobile device when exit or entry points happen to be great but you are out of the office may be fine.

If you're a day trader placing tens or hundreds of orders a day, your muscles will cramp up from entering orders with a teensy keyboard, and your speed could slow down when you least want it to. However, a mobile platform makes a great backup system. If your broker offers phone trading, you can use it to keep in the market — or close out efficiently — if your trading system goes down or you can't get access to it.

Although mobile trading isn't the best idea for your primary trading, mobile technology and the different apps that people develop for it can be really useful. Here are a few great ones to try:

- ✔ **Apps from the exchanges:** Traders need good prices. These apps are published by the different exchanges and give you price quotes and news direct from the source. I list the biggies here, but apps are also available for smaller markets like Warsaw and Dhaka.

  - **CME Group Mobile:** This app takes you to the floor of the Chicago Mercantile Exchange. It's sophisticated, includes market education modules, and is available for both Android and iPhone. However, keep in mind that hardly any floor trading takes place at the Merc anymore.

  - **NASDAQ Q Folio:** The NASDAQ Stock Exchange has always been popular with stock traders looking for small companies, and this app gives you access to portfolio prices, watch lists, and real-time quotes. It's free for both main smartphone operating systems.

- ✔ **News apps:** Apps are a great way to get news and information about the markets. You can use these to supplement your trading outside of trading hours — or for additional insight.

  - **Bloomberg:** Bloomberg is the leading news service for traders, and its news feed is available in app form for both Android and Apple devices.

  - **CNBC Real Time for Phones:** In the olden days, traders often had a TV turned to CNBC going in the background. Now, they can turn to their Apple or Android phones to get real-time NYSE and NASDAQ quotes along with CNBC news headlines. It's free.

  - **Financial Times:** The Financial Times is the United Kingdom's financial newspaper, and it has great information about business from a European perspective. That's especially useful if you trade currencies. The app is free and gives you access to eight stories a month. If you want more news, you have to pay to subscribe.

- **StockTwits:** This service draws a news feed from Twitter and other social-media sources so that you can get an idea of what people are talking about, where the trends are forming, and what new ideas are heating up. The app is free for iPhone and Android users.

✔ **Apps for fun:** The following apps are all about trading, but they are more fun than practical. That's not a bad thing, though, is it?

- **The Game of Stocks:** This is a free stock-market simulator game that lets you start with $22,000 in play money, trade based on real prices in real time, and then see how you do. It's only available for Android.

- **NYSE Euronext Options Quiz:** This app is a good way to learn about options. The quiz app lets you test what you know and earn prizes — virtual prizes, but prizes nonetheless — as you progress.

- **Pirates and Traders:** Okay, this isn't a day trading app, but it's a fun game for the Android system that lets you choose to be a pirate of the high seas or the captain of a trading ship, and you can then try to make money in your chosen role. If you're thinking of day trading because you're bored, you may want to try this instead.

- **Trading Wisdom:** This fun, free app gives you great quotes and advice about trading. It was developed by Sriram Swaminathan and is available for Android.

Chapter 13

Researching Research Services

A lot of people make big money in day trading, but they aren't day traders. They're the people who have profitable businesses selling training services, software, newsletters, and coaching. The problem is, their lessons don't often help their customers make a profit after these education costs are figured in.

Why the discrepancy between the cost of the training and the value it generates for day traders? It could very well be because some traders who buy these services aren't cut out for day trading in the first place; after all, day trading isn't for everyone. In other cases, though, the traders fail to do good research before plunking down the cold cash for training in a system that just wasn't very good.

You've already plunked down the price of this book. Consider that an investment! In this chapter, I cover some of the different services that day traders may want to buy and give you advice on how to determine which ones are worthwhile and which are not.

The Trade of Trading

Day trading is a career. Every career takes time to master, and practitioners have to work to keep their skills up as the field changes. You'll probably find that you need some training to get started and more training to be successful, whether you're trading futures, building bridges, or doing heart surgery. The following sections outline some of the training options available to you.

Let me be frank: Although I put a lot of information in this book about day trading, I don't include everything. This book is a starting point. The fact is, because you can trade so many different assets in so many ways, no one resource can give you all the information you need. A stock trader following a news-based momentum strategy needs different services than a forex trader looking at interest-rate discrepancies. That's why my goal is not to teach you about specifics but to point you to resources that can help you get started and show you how to get the most value from the money you spend.

Enjoying freebies from the exchanges and the regulators

Before you spend more money, check out what several different exchanges and self-regulatory organizations offer for free to help you get started in trading. Through these sources, you can find webinars, online courses, and plenty of reading material that may give you all the information you need to get started. After all, the financial industry wants people to trade — that's how it makes money — and it wants them to be successful, because that keeps the market functioning. (Exchanges are businesses, like any other.) Going through such free material first can give you a great sense of how suitable you are for a given strategy and help you make better decisions about other types of training.

In this section I list a few resources that are particularly good for new day traders.

Chicago Board Options Exchange Learning Center

The Options Institute of the Chicago Board Options Exchange offers a series of great online tutorials, classes, practice accounts, and seminars that cover exchange-traded options in great depth. Many are free, although some of the more intensive programs that include live coaching carry tuition charges. The CBOE also has a two-day seminar for experienced traders who want to come to Chicago (a great city, although the weather is something else). The site includes online toolboxes and calculators, not to mention a simulated trading game.

For more information, go to www.cboe.com/LearnCenter/default.aspx.

CME Group Education

The CME Group, a holding company for several different exchanges, offers extensive and detailed free education programs on just about every aspect of derivatives trading. Whether your interest is currency, grain, or options on futures, the CME Group has videos, online courses, and white papers covering basic vocabulary, advanced trading strategies, and current market commentary.

It has a lot of information that you can use, whatever your strategy. And you really can't beat the price!

For more information, go to www.cmegroup.com/education/index.html.

Institute for Financial Markets

The Institute for Financial Markets is a nonprofit organization that provides basic training programs for people working on the options and futures exchanges. Many of its courses are inappropriate for day traders, who aren't going to be licensed and who do not have mandatory continuing education requirements to maintain those licenses. But some of the options may be helpful to you, so check them out after you see what the exchanges have to offer. Recent offerings include the basics of derivatives and trading strategies.

For more information, go to www.theifm.org.

IntercontinentalExchange

Most of the training programs offered by the IntercontinentalExchange are designed for employees of trading firms and take place at the exchange's offices, but they have offices all over the world. The ICE also has several online seminars that can help you learn more about different products and strategies. These seminars are aimed at traders with a little experience.

For more information, go to www.theice.com/KnowledgeCenter.shtml.

NASDAQ/OMX

Okay, if I'm being honest here, I have to admit that the stock exchanges want to promote investing more than trading, because they want companies to issue stock on their exchanges. The kind of high volatility that day traders love puts off some starchy corporate officers. Hence, much of the information on NASDAQ's site is about how to select stocks for the long term. Still, some information here may be useful to a prospective day trader, including data descriptions that can help you with your strategies.

For more information, go to www.nasdaq.com/investing.

National Futures Association Investor Learning Center

The National Futures Association is the self-regulatory organization for the agricultural and financial futures exchanges. This site includes tutorials on trading futures and foreign exchange. This organization doesn't have a lot of tutorials, but those it does have are free and comprehensive.

For more information, go to www.nfa.futures.org/investor/investorLearningCenter.asp.

New York Stock Exchange

The New York Stock Exchange, like NASDAQ, wants to court investors rather than traders. Still, the exchange's site has information on trading stocks, bonds, and exchange-traded funds that can make you smarter on those topics without spending a dime.

For more information, go to `https://nyse.nyx.com/financial-literacy`.

Hitting the road for conferences

Although day trading is a deskbound pursuit, you may want to get out into the world to learn more about trading and research different companies with products for day traders. Many of the exchanges and larger day-trading brokerage firms have their own seminars and conferences, but a few are open to the public. There is great information to be had, but watch out: The game is sometimes to sell you more than inform you.

Brokerage firms offering many seminars and training programs may have higher commissions than firms offering less service, but the additional expense may be worth it, especially as you're getting started. You can find out more about brokerage firms that work with day traders in Chapter 11.

The Money Show

The Money Show is a series of investment conferences held in different major cities around the country. Some focus on specific topics, such as trading and foreign exchange, while others run the gamut. Registration is free, which means that when you show up people will try to sell you stuff. Although these vendors can be distracting to an established trader, they can be helpful to new traders looking to find out more about all the different software and services available. Just make sure you're getting information, not an opportunity to spend even more money. These conferences also have high-profile speakers, so you can learn from Wall Street celebrities. The Money Show website includes articles, podcasts, and free online courses to help you learn more about trading.

For more information, go to `www.moneyshow.com`.

Trading Forum

The Trading Forum is sponsored by Traders' Library, which sells research materials and investing books. The conference isn't cheap, but it covers specific trading strategies and information. It also offers a good introduction to trading. Although a bit pricey, the information is worth the money, especially if the conference happens to be close to where you live.

For more information, go to `www.traderslibrary.com/conferences`.

Taking training classes

Although not necessary, many day traders learn the game by enrolling in a training program, ranging from a graduate-level certificate program offered by Northwestern University to DVDs hawked on late-night infomercials. No program can guarantee success, nor is any one program right for every trader. I list a few bigger and better-known programs here, but check them out to make sure they're right for you — just as you would check out programs that aren't listed here.

The larger brokerage and research firms offer their own training courses, often at little or no cost. Consider those as a first option, but keep in mind that their introductory sessions may be sales pitches for more products and services. Of course, other training programs may be disguised sales pitches, too. At some point, you're better off trading than training. The markets will school you better than any webinar.

Plenty of great and legitimate training firms are out there — as well as a lot of scammers. Run from anyone who guarantees your success, and don't sign up for a training program until you know what you need to learn. I include some information about due diligence at the end of this chapter.

FX:1 Academy

FX:1 Academy offers in-person training courses in foreign exchange. The bad news is that the courses take place in Asia, mostly in Singapore, which can be an issue if you live in the United States. But if you're interested in trading currencies and find yourself in Asia, you may want to investigate its courses.

For more information, go to www.fx1academy.com.

Kapitall

Kapitall is a brokerage firm, but I list it here instead of with the brokers in Chapter 11 because its services aren't designed for active day traders. However, it has services to help people learn about investing that may also help you learn about trading, including games and competitions. Many of these are free. If you're interested in learning more about the stock market, check it out.

For more information, go to www.kapitall.com.

Pristine

Pristine has a range of books and DVDs, online and in person classes, and coaching services in English and Spanish, covering trading skills that work in most markets. Its courses operate at different levels, with some requiring extensive trading experience using specific software packages.

For more information, go to www.pristine.com.

TopstepTrader

TopstepTrader was founded by a veteran of the Chicago Mercantile Exchange to address the way people learn to trade in electronic markets. (The old method, of working as a runner on the floor of the exchange, no longer works now that the floors are disappearing.) It starts with two weeks of free practice trading. (It also offers paid trading courses.) If you do well enough in the practice account, you can enter its trading combine, which is designed to mimic the National Football League combine: You pay a deposit, which is refunded if your trading adheres to certain risk and other parameters; you receive research and coaching from experienced traders; and your performance is evaluated. If the coaches like what they see, you may be funded to trade for TopstepTrader's parent firm, Patak Trading, or you may be recruited by another firm.

For more information, go to www.topsteptrader.com.

Trading Advantage

Trading Advantage, run by an experienced commodities floor trader, has a ton of training options, ranging from telephone coaching and a virtual trading room to books and DVDs. Some of the company's programs are designed for floor traders at the exchanges who need to learn to trade futures electronically in order to stay competitive, while others work for an average person who wants to get started or who wants to improve his or her trading prowess.

For more information, go to www.tradingadvantage.com.

Trader Kingdom

Run by a group of experienced traders, Trader Kingdom offers webinars, live speakers, and coaching services, as well as a lot of free online educational material on futures trading. If you're considering futures markets, check out the website to see the firm's current offerings.

For more information, go to www.traderkingdom.com.

TradingSchool.com

TradingSchool.com, based in Los Angeles, has a series of online and in-person classes covering trading psychology as well as trading in stocks, options, financial futures, and currencies. The firm works with day traders as well as money managers and other long-term investors.

For more information, go to www.tradingschool.com.

The University of Trading

The University of Trading offers courses in options, equities, foreign exchange, and financial and agricultural commodities online and at its offices in Chicago. Students can hear lectures on different aspects of the markets and have the opportunity to trade alongside experienced instructors. The company trains professional traders, some of whom trade for themselves and some of whom take jobs with others.

For more information, go to www.universityoftrading.com.

Getting the Research You Need

Day traders need a trading system, and they often rely on subscription research services. That's fine, as long as those systems are adding value over and above their cost. Unfortunately, advising day traders is big business, and there may be more money in that than in day trading. Before you call the 800 number given in the infomercial, read the advice I give here, which can help you evaluate the service.

There are three main types of outside services:

- ✔ **Price data** are detailed, real-time price quotes from different markets.
- ✔ **Chart services** help traders identify profitable trends.
- ✔ **Strategic research** helps people develop a system for trading or follow a system designed by someone else.

You may need all three, or none, depending on your knowledge of the financial markets and your trading style.

Many day traders find themselves subscribing to price quote and analytical services. The following section is a listing of a handful of popular ones. It's not a definitive list, and my including them on this list is not an endorsement. Rather, it's a guide to get you thinking about what you may need and where you can go to get it.

If you know you need outside pricing and data services, consider that when you select a brokerage firm. Different firms have different software platforms, and some can handle outside data feeds better than others. For more information on choosing a broker, refer to Chapter 11.

(Price) Quote me on that

Many brokerage firms offer day trading services. They all have services that tell you what the prices are for any security at any time, but this doesn't mean that they have all the prices that you need for your strategy. If, for example, you're day trading common stocks, you may need a system that can signal certain price patterns in any of the thousands of stocks trading at any given day. If you're trading options based on the value of underlying stock, you may need that data as well. If you're day trading international securities, you may need real-time data, and your broker may only offer data with a ten-minute delay in some markets.

Besides needing all the prices and related volume and market-maker data, some strategies involve fast trading. Every second counts, and not all brokers can deliver prices fast enough to make scalping profitable. One solution is to get prices from a separate source that offers faster delivery. Other trading strategies don't require real-time prices on huge numbers of securities, but they may involve a detailed analysis of end-of-day prices. To do that, you may need more information than your broker can give you.

The following sections offer information on some of the different price quote and data services out there.

The quote service can provide the data in real time only if you have enough bandwidth to receive it. Make sure you have the fastest Internet service and modem available in your area and consider having a second way to connect to the Internet if your primary service goes down.

CQG

CQG pulls data from pretty much all of the world's exchanges, making it popular with people who are trading international securities. It also has data on over-the-counter foreign exchange. Traders can buy historical data for backtesting (see Chapter 16 for more), and they can add charting and order routing capabilities to their CQG package. People who want to do even more number crunching on their own can link the data to their Microsoft Excel spreadsheets.

For more information, go to www.cqg.com.

DTN

Trading fuel or agricultural products? Then you may need more research than most brokers can give you. DTN produces a huge range of data for farmers and drillers, and it has plenty of services for traders, too. The company, owned by Schneider Electric, provides pricing and research for commodities traders, including meteorological research and hurricane-related energy supply forecasts. Day traders active in stocks or financial futures are more likely to use the company's IQ data feeds, which allow users to track 1,300 prices simultaneously, and ProphetX, software that combines price data with analytics that can track small market movements and can handle displays on several different monitors at once.

For more information, go to www.schneider-electric.com/products /ww/en/5100-software/5170-market-intelligence-software /61659-dtn-quotes-online/?XTMC=DTN&XTCR=1.

eSignal

eSignal offers detailed prices, news, and trading alerts in most financial markets, delivered to your computer or your phone. Its charting features are more advanced than those offered by most brokerage firms. Especially useful for traders who are looking at several different stocks, eSignal can help identify trading opportunities using a preferred strategy and scan the market for other stocks that meet specified investment criteria. The company also offers backtesting and real-time strategy testing, end-of-day analysis for traders who don't need real-time data, and add-on signals that support different proprietary trading strategies.

For more information, go to www.esignal.com.

InstaQuote

InstaQuote, owned by Bank of America, has data designed for equity options traders. It gives traders price quotes on both options and equities so that they can identify price discrepancies and monitor valuation. It then connects to the exchange's electronic communications networks, allowing for direct access trading. InstaQuote's platform can work with several different brokerage firms' accounts.

For more information, go to www.dafsoft.com.

Oanda

Oanda provides both foreign exchange trading services and data. It has exchange rates for major currencies and small frontier markets. The data is available — for a price — to those who want to use it with another brokerage firm's platform.

For more information, go to www.oanda.com.

Charting your strategy

Almost all day trading strategies rely on technical analysis, which is the process of identifying buy and sell opportunities based on the supply and demand for a security. Technical analysts look at charts of price and volume changes to identify changes in the trend. (I discuss technical analysis in more detail in Chapter 7.) Some technical-analysis strategies are complicated and require sophisticated charting. That's why many day traders use software that can turn price data into the information they need to make decisions.

Many users of these services get tripped up by the symbols and data displays. Take the time to learn as much as you can about how the services work before you trade in real time with real money; most of these providers offer seminars or online tutorials that can help. Yeah, many of the features are obvious, but you want to avoid costly mistakes.

MarketDelta

MarketDelta's software provides detailed charting services that match different strategies over several time periods, in colors that make the data stand out. The goal is to make price information more transparent and thus chart information more accurate. The company mostly deals with professionals, but some of its products are suitable for some day traders.

For more information, go to www.marketdelta.com.

Metastock

Metastock has several different charting and analytical packages, including one for foreign exchange trading, another for people who day trade in stocks, and a third for stock investors who are holding for longer than a single day. It even has some fundamental research tools. Traders following specific strategies recommended by different market analysts can purchase add-ons that give them the tools needed to trade effectively and participate in in-person and online user groups. Some brokerage firms offer Metastock tools as an alternative to the broker's proprietary platform.

For more information, go to www.metastock.com.

NinjaTrader

A trading platform for active traders, NinjaTrader can be used instead of the trading software offered by many brokerage firms, including several of firms that deal with day traders. The service is best known for its charting capabilities in the foreign exchange and futures markets, but it can also handle market scanning, automated trade execution, backtesting, and simulation trading.

For more information, check out www.ninjatrader.com.

OmniTrader

OmniTrader is designed to automate technical analysis (read all about that in Chapter 7), especially for stock traders. Traders can use it to set up automatic trading systems or to help them make their own decisions during the trading day. The system also includes money-management tools (money management is discussed in Chapter 6), as well as simulated trading and backtesting to help you find new strategies.

For more information, go to `www.omnitrader.com`.

RealTick

RealTick combines price data with charting services and market signals for stocks, options, futures, and foreign exchange, making it useful for traders who are working in several markets. Its add-on services let you customize the data if you have an unusual strategy. The service includes direct-access trading through several different brokerage firms, including a few that work with day traders.

For more information, go to `www.realtick.com`.

StockTwits

Social media is a great way to keep up with pop stars and find out local bargains, and it has applications for trading, too. StockTwits is a service that is similar to Twitter. It lets members post trade ideas and market data, and it pulls in streams from Facebook, Twitter, and LinkedIn. It's a way of following market sentiment more than anything, but sentiment drives markets. And StockTwits is free.

For more information, go to `www.stocktwits.com`.

Trade-Ideas

Trade-Ideas is designed for stock traders. The software scans the incoming price data feed to find trading opportunities based on prespecified indicators, and it can also show how much the market is deviating from a trader's style. For traders watching hundreds or thousands of stocks, Trade-Ideas can be a useful addendum to a brokerage firm's offerings.

For more information, go to `www.trade-ideas.com`.

News, newsletters, gurus, and strategic advice

Trading relies on information so that everyone in the market can evaluate what the right price for a security should be. Most of this information can be found from an analysis of the news and the price data, both of which are readily available from brokerage firms and quote services. But many traders follow explicit philosophies or rely on the insight of certain analysts. Here's a list of some of the bigger ones you'll come across.

Many of these market gurus have good ideas, but don't follow any of them blindly. Their techniques don't work in all markets at all times. Besides, anyone with a truly foolproof plan isn't going to give it away. These newsletters are just part of the ongoing conversation in the markets that help traders make decisions.

Briefing.com

If you follow a news-driven trading strategy, you need to know what the news is. Briefing.com offers daily news summaries and live updates on news events and ideas for trades that may suit your style. And unlike the standard news feeds available to anyone with Internet access, it doesn't have any celebrity or human-interest stories to distract you.

For more information, go to www.briefing.com.

Elliott Wave

The *Elliott Wave* is a theory that says markets move in grand cycles over a century or more. Within that grand cycle are subcycles lasting years, months, weeks, days, minutes, and seconds. Given all the layers and analysis required, those who follow the theory usually subscribe to research services to help them. This site is maintained by Robert Prechter, who is one of the leading scholars of the theory.

For more information, go to www.elliottwave.com.

School of Gann

The Gann method of technical analysis looks at the slopes of the charts to predict changes. It's a complicated system, so traders who follow it usually rely on newsletters and research services to help them. School of Gann is one that specializes in this system.

For more information, go to www.schoolofgann.com.

TraderZone

Designed for stock traders working a momentum strategy, TraderZone offers subscribers access to proprietary signal information based on technical analysis.

For more information, go to www.traderzone.com.

TradeTheNews.com

TradeTheNews offers independent traders access to a *squawk box,* the audio news feed and commentary that goes in the background on most professional trading desks. Its staffers work on the floor of different exchanges and provide real-time news and analysis, which is helpful for traders working news-driven strategies.

For more information, go to www.tradethenews.com.

Trending 123

Trending 123 publishes newsletters on technical analysis in the U.S., Canadian, and English stock markets and in foreign exchange. It also offers software and e-mail alerts that point out opportunities in the markets, identified through the company's analytical system. Trending 123 regularly covers psychological aspects of trading to support its customers.

For more information, go to www.trending123.com.

The printed word

Several books cover specific aspects of trading psychology, trading strategy, and research systems in much more detail than I can in the space that the good folks at Wiley have given me. If you turn to the appendix, you can see a list of other resources that can help you in your research.

Just remember: Day trading was a hot topic in the late 1990s, and you may find that a lot of the books and articles on the subject date from that era. Some are lurking in your public library; others are still available for sale or can be found on the Internet. Markets change. So do regulations. SOES isn't around anymore. Don't rely on a system popularized a decade ago unless you've tested it and ensured that it still works.

Doing Your Due Diligence

Trading software, training, and research can get expensive, and some services and seminars are outright scams. Even those that are legitimate (and most are) may not be right for you. Before you spend your money, do your research. Start with the free programs offered by the exchanges (listed in the first section of this chapter) so that you have enough knowledge to understand what a trading-services purveyor is trying to do. Then do research and ask questions. To find out where to go and what to ask, read on.

Where to start your research

You have a ton of tools available to you to do your due diligence. A good place to start is the Internet. Go to your favorite search engine and enter the name of the program you're looking at plus the word *scam* or *rip-off* and see what turns up on the third or fourth page of the search. If nothing of much interest turns up, proceed to the regulatory agencies listed in the following sections.

Anyone with even a little knowledge of search-engine optimization knows this tip. If your search turns up 50 blog posts with lines like "Why Company X is NOT a scam!!!" well, guess what? Company X probably has something to hide, and if you go to the third or fourth page of the search results, you may find out what it is. Or just move on, because plenty of legitimate vendors that you can work with instead are out there.

You may learn very little about any given research firm from an Internet search or checks with the different regulatory organizations. That doesn't mean the firm in question isn't for real, just that it hasn't caused any concerns so far.

Commodity Futures Trading Commission

The Commodity Futures Trading Commission (www.cftc.gov/ConsumerProtection/index.htm) regulates options and futures markets, which are popular with day traders. Although not as well known as the Securities and Exchange Commission, its functions are similar. At its website, you can check out investor advisories, known scams, and recent enforcement efforts to see whether the vendor you're thinking of working with is legitimate or too good to be true.

FINRA BrokerCheck

The Financial Industry Regulatory Authority (FINRA) provides a handy service that lets you check on the current enforcement status of different brokerage firms and their employees, especially in the stock, bond, and options markets.

Some of these firms and people may be offering research services or newsletters, so check to see whether they've had problems in the past. Then you can make decisions based on what you find. Some issues, such as a history of disputes over customer funds, should send you running. Go to `www.finra.org/Investors/ToolsCalculators/BrokerCheck`.

National Futures Association BASIC

Futures are popular with day traders, and they're regulated by the National Futures Association. Its Background Affiliation Status Information Center (BASIC), at `www.nfa.futures.org/BasicNet`, gives you information on people and firms registered with the National Futures Association.

Securities and Exchange Commission

At `www.sec.gov/investor.shtml`, the Securities and Exchange Commission offers lots of great information about every aspect of stock and bond investing, with a special emphasis on problems and scams to avoid. Ponzi schemes involving virtual currencies? E-mail pump-and-dump scams? Don't let the information scare you away from the market; use it to evaluate any services that you're thinking of paying for.

Questions to ask

After you do your basic background checks, you're ready to ask some questions about the service providers you're considering. Talk to the customer service reps, and try talking to other traders as well. This section contains a list of questions to get you started.

- Can I get a free trial to check the service out?
- What training and support do you offer? Do you have a user community?
- How long will it take me to learn the system? Will I need to pay for additional training and coaching, or is your built-in support adequate?
- Who will be teaching me or advising me, and what is this person's background?
- How long have you been in business? Why was the company formed?
- What additional features are available at additional costs? How many customers subscribe to only the basic system?
- Does this system support my trading style and work with the assets I prefer to trade?
- Do you screen traders for your program? Do you ask traders to leave? What are the characteristics of those who do well? Of those who don't do well?

✔ Can I talk to other customers?

✔ Is your software compatible with my broker? With other services I'm using? With my computer's operating system? With my Internet bandwidth?

✔ Are your performance numbers actual, or are they hypothetical and based on backtesting? How were the numbers calculated? (Chapter 16 has more information on performance calculation.)

Hypothetical performance is based on an analysis of what would have happened had the system been in place in the past or of what may happen if market conditions cooperate. It can be subject to *data mining,* which means that the system was developed to generate good performance in backtesting, not because it has any logical or theoretical basis.

Don't trust any promises of performance. Day trading is a difficult business. Many people wash out because it doesn't suit their personality. Others fail because they don't have enough startup capital, they don't take the time to figure out how to do it, or they simply have a run of bad luck. No one can promise that you'll succeed.

Chapter 14

Stress Management in the Trading Day

. . . .

In This Chapter

▶ Reading cautionary tales of traders gone wrong

▶ Finding out how to control your emotions

▶ Checking out the paramount trading plan

. . . .

Day trading can be a ruthless business. Some days, you don't find any trades worth making. Other days, you find trades, but they don't work out the way you want them to. And some days, there are too many good trades, more than you can possibly make, and so you watch profitable opportunities slip away. When you're working with real money, all this stress can be too much to take.

In a money-management or brokerage firm, traders have tremendous camaraderie. They work for the same employer and stick together to blow off the stress. What do you do at home, though? How do *you* keep from panicking, getting depressed, or otherwise letting this business hurt your profits and hurt you?

If you're going to day trade, you need to understand the very real physical and psychological stresses that the market pushes on its participants. In this chapter, I offer some information and advice that can help you avoid a crisis.

Heeding Tales of Those Who Failed

Trader lore is loaded with stories of people who flamed out in spectacular and destructive ways. People who work on trading desks or on trading floors tell tales of colleagues who freaked out, walked off the desk, broke down in the pit, or died at the trading post. They can name colleagues who are alcoholics, who suffered bitter divorces, who committed suicide. Even though day traders usually work by themselves, stories of their self-destructive behavior abound.

Because not that many people day trade consistently, not a lot of good demographic studies have been conducted on just how many day traders end up abusing drugs and alcohol, getting divorced or becoming estranged from friends, and turning to suicide. The anecdotal evidence is pretty strong, though. People in the securities business face high pressure and real dollar losses every day they go to work. Their performance is constantly judged by the market, and it doesn't grade on a curve. If you spend even a few minutes talking to people in the business, you hear horror stories.

Don't be the person who finally gives researchers enough critical mass to report on day trader self-destruction. Stress is a real part of day trading, and not all day traders handle it well. If you know what you're up against and prepare for it, you'll be better off than many.

Many, probably most, day traders lead pleasant lives and suffer no more problems than any other person. That's because they have perspective, balance, and a personality that matches the demands of the business. The following sections offer a few cautionary tales of traders who succumbed to the pressures inherent in the job. I relate them here for this simple reason: Knowing what can go wrong can help you keep in the right.

Jesse Livermore

Jesse Livermore is sometimes considered to be the father of day trading. He's the subject of the book *Reminiscences of a Stock Operator* by Edwin LeFevre, a classic book about trading (see the appendix for more information). Livermore was born in 1877 and started trading stocks when he was in his teens. He claimed to have made $1,000 when he was 15, which may not seem like much, except that he was very young and that $1,000 would be worth more than $20,000 in today's dollars. He made huge fortunes betting against the market in 1907 and again in 1929, and he managed to lose it all both times. By 1934 he was broke and depressed. He attempted suicide in 1935 and succeeded in 1940.

Steve Perkins

Is he a cautionary tale, or the man who learned from his mistakes? Steve Perkins is an energy trader who worked for PVM Oil Futures, a London-based firm. One night in 2009, he got very drunk, got out his laptop computer, and started buying futures; he ended up controlling almost 70 percent of the world's oil market and left his firm with $10 million in losses. He was fired and banned from trading in the U.K. However, in 2010, he was hired by an energy trading firm in Switzerland, and, it is hoped, he will not make that mistake again.

Knight Capital

Knight Capital is a company, not a person, but its story is a good one to keep in mind given how much electronic trading takes place anymore. The company is a major dealer in the stock and equity options markets. It trades for its own account, buying and selling securities from discount brokerage firms to help them execute trades more efficiently. In the wee hours of the morning on August 1, 2012, the company did a software upgrade. When the market opened at 9:30 am New York time, Knight Capital sent a flood of erroneous orders into the market. It turned out that there was a flaw in the software that was installed. Ooops! Before the trading system was shut down, Knight Capital lost $440 million dollars. The firm would have folded if it had not been taken over by a competitor, GETCO.

Unlike Knight Capital, day traders don't get bailed out by competitors. Risk-management techniques can help minimize your risk, and so can having a backup trading method (say, on a laptop or phone) to help you close out quick if your computer does something goofy.

Controlling Your Emotions

The key to successful day trading is controlling your emotions. After all, the stock doesn't know that you own it, as equity traders like to say, so it isn't going to perform well just because you want it to. This can be infuriating, especially when you are going through a draw-down of your capital. Those losses look mighty personal.

Traditional financial theory is based on the idea that traders are rational. In practice, however, most of them are not. In fact, traders and investors are often irrational in completely predictable ways, which has given birth to a growing area of study called *behavioral finance*. It's a hot area generating Nobel Prize winners, and it may eventually help people incorporate measures of investor behavior into buy and sell decisions.

If you can't figure out a way to manage your reactions to the market, you shouldn't be a day trader. Almost all day traders talk about their enemies being fear and greed. If you panic, you'll no longer be trading to win, but trading not to lose. That's an important distinction: If your goal is not to lose, you won't take appropriate risk, and you won't be able to respond quickly to what the market is telling you.

Controlling your emotions is all much easier said than done. Human beings are emotional creatures, constantly reacting (and sometimes overreacting) to everything that happens in their lives. Knowing the emotions that affect trading and having some ways to manage them can greatly improve your overall performance.

Dealing with destructive emotions

In trading, the big emotions can take over and mess up your strategy and your returns. The enemies are doubt, fear, and greed; like any bullies, they have their toadies, including anger, anxiety, boredom, and depression. At this point in your life, you may already know whether you have tendencies toward any of these moods. If so, trading can exacerbate them. If you've never experienced them, you may for the first time. The following sections explain these emotions as they relate to day trading so that you know what you're up against and can plan accordingly.

I include some tips that can help you deal with destructive reactions, but if you are really in the throes of an emotional crisis that affects your trading, seek professional help. And by all means, walk away from the trading desk.

Doubt

Day traders have to act fast. They have to place their buy and sell orders as the opportunities present themselves. The market doesn't give anyone time to second-guess the decisions, but many traders start to do just that. Did the signal really flash? Is this pattern going to continue or reverse? Will waiting a few seconds lead to a better price? Would closing out for the day just be better?

I don't know. And neither do you. That's why traders need to stick to their plans, which isn't always easy. Backtesting (explained in Chapter 16) can help build confidence in a plan, and the use of automated trading tools (refer to Chapter 13) can help overcome the tendency to hesitate before clicking on the mouse button.

Most brokerage firms that offer services to day traders have automated trading capabilities to help you follow your plan. And all brokers can execute stop and limit orders, which can help you get out of positions based on your plans rather than your emotions.

Fear

Fear is one of the worst emotional enemies of the day trader. Instead of trying to make money, the fearful trader tries hard not to lose it. She is so afraid of failing that she limits herself, doesn't take appropriate risk, and questions her trading system so much that she no longer follows it, no matter how well it worked for her in the past.

By the way, failure isn't the only thing that traders fear. Many fear success, sometimes for deep-seated psychological reasons that I am in no position to address. A trader who fears success may think that if she succeeds, her friends will treat her differently, her relatives will try to take her money, and that she will become someone she doesn't want to be.

One way to limit fear is to have a plan for the trading business. Before you start trading, take some time — maybe half a day — to sit down and think about what you want, what will happen to you if you get it, and what will happen to you if you don't. For example, if you lose your trading capital, then you'll have to live on your walk-away fund (see the section "Watching your walk-away money" later in this chapter) until you find another job. If you make a lot of money, then you can pay off your mortgage, and your friends will be none the wiser.

Greed

Greed seems like a silly thing to have on this list. After all, isn't the whole purpose of day trading to make money? This isn't charity; this is capitalism at its purest. Ah, but there's a popular saying down at the Chicago Board of Trade: "Pigs get fat, but hogs get slaughtered."

Traders who get greedy start to do stupid things. They don't think through what they're doing, and they stop following their trading plans. They hold positions too long in the hope of eking out a return, and sometimes they make rash trades that look an awful lot like gambling. The greedy trader loses all discipline and eventually loses quite a bit of money.

If your goal is simply to make more and more money, you may have a problem with greed. Sure, everyone wants to make more, but there are also a basic *need-to-make number* (enough to cover your costs and your basic living expenses) and a *want-to-make number* (enough to cover costs, basic expenses, and extras that are important to you). Your want-to-make can be open ended (as in "as much as possible"), but your need-to-make should be a key component of your risk management. If you know what those numbers are, you're well on your way to preventing the problem.

Limit orders, which automatically close out positions when they hit set prices, are one way to force discipline in the face of greed. You can learn more about limit orders in Chapter 2.

Anger

The markets can be maddening. They don't do what you want them to, and that often costs you real money. And no one wants to lose money. Your rage at the markets can cause you to stop seeing straight.

When anger makes it impossible to think clearly, your best bet is to call it a day, close out your positions, and go somewhere far from your trading screen. Leave your phone at home if you're using your broker's mobile apps, too! Take a long walk and wait for your anger to subside. Otherwise, your rage will interfere with your plans and your profitability. The only way to psych out the market is to be just as mechanical and unemotional as the blips that cross your screen.

Anxiety

Anxiety is the anticipation of things going wrong, and it often includes a physical response: perspiration, clenched jaws, tense muscles, heart palpitations, and so on. Anxious people worry, agonize, overanalyze, and generally stress out. And then they avoid whatever it is that makes them upset. That means that a trader may not make an obvious trade but instead hesitate and miss a market move. He may hold on to a losing position too long because he's worried about the effect that selling it will have on his portfolio. He becomes too nervous to trade according to his plan, and his performance suffers.

One way to combat anxiety is through automated trading and limit orders. If your limits are set when you place the trade, then your anxiety can't override your plan.

Boredom

An ugly truth about day trading is that it can be really dull. In an eight-hour trading session, you may spend seven and a half hours waiting for the right opening. A flurry of trades, and it's all over. To keep yourself entertained, you may start making bad trades, spending too much time in chat rooms, or letting your mind wander away from the task at hand. None of those things is conducive to profitable trading.

One way to reduce the temptations brought on by boredom is to block access to social media on your trading computer. Several companies make software that will keep you from using Facebook, Pinterest, or Addicting Games when you should be trading! A few to consider are Anti-Social (www.anti-social.cc) and Cold Turkey (www.getcoldturkey.com). Keep in mind that they may slow down your system — and that your phone may need a social-media blocker, too.

Depression

Depression is a severe downturn in your mood, especially one that causes you to feel inadequate and lose interest in things you used to like. Although everyone is susceptible to depression, the ups and downs of the market can make traders particularly vulnerable. At best, depression can make it hard for a trader to face a day with the market. At worst, it can lead to alcoholism, alienation, and even suicide.

If you think you may be depressed, check out the self-assessment at www. mayoclinic.com/health/depression/MH00103_D. Or better yet, go to your doctor. He or she will give you a better diagnosis than Dr. Internet.

Having an outlet

Successful day traders have a life outside the markets. They close out their positions, shut off their monitors, and go do something else with the rest of the day. The problem is that a market is always open somewhere. Undisciplined traders work overnight and after hours through electronic communications networks and sometimes move the action to exchanges in other parts of the world. Think about Steve Perkins, losing millions of dollars in the middle of the night! Without something to mark a beginning and an end to your trading day, and without other things happening in your life, the market can consume you in an unhealthy way.

So as you plan your life as a day trader, think about what else you're going to do with your days. Exercise, meditation, socializing, and having outside interests are keys to maintaining balance and staying focused on the market when you have to be. The following sections go into more detail.

Exercise

Exercise keeps your body in fighting shape so that you can stand up to market stress and react to trends when you need to. Many times when you're trading, you have huge rushes of adrenaline that you can't do much about. You have to stay in front of your screen until the trade is over, no matter how much you want to run away screaming. But after the trading day, you can hit the track or pool or treadmill and burn off some of that adrenaline. Figuring out a regular exercise routine can pay off for your trading.

If you aren't an exerciser now, call your local YMCA. It has introductory programs that can teach you how to use the equipment and help you design a workout that suits your current fitness levels and goals.

Meditation

When you're trading, you may get upset and start thinking about everything else that has ever gone wrong in your life, instead of staying focused on the task at hand. Even after you close out your positions and shut down your monitors, your day's trading may keep playing itself out over and over in your head, making it impossible for you to relax. Neither of these scenarios is good for you — or your trading.

Trading requires mental discipline. Good traders can keep their minds clear of everything but their trading system, at least when the markets are at their hairiest. One way to develop that discipline is to take up meditation. Yeah, it may seem goofy, being a big tough trader type doing something woo-woo like meditation, but if you have trouble keeping your focus, you really may want to give it a try. There are an almost infinite number of meditation styles, many of which are associated with different religious traditions, so you can surely find something that works. Research compiled by the Center for Complementary and Alternative Medicine at the National Institutes of Health (`http://nccam.nih.gov/health/meditation/overview.htm`) shows that many people report mental-health benefits from meditation.

Check out the instructions for the Buddhist mindfulness meditation practice at `www.shambhala.org/meditationinstruction.html` as a way to get started.

Friends and family

Day trading is a lonely activity. You work by yourself all day. It's just you, your room, and your screen. This job is really isolating. If you don't get other human contact, you run the risk of personalizing the market in order not to feel so lonely. That's bad, because the market isn't a person; it's an agglomeration of all the financial activity taking place, and it has no interest in you whatsoever.

No matter what you do in life, you want to have the support of the people you know and love. And you need to make time for them, too. Start and end your trading day at regular times and be sure to make plans to see people who are important to you. Going to your kid's ball game, having dinner with your spouse, and seeing your friends for a few beers on a regular basis can go a long way to keeping your life in balance — and that will keep your trading in balance.

If you like pets, consider getting one to keep you company during the day. There's nothing like a dog that needs a walk to force you to close shop for the night.

Hobbies and other interests

A lot of people get into day trading because they have long had a fascination with the market. Trading goes from being a hobby to being a living. In many ways, that's perfect. Going to work is so much easier when you have a job that you love.

But if the market is your only interest, then you're going to be too susceptible to its gyrations, and you're going to have trouble sticking to your trading discipline. Plus, whatever upsets you during the trading day is more likely to carry over. So find a new hobby if you don't have one. Maybe it's a TV show, a sport, or knitting, but whatever it is, you need to have something going on outside of your trading.

Trading is just one part of your life.

Setting up support systems

Exercise and friends and family and hobbies and the like are all well and good, but they don't directly address the mindset of trading. Fortunately, a veritable industry supports traders, and you can tap in to it easily. Many day traders find that reading books, hiring a coach, or finding other day traders helps them get through the day.

Books

A library full of books has been written on the psychology of trading itself. In addition, many traders rely on other self-help and history books for inspiration and ideas. (I think every trader I've ever known owns a copy of Sun Tzu's *The Art of War*, which is about military strategies and tactics. They find that this book helps them prepare their minds to face the market — or at least gives them something interesting to talk about.) I list several books in the appendix that may help you organize your mind and keep your enthusiasm for the market.

Counseling and coaching

Because handling big losses — and big gains —takes a lot of mental toughness, many traders find professional support. They use counselors, psychologists, or life coaches to help them deal with the challenges of the market and understand their reactions to it. You can ask other traders or your doctor for a referral, or check the online directory at *Psychology Today*'s website, www.psychologytoday.com, or the International Coach Federation, www.coachfederation.org. When interviewing coaches or counselors, ask whether they have experience with traders or others who work in finance.

Many day-trading training and brokerage firms also offer coaching services that specialize in helping people learn and follow day-trading strategies. Some day traders find these people to be invaluable, whereas others find they are just glorified salespeople.

Finding other traders

To offset the loneliness of trading alone, many day traders choose to join organizations where they will meet other traders. These may be formal or informal groups (I list a few in the appendix) where traders can socialize, learn new things, or just commiserate.

Many day traders also get together through Internet message boards and chat rooms. I discuss this option in more detail later in this chapter and list a few in the appendix. These groups are less formal, more anonymous, and sometimes as destructive as supportive.

Most day traders lose money and give up their first year. You may find that spending too much time with other traders is more depressing than supportive.

Watching your walk-away money

A lot of traders have a secret that lets them get through the worst of the markets. It's something called *walk-away money,* although traders sometimes use more colorful language to describe it. Walk-away money is just what its name implies: enough money to let the trader walk away from trading and do something else.

And just exactly how much walk-away money does a trader need? Well, the exact amount varies from person to person, but having enough money to pay three months' worth of expenses on hand and in cash is a good place to start. If you know that you can pay the mortgage and buy the groceries even if you don't make money trading today, you're better able to avoid desperate trading. You won't have to be greedy, and you won't have to live in fear.

The more money in your walk-away fund, the better. Then you have more time to investigate alternative careers should day trading prove not to be your thing, and you can relax more when you face the market every day.

Most day traders quit after a year or so. There's nothing wrong with deciding to move on and try something else. If you have some money saved, then you're in a better position to control when you stop trading and what you do next.

If all your trading capital is gone, you may be tempted to tap your walk-away fund to stay in the game. *Don't.* That's the exactly the time that you should use your walk-away money to *walk away,* if only for a short time to clear your head, rethink your strategies, and build up some new trading capital. Otherwise, your trading losses may become financial ruin.

Managing Stress with Your Trading Plan

You may have noticed that trading plans pop up several times in this book. That's because they are so important to maintaining the discipline that leads to trading success. You have to know what you're doing and how to recognize entry and exit points and then go and do it.

In this section, I cover how you can use a trading plan to manage stress and give you a few tips for sticking to your trading plan even as the markets sometimes move against you.

Avoiding problems following your plan

A good, tested trading plan sets out market patterns that work often enough that you can make good trading profits. But some people have trouble following their plan, and that leads to stressful mistakes. Following are some common problems and advice on how you can avoid — or overcome — them.

Prevent choking!

In sports lingo, an athlete who *chokes* starts playing so carefully that he or she looks like a beginner. Choking is often caused by overthinking — by being so afraid of failure that the mind slows down and breaks the play down step by step. Watching a contender break down in a championship game isn't pretty. The fans want to see a good match.

Anyone in a high-performance situation can choke. When a trader chokes, he seems to be following the plan, but it's no longer automatic. Trading becomes so slow and deliberate that obvious trades get missed.

The more you trust your plan, the less likely you are to choke. Has it been tested? Are there parts that you can automate? Chapter 16 has some ideas on how to measure a trading plan's performance before you start to trade with the plan.

Reduce panic

Panic occurs when you just stop thinking. Your most basic survival instincts take over, even when they are totally uncalled for. You're losing money? You start to trade more and more, off-plan, in a desperate gamble to win it back. You're making money? You close out all your trades right now so that you can't possibly lose, even if your plan tells you to hold your positions. When you panic, you can't think straight, and you can't follow your plan.

When your positions are down and you seem to be losing money, you really should be buying and sticking it out so that you can make money later. The problem is that your panicked instincts are telling you to do the opposite. Following through on your plan rather than knuckling under to your instincts is tough to do and requires a lot of discipline. With experience, traders learn to avoid panic.

You're probably going to have more than a few losing trades when you get started. In your trading diary (see Chapter 16), keep notes about how losing money makes you feel. Can you handle it emotionally? If losing upsets you too much, you may not be cut out for day trading. You can't trade with a clear head if you're bogged down with negative thoughts.

Nurture your confidence, not your ego

Day trading requires a lot of confidence because you *are* going to lose money and you *are* going to get beaten up some days. Not only do you have to remain confident in the face of adversity, but you also have to be careful that you do not cross from confidence into an inflated ego. The more your trading success and failure become part of your personal identity, the more trouble you're going to have.

What's the difference between confidence and ego? A confident person would say, "I'm smart enough to figure out what the market is telling me"; an egotistical person, "I'm smarter than the market." The difference is crucial to your success.

Revising and troubleshooting your trading plan

Strong discipline is key to success in trading, but only if you're disciplined in following the right system. If your trading method is flawed, sticking to it is going to hurt you. If something isn't working, don't get mad at the system; take some responsibility and make some changes.

How do you figure out whether your trading system is right and what changes to make? Go through your trading diary (see Chapter 16 for how to set one up) and ask yourself some questions:

- ✔ Why did you choose this system? What is the market telling you about it? Is it telling you that the system works if you follow it, or is it telling you that something is wrong with the underlying assumptions?

  What works for someone else may not work for you. There's no flaw in admitting that you made a mistake and that you need to make a change.

- ✔ Were your mistakes because you followed the plan or because you didn't?

- ✔ What part of the system is causing the trouble? Are you having trouble identifying entry points or exit points? Or are you stuck when the time comes to enter the trade, causing you to miss a point? Or do the trades your system identifies never seem to work out? When you know where the problem is, you can change it.

- ✔ Can you improve your trade efficiency? Is there a way to reduce the number of mistakes? Would automating some or all of your trading help?

One way to get your confidence back while still staying in the market is to trade in very small amounts so that your profits and losses don't really matter. Trade 100 shares, not 1,000 shares. You give up the upside for a time, but you can also get out of the cycle of greed and fear that has destroyed many a trader.

Chapter 15

Taxes for Traders

*T*hink day trade returns come without a catch? Think again, because the IRS has plenty of ways to catch you come April 15. Day trading involves strategies that generate both high returns and high tax liabilities, which can eat away at your total return if you're not careful. Not all your expenses are deductible, and although you may think that you're day trading, the IRS may have a different definition of your activities.

Taxes themselves aren't necessarily bad, because citizens have to pay for things like roads and schools and national defense somehow. But taxes can be devastating to your personal finances if you haven't planned for them. You need to consider the tax implications of your trading strategy right from the start and keep careful records so that you're ready.

Tax issues for day traders are complex and change frequently. And because the federal government is broke, as are most of the states, don't expect the tax rules to get easier. Check the most recent federal regulations at www.irs.gov and work with an accountant or tax expert who has experience in these matters. This chapter is just a guide. I'm a reasonably social gal and all, but I'm not going on an audit with you.

Getting the Lay of the Land: What You Need to Know Based on What You Trade

The Internal Revenue code is complex, with specific rules for specific types of transactions. You can easily get tripped up, and a tax trip-up can be costly. Here I give an overview of different types of day-trading assets and some of the tax implications associated with them.

Commodities and futures

Of the many reasons that day traders work with commodity and futures contacts, one is that the taxes are easy to handle. Under Section 1256 of the IRS code, certain types of contracts — for example, regulated futures contracts, foreign currency contracts, and non-equity options (on debt, commodities, currencies, and stock market indexes) that are marked-to-market in trading — are handled under the *60/40 rule*. This rule stipulates that 60 percent of your total capital gain or loss will be treated as a long-term capital gain or loss, and the other 40 percent of your gain or loss will be treated as a short-term gain or loss. How long you held the position doesn't matter. Why is this rule so nice? Because the long-term capital gains rate is less than the short-term rate, and you as a day trader can take advantage of it, even though, by definition, day traders don't hold positions over the long haul.

Currency trading

If you trade currencies, the tax laws that apply to you can be confusing, and they have gray areas. How taxes apply to you can be impacted by the following:

- **Whether you're an individual or a business:** Small individual currency transactions are usually considered to be like-kind exchanges; for example, if you go on vacation to Mexico, exchange your dollars to pesos when the dollar is strong, and then change whatever remains back at the border a week later when the dollar is a bit weaker, you'll have made a profit. However, this transaction is not a reportable one, because, in essence, you exchanged two identical items: money for money.

  A business, however, can accrue taxable gains and losses due to changes in exchange rates. If a company makes goods in the United States and sells them through its Mexican subsidiary, for example, the amount of profit or loss that the subsidiary has depends on the exchange rate between the dollar and the peso, and that determines the amount of tax that the company pays. In this case, identical objects aren't being exchanged. (The IRS has plenty of rules on how businesses should handle foreign exchange under Section 988 of the tax code.)

✔ **Whether you're trading actual currency or futures and options on currencies:** Futures and options on currencies are taxed under Section 1256 using the handy 60/40 rule described in the preceding section. But you're trading in the spot market. You aren't trading currency contracts; you're trading actual currency. What do you do about profits and losses you may accrue?

The IRS isn't keen on your claiming a tax-free like-kind exchange if your goal is to make a living trading currencies. But you aren't running a business with overseas operations, are you? Unfortunately, there are no clear guidelines here, so you probably want to work with an accountant. The general thought is that you can report your currency trading through Section 988 or Section 1256. Under Section 988, your trading gains and losses are considered short-term capital gains in your trading business. This arrangement saves you money if you lost money trading but costs you if you made money. Under Section 1256, your spot trading is handled as futures contracts, and you pay short-term capital gains taxes on 40 percent of your profits and long-term capital gains taxes on the remaining 60 percent of your profit. This saves you money in the years you made money.

The key? Be consistent. You can't file under Section 988 when you lose money and under Section 1256 in years you make money. That game makes the IRS very unhappy, and you don't want to have the tax guys unhappy with you.

Although you should consider this entire chapter as a guideline and not professional tax advice, this warning holds particularly true for the information on currencies. At the time I am writing this, both the Commodity Futures Trading Commission and the Internal Revenue Service are taking a close look at the forex market to clarify the regulations, so the information may be very different when you do your taxes.

Options

The taxation of options is more complicated than the taxation of other derivatives. The basic information is the same: A gain on an option held for less than a year is a short-term capital gain, and a gain on one held for more than a year is a long-term capital gain. There are two problems, though. The first is that some options strategies offer a combination of short-term and long-term gains and losses. The second is that options trades fall under the wash-sale rule (explained later in this chapter), which limits your ability to make trades of fewer than 30 days in the same securities.

Options have one other wrinkle: You can't use options to manage taxable sales and gains in stocks. An option on a stock is considered to be substantially identical to the stock. That's why the tax treatment is pretty much the same — and why professional tax advice is really important if you're trading options.

The Chicago Board Options Exchange publishes a detailed guide to stock and stock-options taxation. You can download it at www.cboe.com/LearnCenter/pdf/TaxesandInvesting.pdf.

Stock trading

In Chapter 4, I cover the differences between investing, trading, and gambling. Day traders aren't investing; they're looking to take advantage of short-term price movements, not to take a stake in a business for the long term. Unless, of course, you're asking the IRS about it. The IRS defines trading much differently than people in financial circles do. To the taxmen, you are a trader only if *all* of the following apply to you:

- ✔ You seek to profit from daily market movements in the prices of securities, not from dividends, interest, or capital appreciation.

- ✔ Your activity is *substantial;* the IRS code does not spell out what substantial means, but it probably means you're making at least 3,000 trades per year.

- ✔ You carry on the activity with *continuity* and *regularity.* In other words, day trading is more or less your full-time job, you've stuck with it for at least six months already, and you plan to keep trading into the next year.

The 2013 Tax Court case *Endicott v. Commissioner* addressed the issue of *substantial* when deciding whether a person is a trader. The plaintiff made 1,543 trades in 2008, which the IRS said was substantial. The 303 trades made in 2007 did not meet the definition. The taxpayer traded on 75 days in 2006, 99 days in 2007, and 112 days in 2008, and the court ruled that none of those met the requirement for frequent, continuous, or regular trading. This ruling is the clearest guidance issued in a long time.

IRS Tax Topic 429 covers the matter in more detail. If you trade part-time, have other employment, or are new to the day-trading game, the IRS probably won't let you define yourself as a trader. Don't care what an IRS agent calls you, as long she doesn't call you for an audit? Well, understanding the difference between *trader* and *investor* in IRS lingo is important to avoid that audit.

Those who qualify as traders enjoy deductions that regular investors don't. You may quality as a trader for some of your activities and as an investor for others. If you think this scenario applies to you, you need to keep detailed records to separate your trades, and you should use different brokerage accounts to make the difference clear from the day you open the position.

In political economics, taxation serves two purposes. The first is to raise money for the government. The second is to encourage people to do things that the elected officials who amend the tax code want them to do. Much of the investing tax code is intended to promote the formation and growth of businesses. Short-term day trading doesn't do that, so the tax law doesn't offer short-term investors the same benefits that it gives to long-term investors and business owners.

Hiring a Tax Adviser

You don't have to hire someone to do your taxes, but you probably should. Day trading generates a lot of separate transactions to track, and the tax laws are tricky. Mistakes can end up costing you your entire trading profit.

Do yourself a favor and find yourself a tax expert. You can talk to other traders, get references from the attorneys and accountants you work with now, or even do Internet searches to find people who understand both IRS regulations and the unique needs of people who frequently buy and sell securities, whether or not the IRS calls them traders.

The many flavors of tax experts

Okay, you're waiting for me to say there's only one flavor of accountant, and it's plain vanilla, right? Wrong. Tax experts fall into several different categories, and knowing which is which can help you determine who is best for you:

- **Certified public accountants:** *Certified public accountants* studied accounting in college and passed exams testing their knowledge of a wide range of accounting subjects. Because much of accounting involves income-tax preparation, many CPAs specialize in this. CPAs generally have the best combined knowledge of tax laws and tax preparation techniques, but not all of them specialize in or even understand day trading.

- **Enrolled agents:** *Enrolled agents* specialize in tax preparation. They receive registration from the IRS after passing a two-day, eight-hour exam covering only tax topics, which is what they know best. They may not be so good at helping you with other accounting needs, such as preparing payroll for your office assistants.

- ✔ **Tax attorneys:** *Tax attorneys* usually work with CPAs; they are called in to study the legality of proposed strategies or represent a client in tax litigation. They aren't appropriate for most traders, but you may have situations that call for one.

- ✔ **Storefronts and volunteers (probably not a good idea):** Every winter, vacant buildings are turned into tax-preparation centers, and the IRS promotes its cadre of volunteers who help people with their taxes. These services can be a boon to the average person who lacks the time or patience to deal with the tax forms. But if you are trader, you're going to run into complex problems that most of these services are not prepared to handle, such as the many considerations that go with taxes on currency trading discussed previously.

Only CPAs, enrolled agents, and tax attorneys are allowed to represent clients before the IRS in audits, collections, or appeals. Other paid preparers can represent clients in an audit, but they can't handle more complex matters.

Questions to ask a prospective adviser

After you identify a few prospective candidates to prepare your taxes, talk to them and ask them questions about their experience. You want someone who understands things such as the *wash-sale rule* (which can limit the deductibility of your losses and is covered in more detail in the later section "Understanding the wash-sale rule") and the *mark-to-market election* (which can allow you to deduct more losses; see the section "Mark-to-market accounting") and who can help you determine what you owe in taxes and not one penny more.

Here some things you should ask a potential tax preparer:

- ✔ What investors and traders have you worked with? For how long?

- ✔ Have you worked with traders or investors in my state? Can you prepare my state return?

- ✔ Have you helped traders make the mark-to-market election?

- ✔ What is your experience with the wash-sale rule? How will my trading style be affected by it?

- ✔ Who will be preparing my return? How involved will you be?

- ✔ Do you offer tax analysis of trading strategies?

✔ What's your audit record? Why have your clients been audited? What happened on the audit?

✔ What are your fees?

By law, tax preparers cannot base their fees on the size of your tax refund, and they cannot guarantee you a refund. Any preparer who does these things either does not know the law or is willfully breaking it.

You'll feel more comfortable with your tax preparer if *you* have an understanding of the issues at stake. Even if you are hiring someone — and you should — keep reading this chapter and check the appendix for references on taxes and trading.

Doing Your Taxes Yourself

Traders can do their own taxes. If you are comfortable with tax forms, if you are only day trading a little bit, and if I haven't deterred you yet, you may be able to handle your own taxes. Here's what you need: the proper IRS forms and tax preparation software that can handle investment income.

Finding out everything you want to know

The IRS website, www.irs.gov, is a treasure trove of tax information. All the regulations, publications, forms, and explanations are there, and some of it is even in plain English. The site is so vast and detailed that you'll probably be overwhelmed (I'm not sure there is any page in any IRS publication that doesn't mention dividends received under the State of Alaska Permanent Fund).

Curious to know about this State of Alaska Permanent Fund? It's an annual payment made to all residents of Alaska every year, based on the profits of oil pumped in that state. To put this amount into context, Alaska had 731,449 residents in 2012, according to the U.S. Census Bureau. I think there are two pages of IRS publications mentioning the fund for every person who gets a check from it.

The primary publication that covers the tax implications of trading and other investing activities is Publication 550, *Investment Income and Expenses*. It's available at www.irs.gov/publications/p550/.

Making it easier with tax-preparation software

The brave people who do their own taxes know that tax-prep software is a godsend, and it's even more valuable for those do-it-yourselfers who trade a lot. The software fills out the forms, automatically adds and subtracts, and even catches typographical errors. In many cases, it can download data straight from your brokerage account, making data entry really simple.

Most of the big brands, such as TaxCut and TurboTax, publish several editions each year — not all of which are set up to import and manage lots of trading data. Among those that have services for investors are TurboTax Premier Investments (www.turbotax.com), H&R Block at Home Premium (www.hrblock.com), and CompleteTax (www.completetax.com).

Income Categories You Need to Know

Income seems like a straightforward concept, but not much about taxation is straightforward. To the IRS, income falls into different categories, with different tax rates, different allowed deductions, and different forms to fill out. In this section, I cover income definitions you'll run into as a day trader.

Earned income

Earned income includes wages, salaries, bonuses, and tips. It's money that you make on the job. But even if day trading is your only occupation, your earnings are not considered to be earned income. Therefore day traders, whether classified for tax purposes as investors or traders, don't have to pay the self-employment tax on their trading income. Isn't that great?

Well, maybe, maybe not. The self-employment tax, the bane of many an independent business person, is a contribution to the Social Security fund. (Employees pay half of the contribution, and the employer pays the other half. The self-employed have to pay the whole thing.)

The problem is that if you don't have earned income, you are not paying into Social Security. If you are not paying into Social Security, you may not be eligible for retirement benefits. To collect benefits, you have to have paid in 40 credits, and you can earn a maximum of four credits per year. Most employees do this easily, but if you've taken time off work or have a long history of work as an independent investor, you may not have paid enough in.

Any Social Security benefits you do collect are based on the 35 years of highest earned income over your work history. Your years of independent trading show up as years with zero earned income, which may hurt your ultimate benefit.

The Social Security Administration has a handy online calculator, www.social security.gov/planners/calculators.htm, which can help you determine whether day trading makes sense for you right now, given the possible effect on your Social Security benefits.

Investment income

Investment income is your total income from property held for investment before any deductions. It includes interest, dividends, annuities, and royalties. Investment income does not include net capital gains, unless you choose to include them. Do you want to include them? Well, read the next section.

Other than net capital gains, which you may or may not decide to include, most day traders have very little investment income for tax purposes.

Capital gains and losses

A *capital gain* is the profit you make when you buy low and sell high — the aim of day trading. The opposite of a capital gain is a *capital loss,* which happens when you sell an asset for less than you paid for it. Investors can offset some of their capital gains with some of their capital losses to reduce their tax burden.

Frequent traders have many capital gains and losses, though, and they may very well run afoul of complicated IRS rules about capital gains taxation. Day traders get tripped up by capital gain and loss problems all the time. When designing your trading strategy, think long and hard about how much pain taxes may cause. The financial world is filled with horror stories of people who thought they found a clever angle on making big profits, only to discover at tax time that their tax liability was greater than their profit. In the real world, taxes matter.

Capital gains come in two flavors: short term and long term. You're charged a low rate (the current rate is 15 percent) on long-term capital gains, which right now is defined as the gain on assets held for more than one year. Short-term capital gains, which are those made on any asset held for one year or less, are taxed at the ordinary income rate, probably 28 percent or more.

Calculating capital gains and losses: Covering all your basis

Capital gains and losses are calculated using a security's *basis,* which may or may not be the same as the price that you paid for it or sold it at. Some expenses, such as commissions or disallowed wash-sale losses (both of which are discussed later in this chapter), are added to the cost of the security, and that can reduce the amount of your taxable gain or increase the amount of your deductible loss.

For example, if you bought 100 shares of stock at $50 per share and a $0.03 per share commission, your basis would be $5,003 — the $5,000 you paid for the stock and the $3 you paid in commission.

Understanding the wash-sale rule

Suppose you love LMNO Company, but the price of the shares is down from what it was when you purchased them. You'd like to get that loss on your taxes, so you sell the stock, and then you buy it back at the lower price. You get your tax deduction and still keep the stock. How excellent is that?

It's too excellent to be true. This trick is called a *wash sale,* and the IRS does not count the loss. The wash-sale rule was designed to keep long-term investors from playing cute with their taxes, but it has the effect of creating a ruinous tax situation for naïve day traders.

Seeing the rule in action

Under the wash-sale rule, you cannot deduct a loss if you have both a gain and a loss in the same security within a 61-day period. (That's calendar days, not trading days, so weekends and holidays count.) However, you *can* add the disallowed loss to the basis of your security.

Here's an example to illustrate. On Tuesday, you bought 100 shares of LMNO at $34.60. LMNO announced terrible earnings, and the stock promptly dropped to $29.32, and you sold all 100 shares for a loss of $528. Later in the afternoon, you noticed that the stock had bottomed and looked like it might trend up, so you bought another 100 shares at $28.75 and resold them an hour later at $29.25, closing out your position for the day. The second trade had a profit of $50. You had a net loss of $478 (the $528 loss plus the $50 profit). Here's how this works out tax-wise: The IRS disallows the $528 loss and lets you show only a profit of $50. But it lets you add the $528 loss to the basis of your replacement shares, so instead of spending $2,875 (100 shares times $28.75), for tax purposes, you spent $3,403 ($2,875 plus $528), which means that the second trade caused you to lose the $478 that you added back. On a net basis, you get to record your loss. The basis addition lets you work off your wash-sale losses eventually, assuming that you keep careful records and have more winning trades than losing ones in any one security.

To make the calculations easier, several different tax-software packages can download trade data from your brokerage account to keep track of your tax situation. One to check out is TradeLog, www.armencomp.com/tradelog. Even if you hire someone to do your taxes, tracking your potential liabilities as you trade can help you avoid costly mistakes.

The wash-sale rule applies to substantially similar securities. LMNO stock and LMNO options are considered to be substantially similar, so you can't get around the rule by varying securities on the same underlying asset. LMNO shares and shares of its closest competitor, PQRS, would probably not be considered substantially similar, so you can trade within a given industry to help avoid wash-sale problems.

Getting around the wash-sale rule

At an extreme, the wash-sale rule can mean that traders who are in and out of the same securities over and over may be taxed on all their winning trades, without being able to subtract their losing trades for tax purposes. If your winning trades gained $300,000, and your losing trades cost you $200,000, you cleared $100,000 — but the IRS may tax you on the $300,000. Ouch!

There are ways around the wash-sale rule. The obvious solution is to qualify as a trader for IRS purposes and then take the mark-to-market accounting election (covered in the section "Mark-to-market accounting"). Other methods for avoiding the wash-sale rule include trading a given security only once every 60 calendar days and doing all your trading within a qualified retirement account such as an IRA (also discussed later in this chapter). Some securities are handled differently. Futures contracts are considered to generate investment income and losses, not capital gains, and so they are not covered by the wash-sale rule, which makes them a popular alternative for day traders. Profits on options contracts are 60 percent long-term capital gains and 40 percent short-term capital gains, which reduce the wash-sale rule effect.

If you have any more clever ideas about how you can make money without taking a tax hit, be sure to run them through an experienced tax pro first.

Miscellaneous income

Miscellaneous income is money that you received that wasn't earning income, investment income, or capital gains. This kind of income is often payment received in the course of a business or trade. As a freelancer, most of my income is reported to the IRS in the miscellaneous category. Anyone who pays me for my services has to send me Form 1099-MISC at the end of the year, with a copy going to the IRS, to help the agency track my earnings.

Some proprietary traders that provide services for day traders (covered in Chapter 11) report your profits and losses on Form1099-MISC. Miscellaneous income is handled as self-employment income and must be reported.

Tracking Your Investment Expenses

Day traders have expenses. They buy computer equipment, subscribe to research services, pay trading commissions, and hire accountants to prepare their taxes. It adds up, and the tax code recognizes that. That's why day traders can deduct many of their costs from their income taxes. In this section, I go through some of what you can deduct.

You can make your life much easier by keeping track of your expenses as you incur them. You can keep these records in a notebook, in a spreadsheet, or through personal finance software such as Quicken or Microsoft Money.

Qualified and deductible expenses

You can deduct investment expenses as miscellaneous itemized deductions on Schedule A of Form 1040 as long as these expenses are ordinary, necessary, directly related to the taxable income produced, and used to produce or collect income or manage property held for producing income.

Clerical, legal, and accounting fees

You may use the services of a lawyer to help you get set up, and you will almost definitely want to use an accountant who understands investment expenses to help you evaluate your trading strategy and prepare your state and federal income tax returns each year. There's good news here: You can deduct attorney and accounting fees related to your investment income. If your trading operation gets big enough that you hire clerical help to keep track of all those trade confirmations, you can deduct that cost, too.

Office expenses

If you do your day trading from an outside office, you can deduct the rent and related expenses. You can deduct the expenses of a home office, too, as long as you use it regularly and exclusively for business. If your trading room is also the guest room, it doesn't count.

Whether or not you deduct your office, you can deduct certain office expenses for equipment and supplies used in your business. You can usually write off roughly $100,000 in computers, desks, chairs, and the like if you use them for trading more than half of the time. (The limits change every year.)

To get the deduction, you have to spend the money first, and your expenses don't reduce your taxes dollar-for-dollar. If you are in the 28 percent tax bracket, then each dollar you spend on qualified expenses reduces your taxes by $0.28. In other words, don't go crazy at the office-supply store just because you get a tax deduction. It may be helpful to think of deductible expenses as discounts, because in the end that's more or less what they are.

Investment counsel and advice

The IRS allows you to deduct fees paid for counsel and advice about investments that produce taxable income. This advice includes books, magazines, newspapers, and research services that help you refine your trading strategy. It also includes anything you may pay for investment advisory services, such as trade coaching or analysis.

By the way, you can probably deduct what you paid for *Day Trading For Dummies*. Did you save the receipt?

Safe-deposit box rent

Have a safe-deposit box down at the bank? You can deduct the rent on it if you use it to store investment-related documents. If you also keep jewelry that you inherited and never wear or other personal items in the same box, you can only deduct part of the rent.

Investment interest

If you borrow money as part of your strategy, and most day traders do, you can deduct the interest paid on those loans as long as it is not from a home mortgage (because that interest is already deductible) and as long as you are not subject to other limitations set forth in the IRS code, such as the Alternative Minimum Tax. There's always a catch, isn't there? In most cases, the catch is *margin interest* (see Chapter 9 for more information on margin). For most day traders, margin interest is relatively small because few day traders borrow money for more than a few hours at a time.

If you borrow money against your account for anything other than investing or trading, you can't deduct the interest. And yes, most brokerage firms let you take out margin for your own general spending, as a way to let you stay in the market and still get cash.

State income taxes

If you itemize your deductions, you can deduct, as taxes, state income taxes on interest income that is exempt from federal income tax. But you cannot deduct, as either taxes or investment expenses, state income taxes on other exempt income. In most cases, exempt income is related to government bond transactions, and few day traders work in those markets.

The 50 states all have different rules about taxation of investment income. Some states with little or no tax on earned income handle investment income differently. Because there are so many different issues, state taxation is beyond the scope of this book. Check with your state revenue department and a state-savvy tax expert to see what you need to know where you live.

What you can't deduct

As you day trade, you'll probably incur expenses that can't be deducted from your taxes. Disappointing, I know, but if you know what these nondeductible expenses are upfront, you can plan accordingly.

What? I can't deduct commissions?

Every time you make a trade, you have to pay a commission to your broker. It may be small, just a few cents per share or a few dollars per trade, but you have to pay it. And you can't deduct that cost.

Before you splutter in outrage, read this: You can't deduct it, but you *can* add it to cost and subtract it from the proceeds of your trade. Here's an example: You buy 100 shares of Microsoft at $29.40 per share, paying a $6.00 commission on the trade. Your total cost for IRS purposes is ($29.40 × 100) + $6.00, which equals $2,946. Later in the day, you sell all 100 shares for $30.00 per share at a $6.00 commission, so your total proceeds for the deal are ($30.00 × 100) – $6.00, or $2,994. Your total profit for tax purposes is $2,994 – $2,946, or $48.00.

Including the commission in the basis of your trade works like a deduction in terms of the amount of tax you pay, but because it's *not* a deduction, it's not subject to the limitations that affect the deductibility of other expenses.

If your state charges transfer taxes on securities, they are handled the same way as commissions.

Attending stockholders' meetings

Companies hold annual meetings for their shareholders, usually at or near the company headquarters. Sometimes these meetings are deathly dull: The board of directors sits around a conference room in a law office and goes through a boilerplate agenda with nothing to discuss. Others are extravaganzas where the company shows off new products, showcases major accomplishments, and takes questions from anyone in attendance. And a few involve contentious issues that can lead to protests and fighting, which is entertaining to watch if you aren't directly affected.

For long-term investors, these meetings can offer valuable insights on a company's prospects. Day traders probably wouldn't find them very useful, and it's just as well, because the IRS won't let anyone deduct the costs of transportation, hotel stays, meals, and other expenses that may be involved in attending a stockholders' meeting.

Attending investment seminars

The financial-services industry offers all kinds of conventions, cruises, and seminars for day traders. You can spend your days attending training seminars instead of actually trading, if you're so inclined. You're welcome to go to these, and in many cases, you should. You may learn things that would help you trade more effectively. However, you can't deduct the costs. Bummer.

Although you can't deduct the costs of attending seminars, you can deduct the costs of investment counsel and advisory services. Some seminars may qualify as investment advice. These idiosyncrasies are why you need an experienced tax adviser to help you.

Did you notice that two of the nondeductible expense categories have the potential to involve travel? The IRS doesn't want people buying ten shares of Hawaiian Electric Industries stock and then trying to write off a trip to the company's annual meeting in Honolulu, nor does it consider cruises that happen to include a talk by the author of a book on investing to be bona fide investment counsel. It sees these activities as vacations, and vacations are not tax deductible. (Of course, if an author of an investment book happened to be on such a cruise, that may be a deductible cost for book promotion. Most likely. Um, not like I know any authors of investment books who may have looked into this or anything.)

Naturally, there are limitations!

You didn't think the IRS would let you take all your deductions automatically, did you? Of course not. Your deductions may be limited, especially if you don't meet the IRS definition of trader.

At-risk rules

The IRS says that your loss is limited by the amount of property you contribute to your investing activities, including money you borrow. In most cases, day trading losses meet the risk definitions, but if you pursue a naked trading strategy that causes you to lose more than your initial investment, you may fall into this category.

Passive activity losses and credits

The IRS defines a *passive* activity as an investment where the investor does not play an active role but does make money. You can deduct passive activity losses only up to the amount of your passive activity income, and you can use credits from passive activity losses only against tax on the income from passive activities. Day trading is generally considered to be active, because you are materially participating, but if you are generating passive losses from other investment activities, you probably won't be able to use them to offset your day-trading gains.

Interest expense limitations

The IRS allows you to deduct investment interest up to the amount of your net investment income, which is your investment income less all your allowable deductible expenses except for interest. If you lost money trading, you can't use the interest deduction to reduce your taxes. What you can do, though, is carry the undeducted investment interest into next year and use it to reduce your taxes on those profits.

You also can't deduct interest expenses on straddles. A *straddle* is an options strategy that involves buying both a put option and a call option on the same stock with the same strike price and expiration date. In most cases, the nondeductible interest and related carrying charges are added to the basis of the straddle (just as commissions are — see the earlier section "Calculating capital gains and losses: Covering all your basis").

Two percent limit

If you do not qualify as a trader to the IRS, you can deduct investment expenses and other miscellaneous itemized deductions only if they add up to more than 2 percent of your adjusted gross income.

Top Secret Tax Information for IRS-Qualified Traders Only

If you meet the IRS qualifications for being a trader (see the earlier section "Stock trading"), you can avoid some of the tax headaches faced by people who trade but are not considered by the taxman to be traders. If you trade as your job, make thousands of trades a year, and rarely hold any position for more than a day, then you can fill out something called Form 3115, *Application for Change in Accounting Method,* and tell the IRS that you want to use the *mark-to-market election* in calculating your capital gains and losses. Form 3115 isn't an easy form to fill out, so you should have a professional do it for you.

The form has to be submitted with your prior year's tax return. If you want to use mark-to-market accounting in 2012, for example, you need to submit Form 3115 when you send your 2011 tax return in April 2012.

You can't use the election in your first year of trading. You first have to prove that you are a trader before you are allowed to get the tax benefits that go with the title. Consider it an apprenticeship.

If you qualify for trader status, you receive two benefits: mark-to-market accounting and increased expense deductions. I cover both in the following sections.

Mark-to-market accounting

Under *mark-to-market accounting,* you no longer have to track capital gains. Instead, you pretend to sell your portfolio at the end of the year and then pretend to repurchase everything at the beginning of the new year so that all capital gains fall into income.

Because day traders usually close all their positions at the end of the day anyway, mark-to-market accounting may not seem like a big deal, but it is: In effect, converting all capital gains to income means that your trades are no longer subject to the wash-sale rule. For most day traders, this lowers taxes and results in fewer paperwork hassles.

If you use mark-to-market accounting, you can no longer get the 15 percent rate on any long-term capital gains from your trading activities. Unless you work with listed options on market indexes, which are considered to show profits that are 60 percent long-term capital gains and 40 percent short-term capital gains, you may not have any long-term capital gains from your trading activities.

Greater deductibility of business expenses

In general, the IRS allows investors to deduct business expenses only if these expenses exceed 2 percent of adjusted gross income. However, anyone who gets to join the charmed circle of IRS-qualified traders gets to deduct 100 percent of expenses, regardless of their adjusted gross income. They get to deduct all their investment interest, too.

One caveat, though: The IRS assumes that people are in the business of trading because they are making money at it. If you lose money for three out of five years, even if it's because your expenses exceeded your investment profits rather than due to trading losses, the IRS will probably kick you out of the club.

Other Important Tax Info: Forms and Deadlines

Knowing what constitutes income, what expenses you can deduct, and what special rules apply if the IRS considers you a qualified trader is all well and good, but when it comes right down to it, you still need to know the more mundane things like what tax forms to fill out and when they're due. This section has the details.

Using the right tax forms

Many of the differences in income and expenses discussed already in this chapter make more sense when you think about how they are reported on your income tax return. In this section, I give you the highlights of some of the most exciting forms for the modern day trader. Note that they are different for those who qualify as traders by IRS standards (refer to the earlier section "Stock trading") than for everyone else who day trades.

- ✓ **Forms for qualified traders:** If you make the mark-to-market election on Form 3115 (refer to the section "Mark-to-market accounting"), you're considered to be in the business of trading. Business expenses for individual tax filers are put on Schedule C of Form 1040, *Profit or Loss from Business*. Then your trading gains and losses are recorded on Part II of Form 4797. If you have any securities at the end of the year in your trading account, pretend that they were sold on the last business day of the year at current fair market value and then immediately reacquired.

- ✓ **Forms for everyone else:** Day traders who are not considered traders by the IRS should itemize business deductions and investment interest expenses on Schedule A of Form 1040. You should attach Form 4952 if you used it to figure your investment interest expense. You report capital gains and losses from your trading on Schedule D of Form 1040, subject to all the limits on losses.

Paying all year: The joy of estimated taxes

If you have been an employee for years and years, all your tax liabilities may have been covered by your payroll tax deductions. The IRS likes it best that way, because then it gets money all year round. Face it: the easier it is to pay, the more likely you are to do it.

People who are self-employed or who have significant earnings from invest-ments and day trading may generate more income than can be covered from payroll withholding. What you need to do is estimate your tax liability four times a year and then write a check for those amounts. (Otherwise, you could face a penalty at tax time.) Estimated taxes are paid on Form 1040 ES and are due April 15, June 15, September 15, and January 15.

Using Self-Directed IRAs

Much of the tax hassle associated with day trading is eliminated if you trade through a self-directed *individual retirement account,* or IRA. Most brokerage firms can set them up for you and handle the necessary paperwork. Although individuals can contribute only $5,000 per year ($6,000 for people older than 50), the money can be substantial for those who have been contributing for a long time. Also, you can roll over money from an employer's retirement plan, such as a 401(k), into an IRA after you leave.

You don't have to pay taxes in an IRA until you retire, and then withdrawals are generally treated as ordinary income. For this reason, an IRA is a great vehicle for day traders: You can post big gains, count all your losses, and avoid wash-sale rules for trading within your IRA. It's a sweet way to let your profits accumulate and compound for years. Of course, there's a catch: You can't sell short, you can't use all options strategies, and your brokerage firm may not want to clear funds through the IRA.

If you are a full-time trader, consider keeping your retirement fund completely separate from your trading funds. That way, you can pay the bills in your golden years without worrying about what happens every trading day. It's a way to reduce stress, plus many retirement funds have tax benefits that may help the bottom line on your trading business.

You can't withdraw money from an IRA account until you turn 59 ½. If you take money out earlier, you pay a 10 percent tax penalty, and that offsets a lot of the advantages. If you need income from your trading activities to cover your living expenses before then, an IRA is probably not the best way to set up your day-trading account.

Chapter 16

But Did You Make Money? Testing, Tracking, and Evaluating Performance

*A*ny one trade involves a lot of variables: price bought, price sold, commissions charged, volume traded, and amount of leverage used. And each of these affects your overall performance. In the heat of a trading day, it can be hard to juggle all these factors and determine just how well you did or didn't do.

Performance calculation starts before you trade. You want to test your strategies and see whether they work for you, which requires backtesting and paper trading. You want to keep track of your trades in real time with the help of a trading diary. And then, on a periodic basis (at least monthly), you should review your progress to see how much money you're making and whether you need to change your strategy.

Before You Trade: Testing Your System

Performance measurement starts before the trading does. That's because you want to figure out how you'll trade before you start working with real money. Chapter 3 describes some of the different securities that can be traded on a daily basis, whereas Chapters 6 through 11 cover some of the strategies that day traders use. After you figure out the combinations of securities and strategies you want to use, you want to see whether they would have made you money in the past. Then you should try them to see whether they still work now.

The happy news? You can do all this without risking a dime, except of course for the money you may spend on backtesting and simulation software. You knew there had to be a catch, right? Consider it an investment in the success of your business.

Backtesting

In *backtesting*, a trader specifies the strategy that he or she would use and then runs that strategy through a database of historic securities prices to see whether it would have made money. The test includes assumptions about commissions, leverage, and position size. The results give information on returns, volatility, and win-loss ratios that you can use to refine a trading strategy and implement it well.

Starting with a hypothesis

What trades do you want to do? After you figure out what and how to trade, you can start setting forth what your strategy will be. Will you look for high-momentum, small-cap stocks? Seek price changes related to news events in agricultural commodities? Ride large-cap stocks within their ranges? Arbitrage stock index futures and their options?

After you do your research, you can lay out your strategy as a hypothesis, which may be something like this: "High-momentum, small-cap stocks tend to close up for the day, so I can buy them in the morning and make money selling them in the afternoon." Or this: "News events take at least half an hour to affect corn prices, so I can buy or sell on the news and make a profit." With this statement, you can move on to the test to see whether your hypothesis holds.

One of the most valuable parts about backtesting is that you have to be very specific about what your trading rule is. Computers cannot understand vague instructions, and if you find that your trading strategy is too complicated to write out and set into a backtesting program, it's probably too complicated for you to follow.

Running the test

Say you start with something simple: Maybe you have reason to think that pharmaceutical companies that are moving down in price on decreasing volume will turn and close up for the day. The first thing you do is enter that into the software: the industry group and the buy pattern that you're looking for. The results will show whether your hunch is correct and how often and for what time periods.

If you like what you see, you can add more variables. What happens if you add *leverage* (use borrowed money) in your trades? Leverage increases your risk of loss, but it also increases your potential return. How does that affect your trade? Suppose you increase the size of your trades, making fewer but larger ones. Would that help you make more money or less? By playing around with the system, you can get a good sense of the best way to make money with your trade ideas. You can also get a sense of when your rule won't work, which can help you avoid problems.

If your strategy doesn't work in testing, you want to ask yourself why not. Is your theory not as good as you thought, or are the markets different now? And if they are different now, how are they different? Unless you can answer those questions, you're just engaging in wishful thinking, and wishful thinking will destroy any trader, no matter what the test results may be.

Most backtesting software allows for optimization, which means that it can come up with the leverage, position, holding period, and other parameters that will generate the best risk-adjusted return given the data on hand. You can then compare this result to your trading style and your capital position to see whether it works.

Backtesting is subject to something that traders call *over-optimization,* mathematicians call *curve-fitting,* and analysts call *data mining.* All these terms mean that the person performing the test looks at a past time where the market performed well and then identifies all the variables and specifications that generated that performance. Although over-optimization sounds great, what often happens is that the test generates a model that includes unnecessary variables and that makes no logical sense in practice. If you find a strategy that works when the stock closes up one day, down two days, then up a third day, followed by four down days when it hits an intraday high, you probably haven't made an amazing discovery; you've just fit the curve.

People often have elaborate ideas of how the random shuffle feature works on their MP3 players. Ask and they'll give you their own interesting theory for how certain types of songs show up more often than others, how songs with similar titles seem to be played together, and other patterns that they are sure must be there. Why? Because human beings have evolved to see patterns, even when no pattern exists. It's the same with the market. It's entirely possible that, although the results of your test look great, they only show a random event that happened to work once. That's why you need to keep testing, even after you start trading.

Comparing the results with market cycles

The markets change every day in response to new regulations, interest rate fluctuations, economic conditions, nasty world events, and run-of-the-mill news events. (It's like the joke about weather: If you don't like it now, wait a minute, and it'll change.) Different securities and strategies do better in some market climates than in others.

When you backtest, be sure to do so over a long enough period of time so that you can see how your strategy would work over different market conditions. Here are some things to check:

- ✔ How did the strategy do in periods of inflation? Economic growth? High interest rates? Low interest rates?

- ✔ What was happening in the markets during the time that the strategy worked best? What was happening when it worked worst? How likely is either of those to happen again?

- ✔ How does market volatility affect the strategy? Is the security more volatile than the market, less volatile, or does it seem to be removed from the market?

- ✔ Have major changes occurred in the sector over the period of the test? Examples of these types of changes include new technologies that increase demand for certain commodities or changes in regulation that make industries obsolete. Does this mean that past performance still applies?

- ✔ Have there been changes in the way that the security trades? For example, the bulk of trading in most commodities used to take place in open-outcry trading pits. Now, trading is almost entirely electronic. How do your test results look given current trading technologies?

In the capital assets pricing model, which is a key part of academic finance theory, the market risk is known as *beta*. The value that a portfolio manager adds to investment performance is known as *alpha*. In the long run, conventional finance theory says that the return on a diversified portfolio comes from beta; alpha doesn't exist, so investors can't beat the market in the long run. In the short run, where day traders play, this relationship may not be so strong.

Remember the maximum maxim in finance: Past performance is not indicative of future results. A strategy may test perfectly, but that doesn't mean it will continue to work. Backtesting is an important step to successful day trading, but it is only one step.

Simulation trading

With a backtested strategy in hand, you may be tempted to start putting real money on the line. Don't, at least not yet. Start with what is known variously as *ghost trading, paper trading,* and *simulation trading.* Sit down in front of your computer screen and start watching the price quotes. When you see your ideal entry point, write it down. When you see your exit point, write it down. (Or use the simulation functions available from many brokers to save yourself the paper and pencil work.) Do exactly what you plan to do with real money, just don't use the money. Then figure out what your performance would be.

If your strategy doesn't generate a lot of trades, you can probably keep track with a pen and paper and then enter the data into a spreadsheet to calculate the effects of commissions and leverage and to analyze the performance on both a percentage and a win-loss basis. How does it look?

For more complex strategies that involve a large number of trades on a large number of securities, you may want to use a trading-simulation software package. These packages mimic trading software (and are usually added features to trading software packages; see Chapters 11 and 12 for more information). They let you enter the size of your order, let you use leverage, and tell you whether your trade can be executed given current market conditions.

Markets are affected by supply and demand, and your trade can affect that, which is the biggest drawback of simulation trading: It's difficult to take the market effects of your trade into account in any reliable way, especially if you'll be trading large positions in thinly traded markets.

The results of your trading simulation can help you refine your trading strategy further. Does it work in current market conditions? Are you able to identify entry and exit points? Can you execute enough trades to make your day-trading efforts financially worthwhile? Do you want to refine your strategy some more, or are you ready to go with it?

Your tests won't guarantee your results, and they won't show you how you'll react under the real pressure of real markets and real money. However, if your system doesn't work well under perfect conditions, it is unlikely to do better in actual conditions.

Finding a suitable strategy may take a long time. Some traders report spending months finding a strategy they felt comfortable using. Day trading is a business like any other. Consider this part of the market research and education process that you need to go through, just as you'd spend time doing research before opening a store or training for a new career. Be patient. It's better to do good simulation for months than to lose thousands of real dollars in hours.

Backtesting and simulation software

Several vendors have risen to meet the challenge of backtesting, and it is becoming standard on more and more trading platforms. The list in this section is by no means exhaustive, nor is it an endorsement of their services. It's just a good place for you to start your research.

If you're just getting started with trading, you may want to try a cheaper package just to see how backtesting and simulation works. If you already have an account with a brokerage firm, check to see whether backtesting and simulation are among the services offered. You can always move up to a more sophisticated backtesting package as your needs change or if you start pursuing exotic strategies with unusual securities.

The more sophisticated the package, the pricier it is. If you have the programming expertise or if your strategy is not well represented in current backtesting programs, you may want to create your own system. Many software-savvy day traders write programs using Excel's Visual Basic functions, allowing them to create custom tests that they then run against price databases to backtest strategies.

AmiBroker

AmiBroker (www.amibroker.com) offers a robust backtesting service at a relatively low price. For that reason, it's a popular choice with people who are getting started in day trading and who don't have more expensive services. It also allows users to make sophisticated technical charts that they can use to monitor the markets. One drawback is that you may have to pay extra for the market-price-quote data, depending on what securities and time periods you want to test.

Investor/RT

Developed by a company called Linn Software (www.linnsoft.com), Investor/RT allows you to develop your own tests and create your own programs. It has packages for Macs, which makes it popular with traders who prefer Apple computers. Its users tend to be sophisticated about their trading systems and backtesting requirements; this software isn't really for beginners.

MetaStock

As the name implies, MetaStock (www.metastock.com) is designed for traders who work in stocks, although a MetaStock package is available especially for currency traders, and the regular packages include capabilities for futures and commodities traders. It defines traders as *end-of-day* (those who make decisions about trading tomorrow based on numbers at the end of today's trading) and as *real-time* (those who make decisions during the trading day). Most day traders are real-time traders. The company is owned by Thomson Reuters, a major financial-information services company.

NinjaTrader

NinjaTrader (www.ninjatrader.com) is a popular software package used for managing and programming traders. It includes great backtesting capabilities, too. The platform works with many different brokerage firms, for a fee, but the charting and trade testing capabilities are free. That may be why it's become one of the most popular services for backtesting.

OptionVue

If you trade options, you may want to check out OptionVue (www.optionvue.com), which offers a range of analytical tools on the options markets. The software's BackTrader module, an add-on feature, helps you learn more about options markets, test new strategies, and examine relationships between options and the underlying stocks — really useful information for people working in equity markets.

Tradecision

Tradecision's (www.tradecision.com) trade-analysis software package is a little pricier than most retail trading alternatives, but it offers more advanced capabilities, including an analysis of the strengths and weaknesses of different trading rules. It can incorporate advanced money-management techniques and artificial intelligence to develop more predictions about performance in different market conditions. The system may be overkill for most new day traders, but it can come in handy for some.

TradeStation

TradeStation (www.tradestation.com) is an online broker that specializes in services for day traders. Its strategy testing service lets you specify different trading parameters, and then it shows you where these trades would have taken place in the past, using price charts. That way, you can see what would have happened, which is helpful if you're good at technical analysis. It also generates a report of the strategy, showing dollar, percentage, and win-loss performance over different time periods. It doesn't have a trade-simulation feature.

Trading Blox

The Trading Blox software system (www.tradingblox.com) was developed by professional traders who needed to test their own theories and who didn't want to do a lot of programming to do it. It comes in three versions (and price levels), ranging from basic to sophisticated, and the company boasts that it works with some commercial trading firms. Of course, some of its capabilities may be more than you need when you're starting out.

During the Day: Tracking Your Trades

After you put your strategy to work during the trading day, it's easy to let the energy and emotion overtake you. You get sloppy and stop keeping track of what's happening. And that's not good. Day trading is not a video game; it's a job. Keeping careful records helps you identify not only how well you follow your strategy but also ways to refine it. These records can also show you how successful your trading is, and it makes your life a lot easier when tax time comes around. (Refer to Chapter 15 for more information on what the friendly folks at the IRS expect from traders, besides a cut of their profits.)

Setting up your spreadsheet

The easiest way to get started tracking your trades is with a spreadsheet software program such as Microsoft Excel. Set up columns for the asset being purchased, the time of the trade, the price, the quantity purchased, and the commission. Then set up similar columns to show what happens when the position is closed out. Finally, calculate your performance based on the change in the security's price and the dollars and percentage return on your trade. Figure 16-1 gives you an example.

Trade Tracker
2/1/07

POSITIONS Symbol	Description	Purchase Date	Purchase Time	Purchase Price	Lot Attempted	Lot Filled	Comm.	Total Cost	Sale Time	Sale Price	Sale Quantity	Comm.	Total Proceeds	Gain/Loss in Points	Gain/Loss in Dollars	Gain/Loss in Percent
INTC	Intel	2/1/07	9:31	20.98	1,000	1,000	6.00	(20,986.00)	9:52	21.10	1000	6.00	21,094.00	12	108.00	0.51%
NVDA	Nvidia	2/1/07	9:33	30.38	1000	1,000	6.00	(30,374.00)	9:58	30.87	1000	6.00	30,864.00	49	490.00	1.61%
AKAM	Akamai	2/1/07	9:46	57.44	500	500	3.00	(28,717.00)	10:36	56.60	500	3.00	28,297.00	-84	(420.00)	-1.46%
INTC	Intel	2/1/07	10:18	21.08	1000	1,000	6.00	(21,074.00)	10:40	20.95	1000	6.00	20,944.00	-13	(130.00)	-0.62%
AKAM	Akamai	2/1/07	11:08	55.09	500	200	1.20	(11,016.80)	12:08	55.39	200	1.20	11,076.80	30	60.00	0.54%
NVDA	Nvidia	2/1/07	11:08	30.38	1000	1,000	6.00	(30,374.00)	11:28	30.31	1000	6.00	30,304.00	-7	(70.00)	-0.23%
INTC	Intel	2/1/07	11:11	20.91	1000	1,000	6.00	(20,904.00)	11:45	21.03	1000	6.00	21,024.00	12	120.00	0.57%
NVDA	Nvidia	2/1/07	11:55	30.38	1000	1,000	6.00	(30,374.00)	12:15	30.72	1000	6.00	30,714.00	34	340.00	1.12%
INTC	Intel	2/1/07	12:23	20.93	1000	1,000	6.00	(20,924.00)	12:56	21.07	1000	6.00	21,064.00	14	140.00	0.67%
INTC	Intel	2/1/07	13:08	21.05	1000	1,000	6.00	(21,044.00)	13:52	21.04	1000	6.00	21,034.00	-1	(10.00)	-0.05%
AKAM	Akamai	2/1/07	13:22	55.43	500	500	3.00	(27,712.00)	13:41	55.48	500	3.00	27,737.00	5	25.00	0.09%
INTC	Intel	2/1/07	14:05	21.03	1000	1,000	6.00	(21,024.00)	14:26	21.09	1000	6.00	21,084.00	6	60.00	0.29%
NVDA	Nvidia	2/1/07	14:09	30.52	1000	1,000	6.00	(30,514.00)	15:09	30.54	1000	6.00	30,534.00	2	20.00	0.07%
INTC	Intel	2/1/07	15:05	21.10	1000	1,000	6.00	(21,094.00)	15:59	21.11	1000	6.00	21,104.00	1	10.00	0.05%

Starting Capital:		$ 165,239.00
Day's Profit:		$ 743.00
Percent Change:		0.45%
Ending Capital:		$ 165,982.00
Ratio of winning to losing trades:		10 : 4
Hourly Wage:		$ 92.88
Total commissions paid:		$ 146.40

Figure 16-1: You can use this sample to make your own trade-tracking spreadsheet.

Some brokerage firms and trading platforms automatically store your trade data for analysis. You can then download the data into your own spreadsheet or work with it in your trading software, making analysis simple. If you make too many trades to keep track of manually, then this feature will be especially important to you.

Pulling everything into a profit and loss statement

If you refer to the bottom of Figure 16-1, you see some quick summary statistics on how the day's trading went: trading profits net of commissions, trading profits as a percentage of trading capital, and the ratio of winning to losing transactions. This information should be transferred into another spreadsheet so that you can track your ongoing success. Figure 16-2 shows an example of a profit and loss spreadsheet.

Profit and Loss

	Initial Capital	Net Profit (Loss)	Ending Capital	Percentage Change	Hourly Wage
1/3/07	$ 161,298	$ 134	$ 161,432	0.08%	$ 16.75
1/4/07	$ 161,432	$ (268)	$ 161,164	-0.17%	$ (33.50)
1/5/07	$ 161,164	$ 450	$ 161,614	0.28%	$ 56.25
1/8/07	$ 161,614	$ (183)	$ 161,431	-0.1 1%	$ (22.88)
1/9/07	$ 161,431	$ 192	$ 161,623	0.12%	$ 24.00
1/10/07	$ 161,623	$ 598	$ 162,221	0.37%	$ 74.75
1/11/07	$ 162,221	$ (168)	$ 162,053	-0.10%	$ (21.00)
1/12/07	$ 162,053	$ 987	$ 163,040	0.61%	$ 123.38
1/16/07	$ 163,040	$ (196)	$ 162,844	-0.12%	$ (24.50)
1/17/07	$ 162,844	$ 59	$ 162,903	0.04%	$ 7.38
1/18/07	$ 162,903	$ (273)	$ 162,630	-0.17%	$ (34.13)
1/19/07	$ 162,630	$ (124)	$ 162,506	-0.08%	$ (15.50)
1/22/07	$ 162,506	$ 689	$ 163,195	0.42%	$ 86.13
1/23/07	$ 163,195	$ (397)	$ 162,798	-0.24%	$ (49.63)
1/24/07	$ 162,798	$ 967	$ 163,765	0.59%	$ 120.88
1/25/07	$ 163,765	$ (387)	$ 163,378	-0.24%	$ (48.38)
1/26/07	$ 163,378	$ 469	$ 163,847	0.29%	$ 58.63
1/29/07	$ 163,847	$ 798	$ 164,645	0.49%	$ 99.75
1/30/07	$ 164,645	$ (129)	$ 164,516	-0.08%	$ (16.13)
1/31/07	$ 164,516	$ 723	$ 165,239	0.44%	$ 90.38
January:	$ 161,298	$ 3,941	$ 165,239	2.44%	$ 24.63
2/1/07	$ 165,239	$ 743	$ 165,982	0.45%	$ 92.88

Figure 16-2: A sample profit and loss spreadsheet.

Calculate your hourly wage for each day that you trade. Simply take each day's profit and divide it by the number of hours that you worked. That number, more than any other, can help you see whether it makes sense for you to keep trading or whether you'd be better off pursuing a different line of work. If you find that calculating the number daily is too stressful, try doing it monthly.

Keeping a trading diary

As part of your trading spreadsheet or in addition to it, you should track the reasons for every trade. Was the reason for the trade because of a signal from your system? Because of a hunch? Because you saw an opportunity that was too good to pass up? Also track how the trade worked out. Is your trading system giving off good signals? Are you following them? Are your hunches so good that maybe your system needs to be refined? Are you missing good trades because you are following your gut and not the data in front of you?

Over time, some trading systems stop working because too many people figure them out. If you can watch for that, you can tweak your system as you go. The big guys do this, too; the downside of the high-frequency, algorithmic trading that so many hedge funds use is that the algorithms have to be rewritten all the time.

A *trading diary* gives you information to systematically assess your trading. Start by writing down why you are making a particular trade. Do this when you make the trade. (If you wait until later, you'll forget, and you'll change your logic to suit your needs. That's just what people do, you know?) Enter the information in a spreadsheet, jot something quick on a piece of scratch paper, or keep a notebook dedicated to your trading. Your recording system doesn't have to be fancy, as long as you take the time to make the notes that you can refer to.

Some traders create a form and make copies of it and then keep a stack on hand so that they can easily fill them out during the day. They even create predetermined indicators that match their strategies and that they can check off or circle. At the end of the day, they collect their diary sheets into a three-ring binder that they can refer back to when the time comes to evaluate their trading strategy and their performance.

Figure 16-3 offers an example of a trading diary. You can customize it for your own trading strategy, including those indicators that matter most to you.

The trading diary form in Figure 16-3 is just an example. If your trading style is so fast that you don't have time to fill it out, don't fret. Instead, come up with some kind of shorthand that lets you keep a running tally of trades made based on a signal from your system, trades based on your own hunches, and trades based on other interpretations of market conditions. Then match your notes against the trader confirmations from your broker to see how you did.

Trading Diary

Date: _____
Time: _____
Security Name: _____ Symbol: _____ Market: _____

Price entered: _____ Long/short?   long   short
Quantity: _____ Leverage used?   yes   no

Indicators:
Price trend is   rising   falling   rangebound
Volume is   rising   falling   steady
Sector is   rising   falling   rangebound
Market is   rising   falling   rangebound
Technical Pattern: _____

Price closed: _____
Quantity: _____
Time: _____

Indicators:
Price trend is   rising   falling   rangebound
Volume is   rising   falling   steady
Sector is   rising   falling   rangebound
Market is   rising   falling   rangebound
Technical Pattern: _____

I initiated this trade because (check one):
_____ The trading system signalled it
_____ I had a hunch (explain below)
_____ The market looked right, even though the signal didn't go off (explain below)
_____ Other (explain below)

I closed out this trade because (check one):
_____ The trading system signalled it
_____ I needed to cut my losses
_____ I had a hunch (explain below)
_____ The market looked right, even though the signal didn't go off (explain below)
_____ Other (explain below)

Explanation and lessons learned:

_____
_____
_____
_____
_____
_____
_____

Figure 16-3:
A trading diary should be customized to your own preferences.

After You Trade: Calculating Overall Performance

Calculating performance seems easy: Simply use the balance at the end of the year and the balance at the start of the year to find the percentage change. But what if you added money to your investment in the middle of the year? What if you took cash out in the middle of the year to buy a new computer? Before you know it, you're left with algebra unlike any you've seen since high school and you're stuck solving it if you want to see how you're doing.

In addition to the increase in your assets, you want to track your *volatility,* which is how much your gains and losses can fluctuate. Volatility is an important measure of risk, especially if your trading strategy relies on leverage (see Chapter 9 for more information on that).

Reviewing types of return

The investment performance calculation starts by dividing returns into different categories: income, short-term capital gains, and long-term capital gains. Although almost all a day trader's gains come from short-term capital gains, I go over the definitions of each so that you know the differences.

Income

When investors talk about *income returns,* they mean regular payments from their investments, usually in the form of dividends from stock or interest payments on bonds. As a day trader, you may earn income on the cash balance in your brokerage account but probably not from your trading activities.

Capital gains

A *capital gain* is the price appreciation in an asset — a stock, a bond, a house, or whatever it is that you're investing in. You buy it at one price, sell it at another, and the difference is a capital gain. (Unless, of course, you sell the asset for less than you paid, and then you have a capital loss.)

For tax purposes, capital gains are classified as either long-term or short-term. Under the current tax law, any capital gain on an asset held for less than one year is considered to be a short-term gain, and if the asset is owned for one year or more before it's sold, then it's considered to be a long-term capital gain. The difference isn't semantic; long-term capital gains are taxed at lower rates than short-term capital gains. You can read all about that and then some in Chapter 15.

Income in tax terms is different from income in financial terms. Much of what an investor would consider to be a capital gain, such as the short-term capital gains that day traders generate, the IRS considers to be income.

Calculating returns

Give someone with a numerical bent a list of numbers and a calculator, and she can some up with several different relationships between the numbers. After the asset values for each time period have been determined, rates of return can be calculated. But how? And over how long a time period? The process gets a little more complicated because money is coming in and going out while the asset values move up and down. The following sections outline different calculations you can use to figure out your investment returns.

Calculating compound average rate of return (CAGR)

The most common way to calculate investment returns is to use a time-weighted average. This method is perfect for traders who start with one pool of money and don't add to it or take money out. This is also called the *compound average rate of return* (CAGR). If you are looking at only one month or one year, it's a simple percentage. To calculate performance on a percentage basis, you use this equation:

$$\frac{EOY - BOY}{BOY}$$

EOY represents the end of year asset value, and *BOY* represents the beginning of year value. The result is the percentage return for one year, and to calculate it, you use simple arithmetic.

Now if you want to look at your return over a period of several years, you need to look at the *compound* return rather than the simple return for each year. The compound return shows you how your investment is growing. You are getting returns on top of returns, and that's a good thing. But the math gets a little complicated because now you have to use the root function on your calculator. The equation for compound annual growth looks like this:

$$\sqrt[N]{\frac{EOP}{BOP}} - 1$$

EOP represents the end of the total time period, *BOP* represents the beginning of the total time period, and *N* is the number of years that you're looking at.

The basic percentage rate of return is great; it's an accurate, intuitive measure of how much gain you're generating from your trading activities. As long as you don't take any money out of your trading account or put any money into it, you're set.

Calculating performance when you make deposits and withdrawals

You may be putting money into your account. Maybe you have a salaried job and are day trading on the side, or maybe your spouse gives you a percentage of his income to add to your trading account. You may also be taking money out of your day-trading account to cover your living expenses or to put into other investment opportunities. All that money flowing into and out of your account can really screw up your performance calculation. You need a way to calculate the performance of your trading system without considering the deposits and withdrawals to your trading account.

Here's an example: You start day trading on January 1 with $100,000 in your account. On May 1, your income tax refund from last year arrives, and you add $1,000 of the money to your account and start trading with it. On December 1, you take out $5,000 to buy holiday presents. At the end of the year, your account is worth $115,000. How did you do?

As a day trader, you have a few methods at your disposal for calculating your performance when you make withdrawals and deposits:

- ✔ **The Modified Dietz method** loses a little accuracy but makes up for it with simplicity.

- ✔ **The time-weighted rate of return** isolates investment and trading performance from the rest of the account.

- ✔ **The dollar-weighted rate of return** has many flaws but gives a sense of what the account holder has.

Read on to see the return that would be calculated using each of these methods.

Modified Dietz method

The *Modified Dietz method* is related to the simple percent change formula, but it adjusts the beginning and ending period amounts for the cash inflows and cash outflows. The equation for the Modified Dietz method looks like this:

$$\frac{EOY - BOY - deposits + withdrawals}{BOY + deposits - withdrawals}$$

If you plug in the numbers from the example, you get

$$\frac{115,000 - 100,000 - 1,000 + 5,000}{100,000 + 1,000 - 5,000}$$

Do the math and you see that the result is 19.8 percent.

The advantage of the Modified Dietz method is that it's so easy to do. You can use it when you want a rough idea of how you are doing with your trading but you don't have the time to run a more detailed analysis. The key disadvantage is that it doesn't consider the timing of the deposits and withdrawals. It would generate the same answer if you took out $5,000 in May and put in $1,000 in December, even though the amount of money you would have to trade between May 1 and December 1 would be very different.

Time-weighted rate of return

The *time-weighted rate of return* shows the investment performance as a percentage of the assets at hand to trade. This method is the standard of trader evaluation, but the math is much more complicated than with the basic percentage change or the Modified Dietz method. You need to calculate the CAGR for each time period and then do a second calculation to incorporate each of those over a longer period. Using the preceding example, you'd calculate one return for the first four months of the year, another for the next seven months, and then a third return for the month of December. These three returns would then be multiplied to generate a return for the year.

The general equation you use to figure the time-weighted rate of return looks like this:

$$\sqrt[N]{\left(1+r_{p1}\right)\left(1+r_{p2}\right)\left(1+r_{p3}\right)\cdots\left(1+r_{pn}\right)} - 1$$

N is the total number of time periods that you are looking at, and *rpn* is the return for that particular time period. To make the calculations easier, you can do it in a spreadsheet. Figure 16-4 shows the time-weighted return for this example. As you can see, the result is 18.78 percent, a little below the Modified Dietz return.

	January	May	December
Beginning of Period Account Value	$ 100,000	$ 109,000	$ 123,000
Deposit/(Withdrawal)	$ -	$ 1,000	$ (5,000)
Adjusted Beginning Account Value	$ 100,000	$ 110,000	$ 118,000
Trading Earnings	$ 9,000	$ 13,000	$ (3,000)
End-of-Period Account Value	$ 109,000	$ 123,000	$ 115,000
Period Percentage Return:	9.00%	11.82%	-2.54%
Annual Return:			18.78%

Figure 16-4: Here's an example of the time-weighted rate of return calculation.

If you plan on adding to or taking money out of your account, you can make your return calculations much easier by setting a regular schedule and sticking to it. Otherwise, you have to do calculations for fractional time periods. It's not impossible, but it's kind of a hassle.

The time-weighted rate of return gives you the best sense of your trading performance, and its precision more than offsets the complexity of the calculation. You want to look at this number when you are deciding whether to change or refine your strategy.

Dollar-weighted returns

The *dollar-weighted return,* also called the *money-weighted return,* is the rate that makes the net present value of a stream of numbers equal to zero. That calculation is also called the *internal rate of return* or *IRR,* and it is used for other things than just return calculations. You can use it to determine what the return is for a stream of numbers over time and to calculate returns when you're putting money into or taking money out of your trading account. And if you have a financial calculator such as the Hewlett-PackardHP17BII+ or the Texas Instruments BA2+, the calculations are pretty easy.

Ah, but there's a catch! Although useful, the dollar-weighted method can misstate returns and occasionally shows nonsensical results if too many negative returns appear in a series. And yes, day traders often have negative returns. If you get a result showing a ridiculously large positive or a ridiculously small negative return (like −15,989.9 percent, for example), you may want to try another calculation.

Figure 16-5 shows the dollar-weighted rate of return using the same data used in the two preceding examples.

	January	May	December
Beginning of Period Account Value	$ 100,000	$ 109,000	$ 123,000
Deposit/(Withdrawal)	$ -	$ 1,000	$ (5,000)
Adjusted Beginning Account Value	$ 100,000	$ 110,000	$ 118,000
Trading Earnings	$ 9,000	$ 13,000	$ (3,000)
End-of-Period Account Value	$ 109,000	$ 123,000	$ 115,000
Period Percentage Return:	9.00%	11.82%	-2.54%
Annual Return:			12.10%

Figure 16-5: Calculating the dollar-weighted rate of return.

The result is 12.1 percent, lower than the other two examples because the dollar-weighted return overstates the withdrawal and the loss in the last month of the year. The withdrawals affect the account's spending power, offsetting the investment performance. But the overall account balance is up more than 12.1 percent, even considering the deposit at the beginning of May. The weight of the cash flows threw off this calculation.

Because of the problems with dollar-weighted returns, professional investors who analyze investment returns usually prefer the time-weighted, compound average approach. Still, the dollar-weighted return has some value, especially for an investor who wants to know how the asset value has changed over time. Because a day trader is usually both an investor and an account owner, the dollar-weighted rate of return can show whether the investment performance is affecting spending power. This measure is particularly useful if you are trying to decide whether to continue day trading.

Just as you have alternatives in calculating your performance, so too does anyone trying to sell you a trading system or training course. Ask questions about the performance calculation method and how cash flows and expenses are handled. The numbers may not look so great once you grade the math behind them.

Determining the risk to your return

Now that you have return numbers from your profit and loss statements and your return calculations, it's time to perform black-belt performance jujitsu and determine your risk levels. I'm not going to go into all of the many risk and volatility measures out there, because believe me, the good editors of the *For Dummies* books don't want to proofread all the math. In fact, some of these measures may be more math than *you* want to do. That's okay. Even if you look at just a few measures, you'll have more information than if you ignore them all.

Batting average — er, win-loss percentage

Baseball players are judged by how often they hit the ball. After all, they can't score until they get on base, and they can't get on base without a hit or a walk. The number of hits relative to the number of times at bat is the batting average. It's a simple, beautiful number.

Day traders often calculate their batting average, too, although they may call it their *win-loss percentage* or *win ratio*. It's the same: the number of successful trades to the total number of trades. Not all trades have to work out for you to make money, but the more often the trades work for you, the better your overall performance is likely to be. If you have both good performance and a high batting average, then your strategy may have less risk than one that relies on just a handful of home run trades amidst a bunch of strikeouts.

Standard deviation

Want something harder than your batting average? Turn to *standard deviation,* which is tricky to calculate without a spreadsheet but forms the core of many risk measures out there.

The standard deviation calculation starts with the average return over a given time period. This is the *expected* return, the return that, on average, you get if you stick with your trading strategy. But any given week, month, or year, the return may be very different from what you expect. The more likely you are to get what you expect, the less risk you take. Insured bank savings accounts pay a low interest rate, but the rate is guaranteed. Day trading offers the potential for much higher returns but also the possibility that you could lose everything any one month — especially if you can't stick to your trading discipline.

The explanation is a lot easier to understand after you take a gander at Figure 16-6.

Calculating Standard Deviation

	Step One: **Find the expected return**		**Step Two:** **Subtract expected return** **from each reported return**		**Step Three:** **Calculate the square** **of each difference**
	Percentage **Return**		**R-E(R)**		**(R-E(R))^2**
January	(0.02)		(0.0211)		0.0004
February	0.01		0.0079		0.0001
March	(0.00)		(0.0040)		0.0000
April	0.09		0.0849		0.0072
May	0.01		0.0082		0.0001
June	0.01		0.0082		0.0001
July	(0.08)		(0.0818)		0.0067
August	0.02		0.0182		0.0003
September	0.03		0.0282		0.0008
October	(0.04)		(0.0418)		0.0017
November	(0.01)		(0.0118)		0.0001
December	0.01		0.0049		0.0000
Total	0.02			Sum of the squares:	0.0176
E(R)	0.0018	**Step Four:**		Average of the sum of the squares	0.0015
		Step Five:		Square root of the average of the sum of the squares, also known as standard deviation	0.0383

Figure 16-6: Calculating standard deviation.

As this figure shows, you calculate standard deviation through a series of steps:

1. **Take every return over the time period and then find the average.** A simple mean will do. Here, there are 12 months, so I added all 12 returns and then divided by 12.

2. **Subtract the average from each of the 12 returns.** This calculation shows how much any one return differs from the average, to give you a sense of how much the returns can go back and forth.

3. **Square the differences you found in Step 2 (multiply them by themselves) to get rid of the negative numbers.** When you add those up, you get a number known in statistics as the *sum of the squares*.

4. **Find the average of the sum of the squares.**

5. **Calculate the square root of the average of the sum of the squares.** That square root from this step is the *standard deviation,* the magic number you're looking for.

Of course, you don't have to do all of this math. Almost all trading software calculates standard deviation automatically, but at least you now know where the calculation comes from.

The higher the standard deviation, the riskier the strategy. This number can help you determine how comfortable you are with different trading techniques you may be backtesting, as well as whether you want to stick with your current strategy.

In academic terms, *risk* is the likelihood of getting any return other than the return you expect. To most normal human beings, there's no risk in getting more than you expect; the problem is in getting less of a return than you were counting on. This is a key limitation of risk evaluation. Of course, a few periods of better-than-expected returns are often followed by a run of worse-than-expected returns as performance reverts to the mean.

The truism that past performance is no indicator of future results applies to risk as well as to return.

Using benchmarks to evaluate your performance

To understand your performance numbers, you need one more step: what your performance is relative to what else you could be doing with your money. The following sections have the details.

Performance relative to an index

The most common way to think about investment performance is relative to a *market index*. These are the measures of the overall market that are quoted all the time in the news, such as the Standard & Poor's 500 and the Dow Jones Industrial Average. Not only are these widely watched, but many mutual funds and futures contracts are designed to mimic their performance. That means investors can always do at least as well as the index itself, if their investment objectives call for exposure to that part of the broad investment market.

One big problem is that day traders often look at the wrong index for the type of investment that they have. They'll compare the performance of trading in agricultural commodities to the Standard & Poor's 500 when a commodities index would be a better measure. And the indexes assume that the assets in question are held for the long haul rather than traded every few minutes or every few hours.

If you aren't sure what index to use, check a financial website such as Yahoo! Finance (http://finance.yahoo.com/indices) or check out the Market Lab section of *Barron's* (www.barrons.com), a weekly financial publication put out by Dow Jones & Company, the same people who publish *The Wall Street Journal* and the Dow Jones Industrial Average. Both of these have lengthy lists of different stock, bond, and commodity indexes covering the United States and the world. You can find the one that best matches your preferred markets and use it to compare your performance.

In some cases, your trading practices may overlap more than one index. If so, pick the indexes that are appropriate and compare them only to those trades that match. If you trade 40 percent currencies and 60 percent metals, then you should create your own hybrid index that's 40 percent currencies and 60 percent metals.

Performance relative to your time

In the earlier section "Pulling everything into a profit and loss statement," where I talk about tracking your trades and doing a profit and loss statement, I say that you should calculate your hourly wage. There's a reason for that. Instead of day trading, you could put your money in a nice, simple index mutual fund and take a regular job. If your hourly wage is less than what you can earn elsewhere, you may want to consider doing just that.

Of course, there are benefits to working on your own that don't often show up in your bank account. I say this as someone who left finance to be a financial writer. If you enjoy day trading and if you make enough money to suit your lifestyle, by all means, don't let the relative numbers stop you.

Performance relative to other traders

You probably want to know how you're doing relative to other people who are trading. However, you'll probably never know. No central repository of trading returns exists (although wouldn't it be interesting if the brokerage firms or exchanges could report that?). Some academics have done studies of day-trading returns, but they're working with historic data stripped of customer information.

On message boards and at get-togethers, you may hear other traders talk about their returns. Take this information with an entire box of salt. Some people lie. Others exaggerate or obfuscate. Someone who has average or poor returns may want to lie to try to impress others, while those with great returns may not want to call attention to their prowess.

Ignore whatever other traders tell you about their returns. If you are satisfied with your performance relative to your risk and your time, nothing else matters.

Chapter 17

Day Trading for Investors

. . . .

In This Chapter

▶ Developing the trader's discipline

▶ Marking market momentum

▶ Seeing when trading strategies are the best move

. . . .

*I*t takes a special person to be a day trader — one who has quick reflexes, a strong stomach, and a short-term perspective on the markets. Not everyone's meant to parcel out his or her workday a minute at a time. Most people do better with a long-term perspective on their finances, looking to match their investments with their goals and thinking about their investment performance over months or years rather than right now.

But patient long-term investors can learn a thing or two from the frenetic day trader, and that's what this chapter is all about. Many day-trading techniques can help swing traders, position traders, and investors — people who hold positions for days, months, or even decades — improve their returns and make smarter decisions when it comes time to buy or sell. In this chapter, I cover some trading and analysis techniques used by day traders that can help longer-term investors improve their returns. Then I discuss some ways that long-term investors may want to add day trading to their list of tricks as a way to achieve a better total return.

What Investors Can Learn from Traders

In theory, investors may be willing to wait forever to see great stock picks play out, but in reality, they only have so much time and money. A company's stock may be ridiculously cheap, but the stock can languish a long time before everyone else catches on and bids the price up. The investor who buys and sells well can add a few extra dollars to his investment return, and who doesn't want that? In addition, some long-term investors will take a day-trading flyer on a hot idea. Maybe a few will even want to give day trading a try, especially for those securities they've followed long enough to know how the market reacts to news and whether those reactions are appropriate. For a long-term investor, given the time to test strategies and set limits, day trading in known markets may result in some nice incremental short-term returns.

Investors who are interested in occasionally (or frequently) day trading need to adopt not only a few key day-trading strategies but also the key characteristics that make day traders successful.

Being disciplined

Successful day traders have an innate sense of discipline. They know when to commit more money to a trade and when to cut their losses and close shop for the day.

Unfortunately, a lot of long-term investors can get sloppy. They have done so much research and committed so much time waiting for a position to work that they often forget the cardinal rule of the trader: The market doesn't know that you're in it. The stock doesn't know you own it, so it's not going to reward your loyalty. Securities go up and down every day for no good reason, and sometimes you are going to make a mistake and will have to cut your losses. There's no shame in that, as long as you learn from it.

Now, how can you get that discipline? By doing these things:

- **Develop an investment and trading plan, covered in Chapter 2.** Although investing is probably not your primary occupation, you do want to have in writing what your objectives are and how you plan to meet them given other constraints: time, tax considerations, and risk tolerance.

- **Carefully evaluate your performance (covered in Chapter 16).** Keep a trading diary so that you know what you're trading and why. Can you find ways to improve? Are you making mistakes that can be avoided?

- **Set up a sell rule.** A quick way for an investor to improve her trading discipline is to set up a sell rule, a rule that tells her when to cut her losses and move on. For example, if a stock is down 20 percent from where it was purchased or where it traded at the beginning of the year, it may be time to sell, regardless of what you hope it will do.

Traders have to go through these exercises to survive. Investors often skip these steps, but they shouldn't.

Dealing with breaking news and breaking markets

One reason that the markets are so volatile is that they respond to news events. Prices reflect information, changing when any little bit of information comes into the market — even if the info is just that someone wants to buy and someone wants to sell right now. The problem is that sometimes the market participants don't react in proportion to the news they receive. Good traders have an almost innate ability to discern news that creates a buy from news that creates a sell. (You can find out more about market indicators and strategies in Chapter 8.) Sometimes traders want to go with the market, and sometimes they want to go against it.

When your investment idea has been affected by a news announcement, you need to consider how your position — and you — will react. After all, no matter how long your time horizon and how careful your research, things happen to companies: CEOs have heart attacks, major products are found to be defective, financial statements turn out to be fraudulent, and so on. How are you going to respond?

The first point is that you have to respond. The market doesn't know your position, and the market doesn't care. (Have I mentioned that already?) You need to assess the situation and decide what to do. Given the information, is it time to buy, sell, or stay put? Holding your long-term position in the face of long-term news is often okay, but that decision should be an active one, not a fallback. The trick is to be objective, which isn't easy when real dollars are at stake.

Successful day traders are able to keep their emotions under control and keep the market separate from the rest of their lives. Good investors should be able to do the same. Chapter 14 has some ideas that may help.

When evaluating news, day traders look at how the news is different from expectations. Investors can also consider how the news is different relative to the known facts about the company to date. For example, suppose that the Timely Timer Company is expected to report earnings of $0.10 per share. Instead, the news hits the tape saying that earnings will be only $0.05 because of accounting charges. The trader may see that the earnings are below expectations and short the shares to play on the bad news. The investor may know that the accounting charges were expected and quickly buy more shares while the price is depressed. The fact that there is a way for a buyer and a seller to match their differing needs is the whole reason that the financial markets exist!

To a day trader, perception is reality. To a keen-eyed investor, the difference between perception and reality may be an opportunity to make money.

Day traders have to think about the psychology of the market because everything moves so quickly. Investors sometimes forget about psychology because they can wait for logic to prevail. When it comes time to place a buy or sell order, however, understanding the psychological climate that day can give the investor a price advantage, and every bit of profit improvement goes straight to the bottom line.

Day traders keep their sanity by closing out positions at the end of the day so that they can get on with their lives until the next market opens. Investors, on the other hand, may want to know what's happening to their positions at other times. Many brokerage firms offer mobile-phone alert services, which I think are a terrible idea for a day trader but may not be a bad idea for an investor.

Setting targets and limits

Good day traders set limits. They often place stop and limit orders to automatically close out their positions when they reach a certain price level. They have profit targets in mind and know how much they're willing to risk in the pursuit of those gains.

Good investors should set similar limits. It can be harder for them, because they have often done so much research that they feel almost clairvoyant. Why worry about the downside when the research shows that the stock has to go up?

Well, the research may overlook certain realities. And even with thorough analysis, things change. That's why even the most ardent fundamentalist needs to have a downside risk limit. In most cases, stop and limit orders are bad ideas for a long-term investor because they force the sale of a security during a short-term market fluctuation and force the sale when it's really a good time to buy more. Investors have a different risk profile than day traders, so they need to manage risk differently — but they do still need to manage it.

With a *stop* order, the broker buys or sells the security as soon as a predetermined price is met, even if the price quickly moves back to where it was before the order took effect. A *limit* order is only executed if the security hits the predetermined level, and it stays in effect only if the price is at that level or lower (for a buy limit order) or at that level or higher (for a sell limit order).

Day traders close out their positions at the end of each day, so they rarely review their limits. A swing trader or an investor, on the other hand, who holds for a longer period of time, needs to review those limits frequently. How much should a position move each month, quarter, or year before it's time to cover losses or cash out with a profit? How has the security changed over time, and do the limits need to change with it?

When the position is working, an investor thinks of letting it ride forever. But, alas, few investments work that long into the future, so the investor also needs to think in term of relative performance. Has the time come to sell and put the money into something else with greater potential?

When managing money, day traders usually think about maximizing return while minimizing the risk of ruin. For an investor, the goal is maximizing return relative to a list of long-term objectives, including a target for risk. But because long-term objectives change, the portfolio has to as well. That means that a position that has been working out fine may have to be changed in order to meet the new portfolio goals. The discussion is starting to get beyond the scope of this book, but the point remains: Like successful day traders, successful investors have a plan for how they will allocate their money among different investments, and they adjust it as necessary.

Although investing is a long-term proposition and lacks the frenzy of trading, it is still an active endeavor. Instead of putting energy into buying and selling, the investor puts it into monitoring.

Judging execution quality

Day traders rely on outstanding trade execution from their brokers. They need to keep costs as low as possible in order to clear a profit from their trading, especially because their profits are relatively small.

Investors may have a greater likelihood of making a profit, given that they are waiting for a position to work out rather than closing it out every night. Even then, better execution leads to better profits. The magnitude of the few extra cents may be smaller relative to the entire profit, but it still counts.

Looking at total execution costs

Your broker makes money three ways. The first is on the commission charged to make the trade. The second is on the *bid-ask spread* (also called the *bid-offer*), which is the difference between the price that the broker buys the security from customers and the price that the broker sells it to customers.

The third is any price appreciation on the security between when the broker acquired it and when the firm sold it to the customer. Because three sources of profit are available, some brokers don't even charge commission. But note that the broker can still make money — lots of money — even without a commission.

When choosing a broker, consider *total execution costs,* not just commission. Some brokers offering deep commission discounts make money from high levels of trading volume, but others make their money from execution.

Improving execution

The broker has a few tricks for improving execution. The first is to invest heavily in information systems that can route and match orders, because even the slightest delay can make a difference if the markets are moving. The second is to have a large enough customer base to be able to match customer orders quickly. Third, and most important, is to decide that execution is a strategic advantage it can use to keep customers happy. Many brokerage firms would rather concentrate on research, financial planning, customer service, or other offerings to keep customers happy instead of offering excellent execution.

In general, a firm that offers low commissions and emphasizes its services to active traders has better execution than a firm that emphasizes its full-service research and advisory expertise. But there are exceptions, and in some cases, the exceptions vary with account size.

Brokerage firms use several numbers to evaluate their execution, including the following:

- **Average execution speed:** This is the amount of time it takes the firm to fill the first share of an order. Firms also track — and sometimes disclose — how long filling an entire order takes, on average.

- **Price relative to National Best Bid or Offer:** At any time, there is a list of bid and ask prices in the market, and your broker may not have the best spread. The National Best Bid or Offer is the best price in the market. You may not be able to get this price for all sorts of reasons, usually because of the number of shares you want to buy or sell. For example, if the best bid is for 100 shares and you want to sell 500, you won't be able to get all of the order filled. Brokerage firms track and report how close the price you received was to the best bid or offer at the time.

- **Price improvement:** Most brokerage firms buy and sell securities for their own accounts. In fact, working as a trader at a brokerage firm may be a great alternative to day trading. Because the firm may own the security or want it for its own account, it may give you a slightly better price than what's in the market.

✔ **Average effective spread:** This number measures how much the spread between the bid and the offer differed from the National Best Bid or Offer, on average. The lower the average effective spread, the better.

Brokerage firms have to disclose information monthly about the differences between market orders and public price quotes and the size of effective spreads in different securities. You can look up this info to help compare the performance at different firms. Certainly, your results will vary based on what types of securities you're trading, what market conditions are like when you are trading, and how big an account you have with the firm. But investigating the averages for a brokerage firm can help long-term investors decide whether changing firms to improve profits makes sense.

So what can you do to improve your execution? Here are three suggestions:

✔ **Ask the brokerage firm for its policies.** The firm should provide this information, as well as give you some of its recent data, so that you can decide whether the total value of the firm's services matches the total cost.

✔ **Check the weekly "Electronic Trader" column in *Barron's* as well as the magazine's annual review of online brokerage firms.** Execution cost is a key component of *Barron's* evaluation.

✔ **Update your own hardware and Internet connection so that they're as fast as possible.** If you're a day trader, having access to good data is imperative (see Chapter 12 for more information on your equipment needs). If you are not a day trader but actively manage your investment account, you may want to consider an upgrade as well. A few seconds can make a difference.

Applying Momentum

Momentum investors look for securities that are going up in price, especially if accompanied by acceleration in underlying growth. In a sense, they are looking for the same thing day traders are — a security that is going to move big — but they have the expectation of making money over a longer period of time. The thought is that a security starting to go up in price will keep going up unless something dramatic happens to change it. In the meantime, plenty of money can be made.

In momentum investing, instead of buying low and selling high, the goal is to buy high and sell even higher.

Like most investors, a momentum investor starts with careful fundamental analysis (described in Chapter 7), analyzing a security to determine what will make it go up. Then the momentum investor looks for certain technical and market indicators, similar to those described in Chapters 7 and 8 and used by day traders. In addition, some momentum investors rely on chart services, especially the Value Line and William O'Neil charts, to help them identify securities that are likely to have momentum.

Earnings momentum

Earnings momentum is the province of the investor, not the trader. The investor is looking at the earnings that a company reports every quarter to see whether the earnings are going up at a faster rate, say from a steady rate of 10 percent a year to 12, 13, or more. Such an increase often happens because of a new technology or product that turns a decent company into a hot property in the stock and options markets. If the earning growth rate is accelerating, then the underlying price should go up at an accelerating rate, too.

Day traders don't look for earnings momentum, but they do look for price momentum. The two are usually related.

Price momentum

When a security goes up in price, especially at a fast clip with strong demand underneath it, it is said to have *price momentum*. Most day traders are looking for price momentum in order to make a swift profit. Many long-term investors should look for price momentum, too, in order to avoid being stuck with a position for months before it starts to move. After all, patience pays, but it pays even better if your money is working for you while you wait.

Many momentum traders don't care why something is going up in price; they only know that it is going up and that they can profit by being there for even part of the ride. Following are some of the different indicators that these traders look at:

- **Relative strength:** You can calculate relative strength in different ways, discussed in Chapter 7, but the basic idea is that a security that's going up faster than the market as a whole is showing momentum and may be a buy.

- **Moving average convergence/divergence (MACD):** This indicator looks at how the average price of the security is changing over time.

Is the indicator staying relatively level, meaning that the price is moving slowly back and forth, or is the indicator gradually going up, meaning that the price is gradually going up, too? If you plot the moving average against the actual price levels, a wide gap means that the security is moving up or down faster than the average, and if it's moving up, you'd probably want to buy it. (Otherwise, consider shorting the security; you can read more about that in Chapter 9.)

↙ **Stochastics index:** This index is the difference between the high and the low price for a security over a given time period. Some analysts look at days, some at weeks. The idea is that, if the difference is getting bigger, it may be because the security is moving up or down in price at a faster than normal rate, creating an opportunity for a momentum buyer.

At an extreme, momentum investing leads to *bubbles,* like the infamous dot-com bubble in the late 1990s. People were buying the stocks because they were going up, not because they necessarily thought that the businesses were worth much. This run was fun while it lasted, but a lot of people lost a lot of money when reality set in during March and April 2000. The same thing happened in the real estate market. People were playing momentum when they were flipping condominiums in Las Vegas in the first decade of the 21st century, but prices couldn't go up forever — and they didn't.

For investors only: Momentum-research systems

Many day traders rely on different research systems to help them identify buy and sell opportunities in the course of a trading day. These systems usually don't work for an investor, simply because investors are less concerned about short-term movements. They wouldn't see the value in systems that scan the market and identify short-term price discrepancies, for example.

However, many investors use their own research services to help identify good buy and sell opportunities. Two of the more popular ones are Value Line and the William O'Neil charts.

Value Line

Value Line (www.valueline.com) is one of the oldest investment-research services. The company's analysts combine price and trading volume information on stocks with financial data. The numbers are crunched through a proprietary model to generate two rankings: a stock's timeliness and its safety. The higher the stock is on the timeliness ranking, the better it is to buy or hold it now. Historically, Value Line's most timely stocks have outperformed the

Dow Jones Industrial Average and the S&P 500, so people are willing to pay for access to the company's data. In addition, many libraries subscribe to Value Line's print service or online database, so you may be able to get access that way. (Hey, one of the advantages of being an investor is that you have the time to go to the library to look something up, a marvel to a day trader who's too busy to go and get even a cup of coffee.)

Value Line as a company has had some problems, most notably with fraud related to its mutual-fund business, but the charting system was not part of those charges.

William O'Neil

William O'Neil (www.williamoneil.com) started a company to distribute his technical-analysis system on stocks and the stock market, started a newspaper called *Investor's Business Daily,* and wrote a book called *How to Make Money in Stocks* (see the appendix for more information about it). The company's data services are available only to large institutional investors, such as mutual-fund and insurance companies, but between the book and the newspaper, individual investors can learn a lot about identifying momentum to pick good times to buy or sell a stock.

Many traders — in all securities, not just stocks — find *Investor's Business Daily* to be at least as useful as *The Wall Street Journal,* because it looks at the markets from a short-term trading perspective more than from a long-term, business-management angle.

The company's ranking system is based on what it calls CAN SLIM, which is a mnemonic for a list of criteria that a good stock should meet. Note that this system combines both fundamental and technical indicators:

- ✔ **Current quarterly earnings** should be up 25 percent from a year ago.
- ✔ **Annual earnings** should be up 25 percent from a year ago.
- ✔ **New products or services** should be driving earnings growth, not acquisitions or changes in accounting.
- ✔ **Supply and demand,** meaning the number of shares being purchased each day, is going up.
- ✔ **Leader or laggard?** The stock is a leading company in a leading industry and therefore in the best position to do well.
- ✔ **Institutional sponsorship** is in place, meaning that the stock is becoming more popular with mutual funds, pension funds, and other large shareowners.
- ✔ **Market indexes,** such as the Dow, the NASDAQ, and the S&P 500, should all be up.

Of course, not too many stocks out there meet all the CAN SLIM criteria, but the indicators can give an investor a way of thinking about better times to buy (when more criteria are met) or sell (when fewer are being met).

The most serious momentum investors tend to be swing traders, who hold positions for a few weeks or months. Longer-term investors often rely on some momentum signals, though, such as those on the CAN SLIM list, to help them identify good times to buy a stock that has been languishing.

When an Investor Considers Trading

Many day traders are also long-term investors. Sure, they trade for the short term, but they regularly take some of their profits and put them toward investments that have a longer time frame. It's smart risk management for a business that has a high wash-out rate. After all, even a short-term trader has long-term goals.

But does it ever make sense for a long-term investor to take up short-term trading? It may, for three reasons: The idea proves itself to be short-term, the research shows short-term trading patterns that may be profitable, and fundamental analysis supports short selling (which usually has a shorter time horizon than a buy would to an investor). The following sections explain these reasons in more detail.

Don't try riskier trading strategies unless your portfolio can handle the risk. As with full-time day trading, engage in part-time and occasional trading strategies only with risk capital, money that you can afford to lose. Money needed to pay the mortgage this month or pay for retirement in 30 years is *not* risk capital.

The idea has a short shelf life

Certain circumstances turn every long-term investor into a trader once or twice: He buys a security intending to hold it forever, and within a few days or weeks, some really bad news comes out. Or he buys only to see two days later that the company is being sold. That great long-term buy-and-hold idea no longer fits the original parameters, so it's time to sell. Despite the goal of holding forever, the investor decides to get out and move on, even if it's only a day later.

Your research shows you some trading opportunities

Good investors monitor their holdings, and some become intimate with the nuances of a security's short-term price movements even though the objective is to hold the position for the long term. An investor who gets a feel for the trading patterns of a specific holding may want to turn that into swing-trading and day-trading opportunities. Yes, doing so adds risk to the portfolio (and the risks of day trading are covered extensively throughout this book), but it can also increase return.

For example, suppose that an investor who is fascinated with technology stocks notices that the stocks always rise in price right before big industry conferences and then fall when the conference is over. She may not want to change any of her portfolio holdings based on this observation, but she may want a way to profit. So she buys call options on big technology companies before the conference and then sells them on the meeting's first day. That short-term trade allows her to capture benefits of the price run-up without affecting her portfolio position.

You see some great short opportunities

Short selling allows a trader to profit from a decline in the price of a security. The trader enters the order, which automatically arranges the loan of a security from the broker followed by a sale in the market. The trader then waits in hopes that the price will go down. When it does, the trader buys the security back at the lower price and repays the loan, keeping the difference between the purchase price and the sale price.

Because the broker charges interest on the loaned securities, short selling can get expensive. Traders who sell short are usually looking for a relatively short-term profit, not necessarily over a single day but over months rather than years.

In addition to the interest, short selling faces another risk, which is that the security can go up in price while the trader is waiting for it to go down. To reduce that risk, most short sellers do careful research to make sure that they're right about the security being all wrong. And who else does careful research? Many long-term investors.

For the investor who loves to do research and has some appetite for risk, short selling is a way to make money from securities that would make terrible long-term holdings because it seems obvious that they aren't going to do well. When these investors come across securities that are headed for trouble, they can short them in the hope of making a nice short-term profit.

Part IV

The Part of Tens

the part of tens

 For a list of ten alternatives to day trading, check out www.dummies.com/extras/daytrading.

In this part...

- Discover ten good reasons to day trade and ten good reasons to *avoid* day trading. It's not for everyone, and if you realize that it isn't for you, you can save yourself a lot of money and headaches.

- Find out about ten common day-trading mistakes so you don't make them.

- Consider ten different money-management techniques and find one that works for you.

- But wait, there's more! Explore the appendix at the end of this part for lots of resources to help you get started in trading.

Chapter 18

Ten Good Reasons to Day Trade

In This Chapter

▶ Getting ready to be your own boss

▶ Loving the investing business

▶ Figuring out what to expect from the markets

▶ Understanding the importance of financial and personal support systems

Day trading is a great career option for the right person in the right circumstances. It requires a strong, decisive personality who wants to be running the show every step of the way. And because those profits aren't steady, good day traders have some financial cushion and good personal support systems to get them through the tough times. In this chapter, I list ten really good reasons to take up day trading. (For balance, I cover ten bad reasons in Chapter 19.) Think you have what it takes? See how many of these characteristics fit your life right now.

You Love Being Independent

Day trading is like owning any small business. You're the boss and you call the shots. Each day's successes — and failures — are due to you and you alone. The market is irrelevant because you can't control it. Working by yourself all day, you're responsible for everything from the temperature in the office to the functioning of the computers to the accounting for trades.

Good day traders are independent. They don't want someone to tell them what to do; they want to figure it out for themselves. They love a challenge, whether it's finding a good bargain on office supplies or developing a profitable way to arbitrage currency prices.

If you would like to work for yourself and control your own destiny, keep reading. Day trading may be for you.

You Want to Work Anywhere You Like

As a day trader, you have the luxury of setting up shop wherever you please. All you need is an account with an online brokerage firm and high-speed Internet access. You don't even need a computer if you have a smart phone. Nowadays you can find these tools almost anywhere: at home, at the library, in a bar, in a big city, in a small town, in the mountains, or in another country. Day trading offers a lot of geographic flexibility, which few other businesses do. You can trade while traveling as easily as you would trade at home — especially as mobile service improves.

You're Comfortable with Technology

The financial-services industry was one of the first to embrace computer technology in a big way, back in the 1960s, and it is still a technology-intensive industry. The people in colored cotton jackets running around the exchange floor, waving their hands and yelling at each other, are anachronisms.

Day traders use software to develop and refine their trading strategies. They trade online using programs to monitor and automate their trades. They track their trades in spreadsheets and other software. They spend their days in front of a screen, communicating online with other traders all over the world. They interact with computers, not human beings, during the trading day.

Day traders are also self-employed, and many work from home. That means that if their software crashes, they have to fix it. They have to handle the upgrades, install the firewalls, and back up the data. Sure, you can pay someone to do these tasks, but the tech consultant probably won't be able to drop everything to get you up and trading again immediately. Hence, good day traders are comfortable with technology. If you like to mess around with programs, don't mind maintaining your computer, and understand how to set up your hardware for maximum efficiency, you're in good shape for day trading. (Chapter 12 has some more on this, too.)

You Want to Eat What You Kill

You don't have to be a self-employed day trader to trade securities. Brokerage firms, hedge funds, and exchange traders employ people to trade for them. In fact, most securities trading takes place through such larger organizations. But maybe you don't want to share your profits with someone else. Maybe you don't want someone dictating your strategy, placing limits on your trades, or determining your bonus based as much on factors such as teamwork and firm profitability as on what you brought in. You want to "eat what you kill," as they say, and day trading is one way you can do that.

When you day trade, you're responsible for your profits and your losses. That means that you reap the rewards and you don't have to share them with anyone else. It's a powerful incentive for independent people.

You Love the Markets

Good day traders have always been fascinated with the markets and how they move. If you watch CNBC for fun and have been following the securities business for years, no matter what your day jobs have been, then you may be a good candidate for day trading. Of course, I hope you've picked up more than "some people make a lot of money doing this!" A lengthy immersion in the cycles and systems that drive securities prices can help you develop trading strategies and know what you are up against.

And the markets are amazing, aren't they? All the buyers and sellers with all their different needs come together and find the price that gets the deal done. The prices assimilate all kinds of information about the state of the world, the desires of the people trading, and the future expectations for the economy. It's capitalism in its purest form, and watching how it works is almost magical. If you love how the markets work and want to learn first-hand what they tell you about making money, then by all means keep reading.

You Have Market Experience

If you have never opened an account with a brokerage firm, purchased a stock, or invested in a mutual fund, you may not be suited for day trading. It's not that those activities alone are adequate preparation for day trading, but they're a start. They can help you understand all that can happen to cause you to make or lose money.

If you haven't made any trades before, don't quit your day job to day trade. Instead, flip back to Chapter 17 for some ideas on how you can use short-term trading in an investment portfolio. That way, you can learn more and build up your savings before taking the plunge.

You've Studied Trading Systems and Know What Works for You

Much of the work of day trading takes place long before entering the buy or sell order. You have to define your trading system, see how it would have worked in the past, and test it to see how it works now. The preparatory work isn't as exciting as actually doing the day trading, because you aren't making real money, but you're not losing money, either.

Short-term trading has a huge potential for loss, and many traders are chasing the exact same ideas. The more you know about how your strategy works in different market conditions, the better prepared you will be to act appropriately and profitably.

It can take a long time to find a strategy that works enough of the time to make it worth your while. Many day traders spend months developing, testing, and refining their day-trading strategy. You can read more about the process of strategy testing in Chapter 16.

Because backtesting (which lets you test your trading strategy) uses historic prices, you can do much of the work on the side, at night, and on weekends, before you start day trading full time. It's a good way to get prepared for your trading business while you save your money and make other preparations for your new day-trading venture.

You Are Decisive and Persistent

Short-term traders don't have the luxury of thinking too much about what they're doing. Trading has to become intuitive. They have to be able to act on what they see when they see it. There's no room for second guessing, for hesitation, for choking, or for panic attacks.

Good day traders are also persistent. After they find a strategy they trust, they stick with it no matter how things are going. That's how they're able to buy low and sell high.

Even great traders go through bad periods, but if they trust their system and continue to stick with it, they usually pull out of the bad period, often with money ahead. If you've been able to stick it out when things went wrong other times in your life, you know what to expect when day trading.

You Can Afford to Lose Money

Obviously, you want to make money. That's the whole idea of day trading. But day trading is difficult. Most traders quit in the first year. Some can't take the stress, some lose all their money, and some simply don't make enough money to make it worth their time.

Like any small business, you're taking a risk when you set up shop as a day trader. That risk is easier if you can afford to lose money. I'm not saying you need to have so much money that you won't miss it when it's gone, but you shouldn't be day trading with money you need to live on, any more than you would open a store or start a law practice with money you need to buy groceries and pay the mortgage.

If your household does not have a second source of income, be sure to set aside enough money to cover your living expenses while you get started. And you should keep a second pot of money, your *walk-away fund* (see Chapter 14), so that you're free to quit day trading and move on to your next adventure if you decide it's not for you.

It's especially important to have a financial cushion when you're day trading for the following reasons:

- ✔ **You can afford to commit to your trading:** Having your living expenses covered, at least at first, isn't just about dealing with losses. It's also about being able to stick with your trading. If you need cash to pay your bills, you may be tempted to take money out of the market whenever you're doing well. Doing so may keep you from reinvesting your profits. Plus, by not sticking to your strategy, your trading capital won't grow as fast. Think of day trading as a way to build a long-term asset, not a way to generate a steady stream of current income.

- ✔ **You can stay in the market through the rough times:** You know the old saw that the best way to make money is to buy low and sell high, right? Well, this means that the best time to buy is usually when securities prices have been beaten up and you've lost a lot of money. If you can afford some losses, staying in the game will be easier. Plus, you'll be able to stick to your strategy so that you can profit big when the market finally turns.

- ✔ **You can better handle the stress of losses:** Not all your trades are going to work out. Some days, you're going to lose money. If you have enough money that you don't fear loss, you can make better decisions. And you're less likely to panic if you know that you'll still be able to eat, pay your electric bill, and have a roof to sleep under at night. With sufficient funds, you're better able to view the markets clearly and follow a winning strategy.

Trading is very much a game of psychology. Give yourself an edge by waiting to do it until you can afford to.

You Have a Support System

Trading is stressful. The markets gyrate from events that no one can foresee. Things just happen, and no one else who's trading cares how these events affect you. It's enough to make you crazy some days, and unfortunately, some traders do get crazy. Alcoholism, depression, divorce, and suicide seem to be occupational hazards for those traders who have trouble separating what's happening in the market with who they are as people.

The securities markets are wonderful mechanisms for bringing together diverse buyers and sellers. They are not wonderful for propping up your ego, helping you through a rough time in your life, or slipping you a little extra money when you most need it. The markets are not human. They are ruthless machines designed to generate the best price for the aggregate of the buyers and sellers participating that day. Some days, the markets will be in your favor, and some days, they will go against you.

Good day traders are psychologically strong. They understand how their weaknesses come out when they are stressed. They have people (good friends and supportive families) and activities (from exercise routines to hobbies) that help give their brains a break from trading.

Chapter 14 talks about managing the stress of day trading, and in many ways, I think it's the most important chapter in this book.

Chapter 19

Ten or So Good Reasons to Avoid Day Trading

. . . .

In This Chapter

▶ Considering other ways to invest that suit you better

▶ Taking into account your personality and preferences

▶ Recognizing the hard work that successful day trading requires

▶ Putting a damper on unrealistic expectations

. . . .

Day trading isn't right for everyone. In fact, it's a bad idea for most people. It requires a strong personality, someone who can face the gyrations of the markets day in and day out. And it also requires someone with enough attention to detail to run a business. It's a great career option for the right person in the right circumstances. But for people who have trouble keeping cool or who don't have the patience to learn how to trade, and for anyone who has a gambling problem, day trading can be a quick road to ruin.

In this chapter, I list eleven signs that may indicate day trading isn't right for you right now. Take these signs seriously. Most day traders lose money, in part because a lot of people who aren't cut out for day trading try it anyway.

You Want to Learn Investing by Day Trading

Many people want to manage their own investments. Although doing so is certainly possible, you first need to take the time to learn about the basics of finance, such as the relationship between risk and return, proper diversification, and time horizons that are appropriate to your situation. In fact, there's a great book called *Investing For Dummies,* by Eric Tyson (Wiley), that can help.

Some people confuse investing with day trading, though, and these two disciplines are not the same. I list tons of information on the differences in Chapter 4, but here's the condensed version: Day trading involves rapid buying and selling of securities to take advantage of small movements in prices. This can be a successful strategy for part of your investment account, but day trading with all your money is not a good idea.

Buying and selling securities on your own without being a day trader is entirely possible. And if you don't know another good term for "self-employed person managing her own money," just tell people you run your own hedge fund. You'll get better tables at restaurants that way.

You Love Fundamental Research

Fundamental research, discussed in Chapter 7, is the process of analyzing a company to see how good its business is and what the company's securities are worth. Fundamental analysts crunch numbers, build forecasts, check out products, and look for stocks that are going to do well over the long term. They dream of uncovering the next Google or the next Walmart and holding the stock all the way up.

Fundamental research is antithetical to day trading. Day traders look for profit opportunities in short-term price movements. They often do not know what industry a company is in, nor do they care. If you love the fundamentals, you're probably too analytical to be a good day trader.

You're Short on Time and Capital

Getting started in day trading is a lot like buying a small business. It takes commitment of both time and of money. If you don't have enough time, learning technical patterns is difficult. If you don't have the money, you won't be able to work through rough cycles. And there will be rough cycles. That's day trading's only sure thing.

Some day traders are able to trade part time. If you are disciplined, you can be successful as a part-time trader. The key is to close out your positions at the end of your designated trading period as though the market day were ending. If your plan is to trade for two hours a day, then trade for two hours a day and no more. Use an alarm clock as your personal trading bell.

You Like Working As Part of a Group

A decade ago, most large cities had day trading offices, called *trading arcades,* where traders could go each day to buy and sell securities. The big advantage these firms offered was high-speed Internet access. Now almost everyone can get high-speed Internet access at home, so there's little need for day traders to go elsewhere, and most of these offices are closed.

Working at home is great for some people. If you prefer camaraderie during the day, like the support of a team, and want friendly faces around you, you're likely to be miserable day trading. It's just you and the market, and the market doesn't have a great sense of humor.

You Can't Be Bothered with the Details of Running a Business

Day traders are small-business people, and their entrepreneurial flair goes beyond making their own buy and sell decisions. They also buy equipment, shop for supplies, and maintain careful income tax records. To some, this is exhilarating. No more mean office manager who decides how many and what kind of pens must be used. No more going through hoops and bringing in letters from a doctor to get a fancy ergonomic chair. You're the boss, and if you want it, you can have it.

But to others, all this responsibility is overwhelming. Picking out pens? Creating backup procedures? Worrying about accounting software? It's too much. If the mere thought of standing at the office-supply store gives you the heebie-jeebies, you may want to consider trading as an employee rather than trading for your own account.

You Crave Excitement

Trading *seems* so exciting. You've seen the stereotypical picture of the people on the floor at the Chicago Board of Trade, wearing bright-colored jackets and loud ties, screaming and waving their arms. It gets my blood running to just think about it. Of course, they were probably shouting out coffee orders and waving their arms in a debate over the Cubs versus the Sox. And anyway, floor trading is mostly obsolete. Most of the large stock, bond, and derivative exchanges have gone through mergers and reduced the square footage of their trading floors because of changes in how people trade. Nowadays, most traders sit in offices in front of computer screens. They have to stay focused on the little blips in front of them, and it can be deathly dull. Some days few, if any, opportunities come up to trade using your system.

If you crave excitement and have trouble staying focused, you may find that day trading is too boring for you. It can involve intense stress with few opportunities to work it off during the day.

You're Impulsive

With the frenzy of trades and the rapid-fire decisions involved, day trading may seem like a perfect career for an impulsive person. It's all about instinct, about acting on your hunches, about pulling the trigger and seeing what happens. Right? Uh, no. To be a good day trader, you have to trust your trading system more than your hunches. Sometimes you'll make trades when it doesn't seem right and you'll sit out periods even though you are itching to get in. Good day traders are quick thinkers, but they do think. If you like to act now and deal with the consequences later, day trading isn't a good idea for you.

You Love Going to the Casino

Do you get a big rush out of gambling? Do you love trying to beat the odds? Does day trading seem just like a visit to Vegas without the airfare? Then you shouldn't be day trading. Unlike at a casino, no one is going to give you free drinks or Celine Dion tickets in exchange for your massive losses.

A lot of traders like to gamble. Every trader has some crazy story about playing Liar's Poker using the serial numbers on dollar bills instead of with cards, or about a friend of a friend who bet on whether the person walking in front of him would turn right or left. And that's fine, if they keep their gambling in perspective and bet no more than they can afford to lose.

Trading isn't necessarily gambling, but it can be, especially if you get carried away with the market and don't stick to your trading and money-management systems. But remember this: In gambling, the odds always favor the house. When you cross the line, you hand your profit potential over to someone else.

The line between day trading and gambling is thin. Check the questions at www.gamblersanonymous.org/ga/content/20-questions to see whether you may have a gambling problem. Substitute *day trading* for *gambling* and see what you come up with. And by all means, get help if you have a problem. Don't take up day trading.

You Have Trouble Setting Boundaries

Successful day traders are disciplined. They have set trading hours that they stick to and set systems they use to plan trades and manage their money. They took the time to carefully test their trading strategy (see Chapter 16 for more on how you can do that). They understand that if they don't have a system and manage their risk, they are more likely to become one of those numerous day traders who lose everything early on.

The whole idea behind day trading is that you limit risk by closing out your positions at the end of the day. The financial markets are global, though, so in theory, the trading day never ends. If you have a hard time turning off the lights at the end of the day, you may not be the best day trader. If you resent rules, you may rebel against the rules that you've set for yourself.

Good day traders know that they are cut out for day trading before they even begin. They've taken the time to assess how their personality and psychological makeup mix with the demands of the job. And one key trait is discipline.

You Want to Get Rich Quick

Day traders look for short-term profit opportunities, so it follows that day trading leads to big, fast profits, right? Wrong. Day traders make money by collecting a large number of small profits. Those who make money usually do it through patience and persistence. Yeah, one or two day traders out there may have managed to make a killing in a week, but they're the exception.

Research shows that 80 percent of day traders lose their capital and are gone from the business within one year. Instead of getting rich, you are more likely to go broke quick from day trading. If you don't like those odds, try something else with your money.

The Guy on the Infomercial Said It Would Work

A lot of money can be made in day trading, but sometimes it seems like more money is made selling day-trading training systems. Some of these systems are heavily marketed, even through television infomercials. The sales pitch makes day trading seem like an easy, safe, fun way to make money using your own smarts. These commercials leave out pesky details about researching and testing systems, high levels of risk, and the pressure trading can place on a person. And the wash-sale rule (it's a tax thing; refer to Chapter 15) is never mentioned.

Day trading is great for some people. But like anything, if it sounds too good to be true, it probably is. Don't let a strong-arm sales pitch cost you your hard-earned money.

Chapter 20

Ten Common Day-Trading Mistakes

. . . .

In This Chapter

▶ Avoiding other people's trading mistakes

▶ Steering clear of psychological and preparation mistakes

. . . .

Day trading is tough. Many popular markets are *zero-sum games,* meaning that for every winner, there's a loser. Other markets, such as the stock market, have a *positive bias,* meaning they have a tendency to increase in value over time, but you may rarely see big moves in any one day. And the whole point of day trading is to close your positions each night. Most day traders lose money, in part because they make obvious, avoidable mistakes.

This list of ten mistakes can help you avoid the most serious ones. Avoiding these mistakes is no guarantee that you'll make money trading, but it can certainly reduce your risk and improve your odds. And that's half the battle.

Starting with Unrealistic Expectations

Most day traders lose money. Some research shows that 80 percent of day traders wash out in the first year. Brokerage firms that deal with day traders are constantly figuring out ways to attract new customers, because it is so hard to retain the ones they have for the long term.

Yes, some traders make money. A few make a lot of money. But they are the exception. Making money day trading is tough, making enough money to cover the value of your time is even tougher. If you go into trading knowing that it's hard, that you should only risk money that you can afford to lose, and that you need to think about it as a business, you'll have a leg up on those who think that they've found an easy way to make millions from the comfort of their own home — and who are then stunned to discover they are broke.

Starting without a Business and Trading Plan

Trading is a business. When you decide to day trade, you are committing capital to an entrepreneurial business with a high risk of failure. You are no different from your brother-in-law who decided to open a sandwich shop franchise, your neighbor who joined a startup company for little salary and lots of equity, or your college buddy who has been trying to make a go of it as a full-commission life insurance salesman. You are all out on your own, risking your capital in the hope of great success but knowing that many others doing the same thing fail.

Successful businesses have business plans, and your trading business is no different. You need to specify what you are going to trade, when you're going to trade, how you're going to trade, and with how much money — *before* you get started. You need to determine what equipment you need, what services and training you want, and how you will measure your success. Chapter 2 can help you with a business plan, and the rest of the book can help you fill in the appropriate sections of it. Having the plan will keep your expectations in line and create a professional starting point for your new trading venture.

You also need to supplement your business plan with a plan for your trading. How are you going to trade? What signals will you watch for? Under what conditions will you enter a position, and under what conditions will you close it? That's your trading plan. Good traders have trading plans so that they know exactly what they want to do when they see opportunities in the market. This plan reduces the fear and doubt that can unsettle most traders, and it heads off the panic that destroys more than a few. Read Part II of this book for ideas on how to trade.

In addition, good trading plans have to be tested and evaluated. Chapter 16 has good information on testing and evaluation so that you have enough confidence in your system to follow it, even when the market gets squirrelly on you.

Failing to plan is planning to fail, as the cliché goes. You are risking too much of your hard-earned money to skip careful upfront planning. Take responsibility for your trading.

Ignoring Cash Management

Because financial markets can be volatile, you can easily get wiped out. Good cash management can help you stay in the game. Because you never commit all of your capital to any one trade, no one trade can shut you down.

At times — like when you know you've got a great idea — holding back some cash may not seem right, but if you plan to trade for the long run, you need to follow your money-management strategy. Otherwise, you'll never be able to get a winning trade that can offset your losses.

You need to have your wits about you to day trade, but you also need to have capital. Chapter 6 has some great information on cash management, so don't skip it!

Failing to Manage Risk

Day trading is risky business, and most day traders quit because of losses. (Have I told you that already?) Even traders who stick with it have many losing trades. That's why they have risk-management systems in place. Their trading plans include *stops,* which automatically execute buy or sell orders when securities reach predetermined levels. (Stops are discussed in Chapter 2.)

The day trader looking for trouble places orders without thinking about how much of a security to buy or sell at any one time, and she thinks that she'll just know when to sell. And then she second-guesses herself and finds herself with bigger losses than she intended.

If you're going to day trade, be safe. You know what the risks are (that's why you picked up this book), so use the protection offered by stops and sound money management.

Most day traders lose money. Don't risk money you can't afford to lose, and plan for the risks that you take.

Not Committing the Time and Money to Do It Right

Day trading is a job. It's a small-business endeavor that requires research and training well in advance of the first trade. It's not something you can squeeze into an hour a day as a hobby. To do well, you need to set regular hours and have enough money to generate reasonable returns without unreasonable risks.

Many people think day trading is something that they can easily enter into and that they can generate profits while their kids are napping. That thinking is a mistake. If you can't dedicate the time necessary to study the markets and understand how you react to them, you will have trouble staying in the trading business.

Day trading is a business of frequent trades with small percentage gains and a high potential for loss. If you have days of losses, a small account will quickly end up with too little money to meet minimum order sizes. Therefore, successful traders start with enough money to last through periods of drawdown and are still able to generate meaningful dollar returns. Consider this: A 1 percent return on $1,000 is equal to $10, but a 1 percent return on $100,000 is $1,000.

If you have more money to begin with, the dollars you make from day trading will seem more real to you. The U.S. Securities and Exchange Commission and the National Association of Securities Dealers define day traders in part as customers with $25,000 in their accounts. If you have $25,000 you can afford to lose, you are more likely to be a successful day trader than if you have only $2,500 — and you'll be considered to be a day trader, not a dilettante.

You are going to lose money. All day traders have bad days, and they are more likely to lose money early in their trading careers before they get a feel for the markets and their own reactions to it. If you have enough money when you begin, you can consider these losses to be part of your apprenticeship.

Chasing the Herd

Everyone in the market is looking at the same data and the same technical indicators (like those discussed in Chapter 7). Good day traders follow market trends but with the goal of being early or on time. Those who get in late get crushed: They buy too high, or they sell too low. Chasing the herd is tempting, because it's so hard to watch the market move away from you.

Day trading requires quick reactions. It's video games and psychology, some people joke, because the trader who can figure out what others in the market are doing and then click on the mouse button fastest has a huge advantage. The trader who hesitates or goes along for the ride is likely to be ruined.

There's no easy solution for this. It helps if you know that you are psychologically cut out for day trading (covered in Chapter 14) and have confidence in the long-term performance of your trading system (covered in Chapter 16). But to a big extent, you just have to have some experience in the markets to know how your trading system matches what's in your head.

Switching between Research Systems

Day traders lose money, at least part of the time. And losing money can cause a day trader to lose trust in his trading system. And many do what seems logical, which is move to a trading system that seems to be working. The problem is that no system works all the time; if one did, everyone would use it. And sometimes things look worst before they turn. By switching systems whenever things look bad, the trader never learns the nuances of how a given system works for him. And he's likely to get stuck on another downtrend, picking up the new system right when the old one starts to work again.

Markets go in cycles. No system works all the time, but if you panic and start trying new things without doing a lot of upfront work, you're likely to make things worse. Chapter 16 covers performance evaluation and system testing in great detail. The more you understand your system and how it works, the less likely you are to be brought down by floundering around for new systems all the time.

Bottom line: Anyone who has a magic trading system that works in all markets is retired and living on a beach in Maui. Everyone else has to live through a few rough stretches.

Overtrading

Because day traders don't hold positions for long periods of time, they rarely enjoy big and profitable price moves. Instead, they make money from lots of transactions with small profits. They are crazy people, moving in and out for short periods. But believe it or not, the day trader who trades *too* much loses out. She won't be in the market for large intra-day moves, and she'll get killed on commissions and other transactions costs.

As paradoxical as it seems, many day traders do better by making fewer trades each day. That way, commissions and fees take a smaller bite of the profit. One way to profit from fewer trades is with better money management, discussed in Chapter 6. A trader who puts money to work appropriately can often make more money than one who trades frenetically.

Sticking Too Long with Losing Trades

Day traders are often overcome with fear, doubt, greed, and hope. They are afraid to recognize a loss. They wonder whether they're good traders. They don't want to pay the commission to get out of the loser. And if the security was a good buy at the higher price, it's surely a better buy now that the price has gone down. These traders think that if they just keep a positive mental attitude, everything will work out all right in the end.

Good traders have systems in place to limit their losses. They use stop orders (Chapter 2) to force themselves out of bad trades. They would rather put the money to work on a good trade than stick out a bad one.

The market doesn't know your position; even if it did, it wouldn't care. Therefore, no amount of wishing and hoping will cause the market to reward you for your patience. If a trade isn't working, get out. As the man in the musical sings, tomorrow is a latter day.

Getting Too Emotionally Involved

Trading is a stressful business. You're up against an impersonal market that moves seemingly at random (and many academics would say that it moves truly at random). It involves money, which to some people is a way to keep score in life and to others is their primary source of security. Losing trades mean a loss of status and a loss of safety. It's no wonder that so many traders are head cases when the entire market sometimes seems to be conspiring against you — you specifically.

The best traders are almost Zen-like in their lack of attachment to the market. They are able to remove themselves from the frenzy of the trading day so that they're not susceptible to fear, doubt, greed, and hope. Chapter 14 has some advice that can help you approach the trading day in a calmer manner. Only you know whether you are capable of that.

Chapter 21

Ten Tested Money-Management Techniques

The key to success in day trading is discipline. That starts with good money management: determining how much money you will trade, when you will cut your losses, and when you will walk away with money in your pocket. If you don't manage your money, you won't be trading long.

Here, you get an overview of the key money-management techniques that you should consider as well as one that is a very bad idea. Some of these techniques are simple; no calculation is required, and you can use them right away. Others involve a little workout with your calculator. A few of these techniques need your performance history to work, so you can't use them right away, but you can experiment with them as you build your trade data. (And yes, this is one of the many reasons that traders should keep records of trading activity; see Chapter 16.)

These days, many brokers include money-management calculators and apps in their trading systems, so you can enter the parameters that reflect your trading style and your account balance to get the right amount to trade, right away. These calculators remove the guesswork and mystery associated with some of these techniques — if you use them. Chapter 11 has more information.

Taking Money off the Table

Here's the simplest form of money management: When you're up, take the profit rather than waiting to make even more money. Fight the greed, take the cash, and call it a day.

If you have a week, month, or year with particularly strong profits, take a little money out of your trading account and put it in a retirement fund, use it to pay off a debt, or move it into a low-risk investment to help diversify your high-risk trading activities.

Even if you do nothing else, taking profits when you have them can help keep you in the game longer.

Using Stops

Unless you're a machine, staying disciplined all the time can be difficult. Humans do goofy things. That's why there's a simple way to force discipline on your trading to keep your losses from destroying your trading account: a stop order.

A stop order, also called a stop-loss order, is an order to buy or sell a security as soon as it hits a given price, known as a stop price. The order sits dormant in the broker's computer until the market price hits the stop, and then the order is executed. This automated action helps you lock in a profit or cut a loss. Some traders don't like stops because on occasion one will be executed on a one-time down trade or while a stock is shooting up at price, causing them to leave some money on the table. However, stops are an easy way to force discipline into trading. They can help you manage your money with very little extra effort.

Yes, some brokers charge an extra commission for a stop order. But it may be worth it.

Applying Gann's 10 Percent Rule

The Gann money-management system is part of a complicated system of technical analysis used to identify good securities trades. The chart system is complex, but the money-management system is simple. The core of it is a limit on the money placed on any one trade to 10 percent of the account value, never more. The dollar value of that 10 percent goes up or down as the account value changes, but the 10 percent limit ensures that you always have some powder dry to stay in the market.

Most traders who follow Gann's 10 percent rule combine it with stops to limit losses.

You can't take advantage of a profitable opportunity if you have no money to trade. You can lose everything in your account if you let your losses run.

Limiting Your Losses with the Fixed Fractional System

The fixed fractional system is misnamed; it's actually a range of fractions that determine how much of your trade capital to risk on any one trade. A larger fraction is allocated to less risky trades; a smaller fraction to more risky ones. The calculation can be found in Chapter 6.

To do the calculation, you need to know how much money you can lose on any one trade. The study needed to determine that amount can go a long way toward improving your trading without getting into the math. Fixed fractional takes the stop a step further; it helps you limit your losses and pick up more from your wins by considering how much to trade along with the potential value of losses and gains.

Increasing Returns with the Fixed-Ratio System

The fixed-ratio system of money management is related to fixed fractional trade sizing. The key difference is that it looks at accumulated profit rather than total account size. (Accumulated profit is the value of the account less the capital that you put into it when you started trading.)

This system was specifically designed for options and futures trading by Ryan Jones, a trader himself. The goal is to increase returns from winning trades and protect profits from losing ones. The basic calculation is in Chapter 6.

Following the Kelly Criterion Formula

The Kelly Criterion is based on some statistical work by mathematicians working at Bell Labs in the 1950s. They realized that it had applications to gambling, so they went to Las Vegas and made a lot of money at blackjack. I kid you not. The casinos changed the rules so that it no longer works at Vegas, but it does work in securities markets.

What this formula does is ensure that you will never run out of money, so you will always be able to place yet one more trade. In the real world, of course, you can reach a point where you still have money but don't have enough to place a trade.

$$\text{Kelly \%} = W - \left(\frac{1 - W}{R} \right)$$

The equation looks at the percentage of trades that are expected to make money (W), the return from a winning trade, and the ratio of the average gain from a winning trade relative to the average loss of a losing trade (R). You may not be able to use the Kelly criterion until you have been trading long enough to amass data to use in the equation, but that's okay — you have other choices here!

The Kelly criterion often generates a trade size larger than many traders are willing to use. One alternative is a *half Kelly* trade, using half of the amount recommended by the equation.

Figuring the Amount to Trade with Optimal F

Optimal F is another money-management system that needs performance figures to generate an ideal trade size. It was developed by Ralph Vince, a trader, and it comes up with the ideal fraction of your account to trade based on your past performance. The calculation changes with every trade, so it's usually done through a spreadsheet or an app.

Measuring Risk and Sizing Trades with Monte Carlo Simulation

The Monte Carlo simulation is another money-management system drawn from gambling. It's used for risk management in many different businesses, including trading. You enter risk and return parameters into a computer program, and it tells you the likelihood of total loss and the optimal trade size.

The system can't account for every possible thing that can go wrong, and it requires a lot of computer power — even nowadays. That being said, many trading and brokerage platforms have Monte Carlo applications that can be used to help you measure risk and size trades.

Taking a Risk with the Martingale System

Martingale is another simple money-management system, no calculator required. It's popular with gamblers and traders alike. You start with a small amount per trade — you get to pick it yourself, but it should probably be less than 5 percent of your account value. If the trade works, your next trade should be the same amount. If the trade does not work, then you close it out and place double the amount (*double down,* as they say) on the next trade so that you win back the loss. That doesn't work? Double again. After you have a winning trade, go back to the initial amount for your next trade.

If you have to double down for a long series of trades, the money involved quickly grows: from $2,000, for example, to $4,000, $8,000, $16,000, $32,000, $64,000, and even $128,000 if you have six losing trades in a row. This is the problem. If you have an infinite amount of money, you will come out ahead using martingale. Of course, if you had an infinite amount of money, you probably wouldn't be reading this book.

With martingale, you can run out of money before you have a trade that works. The method works best for aggressive traders with large accounts who start with small initial trades. It's a risky money-management strategy, but it's also far preferable to having no strategy at all.

Throwing It to the Fates

Many traders have a logical problem with money management. If you have a sure thing, why shouldn't you put all your money on it? If you know the next trade is going to be great, why should you close out the day with a balance decline? Ah, but your logic is colored green with greed.

Few sure things are as sure as they seem. Lose on the sure thing, and you won't be around for the next trade. Exceed your daily loss limit, and you'll have even greater losses.

The wise sage Bart Simpson once said that years of watching television taught him that miracles always happen to poor children on Christmas Eve. Knowledge of money management is more of a sure thing than believing that you will be the beneficiary of a miracle today.

Appendix

Additional Resources for Day Traders

· ·

*A*s much as I hate to admit it, *Day Trading For Dummies,* 3rd Edition, doesn't tell you absolutely everything there is to know to get started in day trading. This appendix lists books, websites, periodicals, and other resources offering trading strategies and techniques and ideas on managing risk, taxes, and stress.

Great Books for Great Trading

Have a shelf that looks a little bare? Fill it up with a few of these beauties.

Basic trading guides

The following books offer nuts-and-bolts information on day trading:

- ✔ *Algorithmic Trading and DMA: An Introduction to Direct Access Trading Strategies,* **by Barry Johnson (4Myeloma Press):** This is the textbook on algorithmic and program trading. If you want to trade this way, you'll need the book; if you want to learn more about what other traders are doing, you'll probably want it. The downside is that this volume is as much doorstop as book.

- ✔ *The Bible of Options Strategies: The Definitive Guide for Practical Trading Strategies,* **by Gary Cohen (FT Press):** Many traders prefer options to stocks, and this book covers the main strategies as well as some of the more esoteric ones that may work for you.

- ✔ *Day Trading the Currency Market: Technical and Fundamental Strategies to Profit from Market Swings,* **by Kathy Lien (Wiley):** The foreign exchange (forex) market is popular with day traders, but it's a little different from the stock and futures markets. Trading in currency relies heavily on leverage, and market participants have more motivations than simply hedging or speculating. If you are interested in trading currencies, this book can help you get started.

✔ *Mastering the Trade,* **2nd Edition, by John F. Carter (McGraw-Hill):** The author, an experienced trader, walks day traders and swing traders through the ins and outs of the markets, offering specific advice on different trading opportunities. He includes charts and data that explain when to place a trade and when to close it out. This book is practical, useful, and detailed.

✔ *The New Money Management: A Framework for Asset Allocation,* **by Ralph Vince (Wiley):** Money management can keep traders in the game longer while maximizing potential returns. It's a key discipline that can mean the difference between long-run success and failure. Unfortunately, many day traders completely overlook money management. This book reviews Vince's money-management system in great detail.

✔ *Trading Rules that Work: The 28 Lessons Every Trader Must Master,* **by Jason Jankovsky (Wiley):** If it were possible to get rich from knowing just a handful of specific trading indicators, every trader would retire and run huge charitable foundations. But it's not that easy. Instead, a disciplined, professional approach to the market makes a difference over the long run. This book is a useful overview of different trading rules, why they work, and how traders should apply them.

✔ *Trading Systems and Methods,* **5th Edition, by Perry J. Kaufman (Wiley):** This textbook on trading systems provides a detailed analysis of the popular and the obscure alike. What makes it especially nice is the book has a companion website with actual trading programs on it. You can use them as a starting point for developing your own trading systems.

Technical analysis guides

Technical analysis is a system of looking at price and volume trends to determine supply and demand levels in the market. Supply and demand, of course, drive price changes, so understanding the dynamics is pretty darn useful. Here are a few books that cover technical analysis in detail:

✔ *Candlestick Charting For Dummies,* **by Russell Rhoads (Wiley):** Candlestick charts were developed in Japan and are the basis of a system of technical analysis that's popular with short-term traders, including day traders. This book explains how to identify and use candlestick patterns.

✔ *Mind Over Markets: Power Trading with Market Generated Information,* **by James Dalton, Eric Jones, and Robert Bevan Dalton (Traders Press):** Don't let the title fool you. This book is not about trading psychology. Instead, it covers a price-charting and technical-analysis system in great depth, especially the relationships between price changes and volume changes. The system, called *market profile,* is especially useful for day traders working in futures markets.

✔ *Tape Reading and Market Tactics,* **by Humphrey B. Neill (Marketplace Books):** In the early part of the 20th century, traders looked at price and volume information that came across ticker tapes. Traders still rely on an analysis of price and volume information, just with different tools. This book was originally written in 1931, but many day traders find that Neill's advice on what to look for and what to avoid when looking at price data still holds true.

✔ *Technical Analysis For Dummies,* **by Barbara Rockefeller (Wiley):** Day traders use technical analysis to help gauge market activity, and this book is a detailed guide on reading charts and applying the information to trading in an intelligent way. What else would a *For Dummies* book offer?

Schools of price theory

Most day traders take an eclectic approach to the markets. They find a few indicators that help them and then apply those indicators to the situation in the market. Over time, they refine their systems. Some traders, however, rely on specific theories for how prices should move. Here are some basic texts on the different theories.

✔ *Dow Theory Unplugged,* **by Charles Dow, Richard Russell, et al. (W&A Publishing):** The Dow Theory, developed by Charles Dow, publisher of *The Wall Street Journal,* predicts overall market performance based on the performance of different industry sectors. It doesn't work quite the same way it once did, given how much less industrial the U.S. economy is than in Dow's time. This book includes Dow's essays as well as commentary and analysis from different experts.

✔ *Elliott Wave Principle: Key to Market Behavior,* **by A.J. Frost and Robert R. Prechter, Jr. (Wiley):** The Elliott Wave theory is a strange animal. It looks for really long-term patterns in the markets — over decades and even centuries — based on the *Fibonacci series,* a number series found in nature. It's not widely used, but some traders swear by it.

✔ *How to Make Profits in Commodities,* **by W.D. Gann (Lambert Gann):** This book isn't exactly an easy read, but many analysts believe that Gann's system can help them figure out how prices change over time. The original text dates from the 1940s. Some people find it dated; others think it's timeless.

- ✔ *How to Make Money in Stocks: A Winning System in Good Times or Bad,* **by William J. O'Neill (McGraw-Hill):** William O'Neill's system is of most interest to people who are swing trading or investing in common stock, but it may help day traders understand what other participants in the market are looking at when they place orders. The book explains *momentum* investing, which looks for stocks of companies with improving business trends and performance.

Trading psychology

Good traders are mentally tough. They need the confidence to face the market, the decisiveness to place orders, and the fortitude to take losses — and do it against a faceless mix of everyone else trading that day. Several books address trading psychology specifically; others on mental strength are also popular with traders because their lessons can be applied to the markets:

- ✔ *The Art of War,* **by Sun Tzu:** It seems like every trader I've ever met has a copy of *The Art of War.* It's a Chinese text describing military strategy, including the importance of mental toughness and strict discipline. First translated into a European language in 1782, several different versions and translations are in print.

- ✔ *Awaken the Giant Within,* **by Anthony Robbins (Pocket Books):** This basic self-help book is popular with all sorts of folks. Many traders find that Robbins's methods give them confidence and help them control their minds when they're trading.

- ✔ *The Crowd: A Study of the Popular Mind,* **by Gustave LeBon (Dover Books):** In the 19th century, Gustave LeBon wrote this treatise on crowd psychology. He didn't think much of his fellow human beings, but many traders have found that his insights explain some short-term irrational behavior in the markets. Understanding why traders make mistakes can help you make profits.

- ✔ *The Disciplined Trader: Developing Winning Attitudes,* **by Mark Douglas (Prentice Hall):** Mark Douglas is a trader who lost a lot of money and tried to figure out why. As he did that, he developed a great deal of insight into the psychological aspects of trading. Namely, the market doesn't care about who is trading in it, so every trader is responsible for his or her own results. Many experienced day traders swear by the information in this book.

- ✔ *Trading in the Zone,* **by Mark Douglas (Prentice Hall):** This book covers the mental discipline of trading, emphasizing the practices and routines that take the emotion out of it. A trader has a short time to make a profit, and some panic at the idea. This book has helped many traders focus on the key elements of trading rather than the fear, doubt, and greed that can undo the best of them.

History and memoir

I'm not willing to accept the Elliott Wave and say that all market movements are part of overarching trends, but market history — like all history — tends to repeat. Why? Because people are people, and no matter how commerce and the economy changes, people do the same things over and over again:

- ✔ *Double Down: Reflections on Gambling and Loss,* **by Frederick and Stephen Barthelme (Harvest Books):** Want to see what a gambling addiction looks like? The Barthelme brothers are writers and English professors who inherited $250,000 from their father's estate and then lost it all playing casino blackjack. It's a story of how complicated relationships with money cause people to make bad decisions. For a day trader, this book tells what happens when people cannot place limits for emotional reasons, a route to ruin in the casino or during the trading day.

- ✔ *Fortune's Formula: The Untold Story of the Scientific Betting System that Beat the Casinos and Wall Street,* **by William Poundstone (Hill and Wang):** Claude Shannon and John Kelly were Bell Labs scientists working on queuing theories for long-distance calls when they stumbled on what is known as the Kelly Criterion: The ideal proportion of money to bet can be found by the ratio of your edge in the market divided by the odds of winning. Day traders can use this *edge/odds formula* to figure out how much money to allocate to a trade. This book explains how the system works, though it never quite proves that it works when applied to legitimate casinos or to trading.

- ✔ *Reminiscences of a Stock Operator,* **by Edwin LeFevre (Wiley):** This classic, written before the 1929 market crash, tells of the adventures of Jesse Livermore, one of the most successful traders of his time. It's a disguised memoir of speculation, with a character named Larry Livingston standing in for Livermore. Some traders like it for the lessons they can learn from Livermore; others are just amused by how unchanged the art of day trading is despite dramatic changes in technology.

The Trader's Internet

Day trading was made possible by the Internet. When high-speed connectivity to market data became affordable, almost anyone could trade with the same speed as folks working on the exchange floor or a brokerage trading desk. And yet the Internet can be a terrible distraction to a day trader or to anyone else working alone. Here are some good websites for day traders, but you may want to limit your use of them to before and after trading hours.

- ✔ **Cara Community:** Bill Cara isn't a day trader, but he is a full-time investor who pays careful attention to the markets. Each day, he records his observations about what's happening on his blog, www.caracommunity.com. It's good reading.

- ✔ **Elite Trader:** Elite Trader, www.elitetrader.com, is one of the big trader communities online, with forums, book and software reviews, and broker ratings. The participants can be passionate, but the information is often great.

- ✔ **IndexArb.com:** Interested in trading futures on the market indexes? This site, http://indexarb.com, has useful information. It lists the premiums on different contracts, offers strategies for different market conditions, and gives you some good background information to help you make your own decisions.

- ✔ **TraderInterviews.com:** Looking for something educational and inspirational for your MP3 player? TraderInterviews.com (www.traderinterviews.com) features discussions with different traders.

- ✔ **Trader Mike:** Every day, Michael Seneadza, a day trader, updates his blog at www.tradermike.net. It includes his trading journal, thoughts on the markets, and advice on day trading, which he admits is not definitive. This blog is often thought-provoking.

- ✔ **Trade2Win:** Are you looking for forums about trading? Want to find out what other traders think about a service or a strategy? Looking to learn more? Check out Trade2Win, www.trade2win.com, one of the most comprehensive trader sites in cyberspace.

- ✔ **Traders Laboratory:** If you are interested in meeting other day traders online, finding web-based seminars, reading traders' blogs, or checking out economic release calendars, then Traders Laboratory, www.traderslaboratory.com, is the site for you.

Other Mainstream Media

Even though traders are hooked to real-time market data through the Internet, they still look to some old-style sources for information. Believe it or not!

- ✔ **Barron's:** *Barron's* (www.barrons.com) is a weekly financial newspaper published by Dow Jones & Company. The primary emphasis is on long-term investing, but it carries in-depth market analysis and often interviews outstanding traders. In addition, the regular "Electronic Trader" column carries news and ratings of online brokerage firms, many of which specialize in services for day traders.

✔ **Bloomberg TV:** Bloomberg TV (www.bloomberg.com/tv) is a cable channel that carries news and information about the markets. Some traders keep it running in the background while they trade. Others watch the shows before and after market hours.

✔ **Investor's Business Daily:** This newspaper, www.investors.com, is published by the William O'Neill Company, which also publishes charts and technical analysis systems used by stock investors. Every morning, *IBD* has new trade ideas and market analysis for active traders, especially those in the stock market.

Index

• C •

• D •

● **H** ●

● **I** ●

● *J* ●

● *K* ●

• *N* •

About the Author

Ann C. Logue, MBA, is the author of *Hedge Funds For Dummies, Socially Responsible Investing For Dummies,* and *Emerging Markets For Dummies* (all published by Wiley). She has written for *Barron's, The New York Times, Newsweek Japan, USAToday,* and the International Monetary Fund. She is a lecturer at the Liautaud Graduate School of Business at the University of Illinois at Chicago. Her current career follows 12 years of experience as an investment analyst. She has a BA from Northwestern University and an MBA from the University of Chicago, and she holds the Chartered Financial Analyst (CFA) designation.

Dedication

Once again to Rik and Andrew, for their love and support.

Author's Acknowledgments

So many wonderful people helped me on the different editions of this book. I talked to many day traders, brokers, and others in the investment business, including Jack Alogna and Beth Cotner; Michael Browne of DTN Inc.; Nihar Dalil, Glenda Dowie, Greg Gocek, and Robert Cohen of the CFA Society of Chicago; Mary Haffenberg and Curt Zuckert at the Chicago Mercantile Exchange; John T. Hoagland, Conor Meegan, and Michael Patak at Topstep Trader; Anil Joshi of NuFact; Karen H. at Gamblers Anonymous; James Kupfer of Waterston Financial; James Lee of TradersLaboratory.com; Wayne Lee of NASDAQ; Michael Lindsay, Khurram Naik, and James Cagnina at Infinity Brokerage Services; Casey Nicholson, Erika Olson, Don Padou, Karina Rubel, Mario Sant Singh, Chris Tabaka, Elizabeth Tabaka, and Allen Ward. I also talked to several other traders who asked to remain anonymous; they know who they are, and I hope they also know how much I appreciate their help. As for the mechanics of putting together the book, Alissa Schwipps and Stacy Kennedy of Wiley were great to work with this time around. Finally, my agent, Marilyn Allen, made it all happen.

Thanks, everyone!

Publisher's Acknowledgments

Acquisitions Editor: Stacy Kennedy

Senior Project Editor: Alissa Schwipps

Copy Editor: Caitlin Copple

Technical Editor: Russell Rhoads

Project Coordinator: Erin Zeltner

Cover Image: ©iStockphoto.com/vasabii